M.KIRST

SCHOOL EVALUATION

The Politics & Process

edited by

ERNEST R. HOUSE

University of Illinois

at Urbana-Champaign

McCutchan Publishing Corporation

2526 Grove Street
Berkeley, California 94704

ISBN: 8211-0750-X
Library of Congress Catalogue Card Number: 72-91622

To my best resources—Kristin, Colby, and Donna

CONTENTS

CONTRIBUTORS

RICHARD BODINE is Director of the Area Service Center, Champaign, Illinois.

ROBERT BURNHAM is a member of the Educational Administration Department, University of Illinois at Urbana-Champaign.

REGINALD K. CARTER is Assistant Professor in the Division of Social Sciences of the University of Wisconsin-Parkside.

DAVID K. COHEN is a member of the education faculty at Harvard University, and Executive Director of the Center for Educational Policy Research.

FREDERICK R. CYPHERT is Dean of the School of Education at the University of Virginia.

DAVID A. ERLANDSON is a member of the Educational Administration Department, Queens College, City University of New York.

WALTER L. GANT is Director of the Department of Adjustive Services, Norfolk City Schools.

DENNIS GOOLER is Director of the Instructional Technology Area at Syracuse University.

HARRY J. HARTLEY is Dean of the School of Education at the University of Connecticut.

J. THOMAS HASTINGS is Director of the Center for Instructional

x

Research and Curriculum Evaluation at the University of Illinois at Urbana-Champaign.

GORDON HOKE is a member of the Center for Instructional Research and Curriculum Evaluation at the University of Illinois at Urbana-Champaign.

ROBERT J. HUYSER is a member of the Michigan Department of Education.

C. PHILIP KEARNEY is Associate Superintendent of the Michigan Department of Education.

EDWARD F. KELLY is Associate Director, Center for Instructional Development at Syracuse University.

THOMAS C. KERINS is Director of the Service Coordinating Unit, in the Office of the Superintendent of Public Instruction of the State of Illinois.

DAN C. LORTIE is a sociologist and the Acting Director of the Midwest Administration Center at the University of Chicago.

BARRY MacDONALD is a member of the Center for Applied Research in Education, at the University of East Anglia, England.

BARRY McGAW is a Senior Research Officer in the Research and Curriculum branch of the Department of Education, Brisbane, Australia.

THOMAS R. OWENS is Director of the Center for Planning and Evaluation in the Santa Clara County Office of Education, San Jose, California.

LAWRENCE F. READ is Superintendent of Schools in Jackson, Michigan.

BARAK ROSENSHINE is a member of the Bureau of Educational Research at the University of Illinois, Urbana-Champaign.

MICHAEL SCRIVEN is a member of the Philosophy Department, University of California at Berkeley.

ROBERT E. STAKE is Associate Director of the Center for Instructional Research and Curriculum Development at the University of Illinois, Urbana-Champaign.

ROBERT L. WOLF is a graduate student in the Center for Instructional Research and Curriculum Evaluation, at the University of Illinois, Urbana-Champaign.

PROLOGUE

Evaluation in a Pluralist Society

The primary purpose of this book is to acquaint the practicing administrator, the decision maker, and the educational consumer with the world of evaluation. Evaluators will find the book useful for its unique approach to evaluation. Some of the best, most current evaluation writings are included. But it is the administrator and the teacher who are most victimized and most confused by the swirl of pressures. Increasingly, they are being called upon to criticize, defend, and improve their programs. Doing that is what evaluation is about.

The book will not make the administrator an evaluator. No book could do that. Only considerable training and experience can teach the skills necessary to make one a competent technician. There is no need for the administrator to have such skills since there are many people who do. The administrator does need to know how to initiate an evaluation and, just as important, when not to start one. He needs to know where a particular evaluation is likely to lead him, for there are many different kinds of evaluation, all likely to produce wildly different results.

The administrator does not need to know the technology itself but what the technology can do for him or to him. Evaluation is one of the most technical aspects of education: it traffics in such concepts as statistics, reliability, and experimental design. As with other technologies, one does not need to know the technical details to make use of it, just as one need not be an engineer in order to drive a car, and certainly one need not be a nuclear physicist in order to contemplate the ramifications of nuclear power. In fact, not being a specialist often helps one grasp the implications of the technology better than the specialist who is often a slave to his own skills.

1

It is possible for evaluation, like other technologies, to produce disastrous consequences from good intentions. Technologies have a logic of their own that is oblivious of undesirable ends. We are already suffering the ravages of several unchecked technologies as well as reaping their benefits. The wise man will proceed with some trepidation, carefully weighing the fruits of a new technology against its inevitable side effects, in itself a delicate evaluation task that must be performed by nonspecialists working through our political institutions.

Viewing the field of evaluation and the "accountability" movement, I feel that there is good reason to be concerned. The religious dedication to certain techniques, the promise of utopian rewards if we will but believe, are familiar signs of another educational stampede. With few exceptions, the techniques are uncritically accepted, the assumptions unquestioned, the future guaranteed. In fact, most books on evaluation offer the one sure prescription of how it should be done. In a counterspirit the material in this book has been selected. The administrator should have the basic alternatives laid out before him, along with some intelligent discussion of where each choice is likely to lead. This book assumes that the administrator is a consumer of evaluation: he is not going to conduct the evaluation; he is going to decide whether he is going to use an evaluation and what kind to initiate or accept. These readings were selected to present the basic alternatives in evaluation, to examine underlying assumptions, and to describe what has happened when various approaches have been tried. Several examples of evaluation attempts are provided in the belief that examples carry more weight than generalizations about them.

This book must be of practical help to the administrator, not by telling him what he must do (no one knows enough to tell him that), but by alerting him to real problems, the values underlying them, and the alternatives he must face in a complicated, confused world. If the administrator does not recognize these examples as something that could happen in his own setting, he should immediately toss the book aside.

Much of this work represents the accumulated experiences of the Center for Instructional Research and Curriculum Evaluation (CIRCE), and particularly the sage counsel of people such as Bob Stake and Tom Hastings. CIRCE is the oldest, probably the most innovative, and certainly one of the most respected evaluation organizations in education. Through many years and painful projects, the Center's work has confirmed the belief that awkward techniques though useful, are seldom the equal of human judgment, that intuition is as indispensible to human thought as is analysis, and that intellectual humility is particularly appropriate in a world where complexity outstrips understanding. Based on extensive interaction with practitioners, in listening as well as telling, this viewpoint may be more congruent with the administrator's world than are the prescriptions to which he is usually subject. I believe that its claims for evaluation are more modest, more realistic, and more useful.

THE THEMES OF THE BOOK

The major theme of the book is the political nature of evaluation. Contrary to common belief, evaluation is not the ultimate arbiter, delivered from pure objectivity and accepted as the final judgment. Evaluation is always derived from biased origins. When someone wants to defend something or to attack something, he often evaluates it. Evaluation is a motivated behavior. Likewise, the way in which the results of an evaluation are accepted depends on whether they help or hinder the person receiving them. Evaluation is an integral part of the political processes of our society.

At its simplest, evaluation is the process of applying a set of standards to a program, making judgments using the standards, and justifying the standards and their application. But there are many standards, especially in a pluralist society: which to apply? There are many ways of using the standards. Often the initiator of the evaluation determines the standards: if a school superintendent wants to defend a program, he usually chooses the ground on which it is evaluated; if a school critic wishes to attack the program, he chooses different standards. Whichever side the results favor will use them to gain political advantage. Evaluation becomes a tool in the process of who gets what in the society.

A second theme is that both one's administration and one's evaluation are intimately related to whether one believes that the goals of the class, school, district, state, or nation are already established or are yet to be arrived at through negotiation between groups. If one believes that the goals are already set, or that it is the prerogative of a designated group to set them, evaluation is usually taken to be a comparison of the program's goals with its outcomes to determine how well the goals were met. Most evaluation is derived from this model, beginning with the "behavioral objectives" approach and extending through PPBS (Planning-Programming-Budgeting-Systems) and other, more recent "systems" approaches. The administrator who sees his organization this way is apt to prefer administrative to political tasks, to see administration as the efficient use of resources.

More recently, the goals of the organization have been seen to be not set but constantly negotiated among different power groups. The organization is not a monocratic expression of one person's authority but an ever-shifting coalition of groups influenced by powerful forces both within and without. Shifting goals and priorities greatly complicate the job of the evaluator and, indeed, that of the administrator. Goals and standards beneficial to one group may not be acceptable to all groups. The goals themselves often become the object of empirical investigation, as in "needs assessment." The administrator is likely to see his task as "political," to organize coalitions to achieve certain ends, to keep groups working with one another, and to help negotiate the differences between the Birchers and the ADA. I believe that a general discord about goals is prevalent in the schools today, but both views are well represented in the book.

A third theme is the relationship between decision making and evaluation: the delicate relationship between the administrator and the evaluator. How much the administrator currently attends to formal evaluation data is easy to gauge—not much. How much he should attend to is more difficult to establish. Rational decision models would have the administrator diligently searching the horizon for answers to various questions, weighing the evidence, and heroically, if mechanically, basing his decision on hard data.

Decision making is never like that. The administrator does not have time to search, nor does the organization ordinarily generate more than one new way of doing something. In fact, the image of the organization as an integrated, problem-solving mechanism, unanimous about its goals, is difficult to maintain. Seldom are hard data available, and even if there were, there are many other kinds of information to which the administrator must attend. A few test scores are not infallible guides in a complex world. Evaluation data, like other data, must compete for the administrator's attention. Under favorable circumstances, evaluation data might account for 20 percent of a decision. The proper role of evaluation data is to be useful, not determinate. Ultimately, human judgment must resolve the issues insofar as they are ever to be resolved.

THE STRUCTURE OF THE BOOK

The first part of the book, *Decision Making and Evaluation: A Tenuous Relationship,* attempts to draw a line between the evaluator and the administrator. Schools are extremely vulnerable to public pressure, and the consequences this has for evaluation are discussed. It is often to the administrator's advantage to keep school activities hazy and vague, and thus reduce conflict. Many administrators see evaluation as potentially valuable but too dangerous for them to try. Nonetheless, pressures for evaluation are building up and already much is done covertly. It is to the administrator's advantage that he be at the center of such activities so that he can reap the benefits and prevent the disasters. Different evaluation approaches can lead in quite different directions.

The second part of the book, *Politics as Usual,* illustrates the political nature of evaluation. Often it is used by the higher levels of government to shape the behavior of the lower. The statewide Michigan assessment program, described in chapters 5 and 6, is a good example of the political fire that can result. Evaluation findings are often ignored or buried if they do not agree with the client's preconceptions. The last few selections try to define the proper role of the evaluator in such a political maelstrom: he must be sensitive to the vulnerability of the organization he is assessing, yet responsible to the audience who will read his report; ultimately, he must be both fair and honest. It is not an easy role to maintain.

The third part of the book, *Evaluating Teachers: Does Anyone Really Want to be Evaluated?* attacks the issue of the evaluation of teaching. There is a difference between evaluating to improve something and evaluating to reward or punish individuals. The evidence is that the latter is on very shaky ground. Technically, it is difficult to substantiate single measures of teacher performance as being particularly effective. Politically, teachers are threatened by evaluation and not encouraged by the school environment to expose their teaching. Possible alternatives are evaluations of programs rather than of individuals, and in-service programs revolving around "self-assessment" techniques.

The fourth part of the book, *If Everyone Agrees . . .* deals with approaches that are currently in vogue in educational evaluation: the behavioral objectives and systems analysis approaches. Both assume that, initially, agreement can be reached on the goals and objectives that are to be pursued. Both demand that the objectives be prespecified and that the evaluation measure the achievement of the goals. Other articles in the section attack the assumptions, efficacy, and benefits of such approaches. Special attention is paid to performance contracting, which represents the apotheosis of the systems approach. It is found wanting.

The fifth part of the book, *If Nobody Agrees* . . . explores courses of action that may be pursued when there is no goal consensus, as increasingly seems to be the case. One approach is to search out goal consensus or try to create it. One can explore what various publics think and how they, as independent groups, judge educational programs. Another strategy is to create radically different modes of evaluation. In the face of a lack of consensus about goals (and perhaps values), one might establish an educational consumers' agency, rely on the critical intelligence and techniques of the professional evaluator, or resolve goal conflicts judicially. The book ends with some interpretations and generalizations by the editor.

I

DECISION MAKING
AND EVALUATION

A Tenuous Relationship

What is the relationship between the evaluator and decision maker? Lortie's discussion of school structure is essential to an understanding of the role of evaluation within the school. Lortie sees the school as being vulnerable to political pressure. The vulnerability of school boards and the uncertain position of the superintendent lead to very conservative school systems. Goals and objectives for the school are usually stated in general, hazy terms in order to protect the system from the deep splits in the American value structure. The schools are organized to avoid trouble. Political pressures are more likely to have an effect if there are no commonly agreed upon goals and no clear link between objectives and outcomes that could justify behavior.

What is the role of evaluation in this structure? Clear evaluation results lead away from the vagueness and compromise on which the system is based and which are possibly resulting in a crisis. They emphasize value conflicts rather than submerge them. In this atmosphere rational decision making must be subservient to political decision making. The administration must be sensitive to political coalitions. Lortie sees two rational plans as possible. One is a movement toward a tight managerial model, a master plan that is the duty of administrators and teachers to implement; the system becomes highly centralized and evaluation sees that the plan is implemented. The second is a separation of power. Each group in the school would have certain powers; some control would be allocated to specialists; groups, such as teachers, would retain some autonomy; the system would remain somewhat decentralized, and evaluation would concentrate on justifying behavior and communicating to other groups. Both forces are currently implicit in the structure of the schools.

What stance should the administrator assume about evaluation in such a maelstrom of forces? Erlandson tackles the problem from the position of the practicing administrator. He confirms the power of evaluation itself to structure a situation. Evaluation often defines both the problem and the solution. It is an essential part of the power required to run a school. Evaluation is going to occur, indeed occurs covertly, whether the administrator likes it or not. The issue is whether the administrator should merely react defensively or should seize control of the evaluation process itself. The more the administrator uses overt evaluation procedures, the less his educational program is subject to momentary whims and circumstances. Without being a technician himself, he must have a working knowledge of evaluation. Otherwise, he diminishes his own control of the school.

For the evaluation to be effective he must know precisely what he wants from it. The more specific are the questions he wants answered, the better. He must also realize that not all evaluation experts are the same and will not give him what he wants. The administrator should ask himself:

1. "What do I need to evaluate?" The usual temptation is to concentrate on too narrow a range of issues. He should concentrate on evaluating programs and not people.
2. "What do I want to evaluate?" This question serves as a screen between relevant and irrelevant data. The answer must be as specific as possible since it can help determine the design of the evaluation. It should lead to realistic problems. What is bugging the administration?
3. "What do I intend to do with the results?" Most results are never used. Test scores are collected and forgotten. The honest administrator admits that he wants data to impress the public. He should also be aware that any evaluation will reveal many program weaknesses because no program is perfect. He must stand ready to redress the weaknesses he finds as well as to publicize the good results.

Of course, the administrator cannot concentrate only on his own concerns in building a successful evaluation. He must also consider the criteria that other people use to evaluate him and the relative political potency of these judges. In fact, this concern often prompts evaluation to focus on what people think about the schools.

Erlandson proposes a strong, central, aggressive role for an administrator in the conduct of evaluations. He sees evaluation as a critical tool in governing the school. Apparently he has less fear than Lortie about the potential damage an evaluation might do—although he cautions against the wrong kind of evaluation and thinks a continuing role for the administrator essential.

The survey of needs conducted by Hoke confirms many of the contentions made by Erlandson. The political nature of the school, the "day-to-day survival in a sea of conflicting forces," was emphasized by the different types of school personnel whom Hoke interviewed. Generally there was confusion over how evaluation would fit into everyday operations. All agreed that something should be done, that local districts needed help. Yet all agreed that, traditionally, evaluation has had little effect on life in the schools. Hoke found no use made of the national information systems now in operation and very little enthusiasm for a translator of data to work with the schools, a role proposed by various reformers.

In Hoke's interviews one can read a plea for help and, at the same time, a suspicion of how that help might be delivered and an uncertainty about how it could be used. A few clues about what kind of evaluation would be useful were given. In his role as a power-broker, one suburban superintendent saw the art of discerning public opinion (one type of evaluation) as "politics in its parent form." Another said that evaluators must realize that their opinions are only part of the picture. The mismatch between what these practitioners saw as their problems and what they saw evaluation as being able to provide them led Hoke to conclude that not much evaluation is going to be done until there is some way of helping school people deal with the consequences of evaluation.

Surely this is correct. As long as administrators perceive evaluators as researchers out of contact with the political world and trying to tell them what to do, not much is going to happen. The evaluator must realize that his data account for only part of an administrator's decision. Other important inputs for decision making are the conscience of the administrator himself and the opinions of those whom the decision affects. Attempts to provide unequivocal answers to problems with evaluation data are mistaken. Evaluation does not replace the decision maker's intuition; it informs it. No administrator should be able to run his district in good conscience without the guidance of some data.

Can evaluation be used in a practical decision-making fashion? Can it cut costs? These are the questions to which Kelly addresses himself. His answer is a qualified yes. He points out that, although there is no necessary relationship between evaluation and cost cutting, pressures push in that direction. He gives an extended example of one such evaluation at a university. Universal dissatisfaction with the freshman composition course led to a drastic overhaul. A development team, working closely with evaluation specialists, redesigned the course. Use of faculty hours quickly became a primary focus. The outcome of the overhaul was that the faculty thought students were performing better, the students thought the course was better, and costs were reduced significantly. Kelly warns, though, that there is no single criterion of cost effectiveness, such as dollars and cents: many costs are hidden.

1

RATIONAL DECISION MAKING: IS IT POSSIBLE TODAY?

A conversation between Dr. Dan C. Lortie and EPIE Forum, November 1967

EPIE: Dr. Lortie, you and your colleagues—particularly the ones who specialize in the sociology of education—have not often emphasized the need for a rational model of school organization and school decision making in your work. Is this because your own models and theories do not require it or because the decisions arrived at in a school system are really not formulated in a rational fashion?

Lortie: To answer this question, we would have to consider a model of the way schools work. When a sociologist looks at the organization and studies the way it really works, he's interested in the distribution of power that exists within the structure, the varying orientations of people to it, and the constraints that emerge for any given person or group of persons in the organization as a result of the interplay of these varying orientations and attitudes. The way in which we have organized our public schools makes it difficult for decisions to be made within an entirely rational framework. It is more difficult for school officials publicly to announce and align specific objectives with a clear conception of output than it is to organize to avoid trouble.

If you examine the statements of objectives of most school systems, you'll find that they are vague, unranked, and have very little directive power for persons within them. This is a special situation to education I think, because if you look at the legal distribution of power in schools, you will find that it is concentrated—officially—in the hands of the board and, to a lesser extent, the superintendent.

Reprinted from *EPIE Forum* 1 no. 3 (November 1967): 6-9. Copyright 1967 by EPIE Institute.

No one else in school systems has any autonomous, official, authority—not the curriculum director, or the assistant superintendent in charge of plant, or the high school principal, or the teacher of physics in the high school. Anybody else's authority is derivative—in official terms—from that invested legally in the board.

What we have, then, is a situation in which individual choices, political pressures, and such, are likely to have much more effect than if there were a clear link between organizational objectives and the actions of those who are delegated to take them and put them into action. What happens in schools at any given moment, it seems, is a mixture of the board's political concerns, its relationship to the local community, the superintendent's own immediate sense of priorities, the relative aggressiveness of a given principal or department head, and the informal relationships that determine whether or not teachers are acting with a fair degree of autonomy.

As far as curriculum planning is concerned, I think that most of the rationales that one encounters tend to presuppose a detached, autonomous group of professionals sitting around with clear authority to set goals and specific means. And legally this isn't so. In hierarchal terms, where this autonomy exists it is always fragile. I'm convinced there is great autonomy in the schools on a day-to-day basis, but it has fragility because of its lack of official sanction. Superintendents are nervous men. Their position is an extremely ambiguous one, they are subject to loss of their jobs, and so forth.

By virtue of their role, they are forced into very heavy concern with political matters. So I think that what we tend to end up with is a situation in schools in which it is difficult to get either concerted rational action in the sense of the clear demarcation of goals or the clear delegation of authority to others to align goals and means— because there is the risk that conflict and trouble will arise in the community or school. Schools are not that well-protected from trouble and all kinds of political repercussions.

EPIE: Yet there is a continuing motivation among a number of professional administrators to implement a rational procedure, even though these difficulties exist.

Lortie: Yes, I think this is true. I think you would find that it varies a great deal, depending upon the kind of constituency which schools serve. If you go up to one of the prosperous suburbs north of Chicago, you'll find skillful administrators coupled with a high community evaluation of the importance of education. There is a good tradition of autonomy. This means that, in some of those systems, the superintendent and staff have opportunity for clear goal setting and careful derivation of means in terms of curriculum choices, procedures, and what-have-you. I'm not saying that it is never this way but, generally speaking, you look at schools and it's curious that there is an absence of clearly constraining goals—(as in the case of business, for example, where you've got to make a profit)—and that the absence of such goals in schools actually inhibits freedom! You'd think it might be the other way around. But it is difficult for subordinates in school to tie their decision making to a clearly demarcated set of goals. This, of course, is a factor that will vary with the political context.

EPIE: Suppose we were able to measure the outcomes of education more fully—as we might say that we are able to measure the outcomes of business—not just short-run profit, but long-run profit, public confidence, and the like—things we feel we can get some measure of. Do you feel that then it would be easier for the schools to adopt a policy that permitted them to approach their goals in a more rational fashion?

Lortie: That's a fascinating question because in some ways I think we are inhibited from using a rational model in schools by the fuzziness of our thinking. The question is, "If our thinking becomes more precise, if our technology becomes keener so that we have a better understanding of the relationship between objective A and alternative means 1, 2, and 3, and which has the greater likelihood of producing output A, will we, in fact, move toward systems that are more rationally organized?"

In looking at it from some points of view, I think that this will create a crisis. I think the fuzziness that we find at the highest level of school systems is politically caused in a very particular fashion. Many American communities have very deep internal cleavages—this is what we mean by a pluralistic society. Schools, because they are modes of socialization, are involved in perpetuating somebody's core values.

I think we have been able to build public schools and to get them working on a day-to-day basis largely by ignoring such cleavages. Now, if we come along and say, "Look, we can measure objectives 1, 2, and 3. Your job is to lay down the line as to which is the most important—which should be controlling which?" I think we will have a very sharp reversal of the major modes of political action that have been used up till now, which have been those of vagueness and compromise and of avoiding the substantive choices.

EPIE: If there were a "sharp reversal," what might we expect to come about?

Lortie: Of course I'm guessing, because we don't have the studies to document this, but the way it looks to me at this moment is that the average school board puts out a fuzzy, meaningless statement of objectives. The superintendent makes specific recommendations from time to time to the board, and they decide to vote for or against them. When they talk about policy they tend to talk about procedures, not about what persons in instruction consider objectives. This tends to lower the political vulnerability of the board and the superintendent. It does not exacerbate the public. There are so many potentially explosive issues in education that it's easier if you avoid substantive commitments and focus on single individual actions. And boards will frequently avoid substantive decisions in areas that they *know* are sensitive—religion, athletics, racial integration. These are hot, tough, miserable issues—particularly when seen from the perspective of somebody serving on a board in an essentially political office with little remuneration. At what point does the balance of benefits and costs lead board members, for example, to resign their posts?

In any event, we are concerned about a more rational model—we *want* a more rational model, in a sense. We want to feel that we are setting clear objectives and that we are maximizing our means of attaining them, and we want a feedback system. All presuppose a kind of freedom from these fears on the part of persons running schools, and I think that, before we are going to get rationality of this sort accepted by people in schools, there are going to have to be some changes in the relationship between schools and the community.

EPIE: Are there any alternatives to our present situation?

Lortie: Yes. I believe there are two. What we do now is to hide these problems with a complex series of informal understandings between the different layers of the system and keep our fingers crossed that trouble won't arise so that the board has publicly to acknowledge the errors of its subordinates. Instead, we could move toward a tight managerial model where we try to institute close, steady controls over the behavior of people within the system. So we could say the curriculum in third grade is as follows:

Ritual observances	9-9:20
Arithmetic	9:20-10

and specify particular topics to be taught in such-and-such a fashion and to be tested at regular intervals. We could, in short, use a kind of modern industrial manager model that places the plan first and sees teachers and others as essentially "agents" of that plan.

In this kind of managerial model, when I talk about the plan, I don't mean to suggest that the plan is rigid or permanent. It can be an extremely rational procedure in that you start off with objectives, you have a commitment to plan A, and you keep testing it and revising it. But it does necessarily involve centralization so that when we are talking about say, the curriculum or instruction area, we would necessarily grant a great deal of power to those who are in charge of curriculum at the central office level, given the current structure of schools. There are costs and benefits associated with this kind of plan. I'm uneasy with it—perhaps because I'm a professor and tend to place a high value upon individual autonomy, but I think there might be an objective way of finding the consequences of moving this way.

The second alternative would move us toward a model of separation of powers within the school system—much like, say, a great university, where the board would have certain legislative and review powers. The superintendent would become more like the president of Harvard or the University of Chicago, who has certain statutory rights, who is perceived as an independent executive, and the faculty would be given certain kinds of policy-making areas, primarily having to do with instruction. It really raises a question as to whether what we do in a modern university is rational? What is done there is to allocate control of instruction to specialists both in terms of collective attempts to regulate programs (programs are really accretions of individual professors' efforts arranged in some kind of pattern), and in terms of individual efforts, in the sense that we have no supervision over the individual professor. He is perceived as capable of planning an entire course, and there is no procedure for reviewing his plan.

Thus we have a choice of two rational plans. In the first we move primarily toward a centralized managerial model, which has the advantages of incorporating into the plan the most recent knowledge and information about learning techniques and similar procedures, but which, in a sense, reduces the status of teachers and principals and others to implementers. This plan places a very heavy emphasis upon control and having to make your people do what is specified. The real question is how feasible this is, given the geographical and social dispersion of schools and teachers. Schools themselves are isolated from the central office, and within schools we have built up an elaborate etiquette to protect individual teachers—particularly those who have tenure and seniority—from intervention. The principals are very loath to intervene. Central office supervisors are normally few in number, limited in power, and rarely get to see more than a fraction of the teaching force's work in any given year. There is, of course, the possibility of testing by results. We might get much more elaborate in the use of achievement tests, etc., so that rather than emphasizing the teacher's compliance with the given process we go around this and test what's happening to students.

The second alternative is a very expensive one, if taken seriously. I don't expect that we could ever get a professionalized teaching force in the same sense as the university professors are professionalized. How did they get this way? Years of preparation, a light teaching load, allowance for privacy, opportunity for professional recognition. Teachers in the public schools get less of these. Teachers today receive relatively little return for their heavy investment in a career in education. The professionalization of the classroom teacher would require considerable changes in the entire career line and work organization of school personnel. For example, to professionalize teaching would require expensive rearrangements in the allocation of teacher time. They would need time to record and analyze their teaching experiences, and so forth. But it is possible to move in that direction. I believe you can get people to make the necessary investment in their careers *if* the rewards warrant it.

EPIE: Oriented by habit and principle to his own standards, the classroom teacher makes unconscious decisions all day long. Some decisions will be enormous errors, of course, but thousands of others are right. Would we be better off to call for more conscious decision-making processes, oriented to a less personalized schedule of values?

Lortie: The problem here is that we do not only have pluralism in the community, and at the board, and superintendent level, but we have pluralism within the school itself. My interviews with teachers show considerable variation in what they consider to be the important product of their efforts. The most dramatic instance of this, I think, was in one high school where I interviewed three social science teachers, all working in the same department. My interview included the chairman. The chairman, teaching twelfth grade, clearly saw himself countervailing the strong, as it happened in this case, Republican, conservative nature of this community—preparing his students for university work by trying to instill in them a kind of skeptical liberalism toward what they heard and read. He had, in a way, a sophisticated conception of the Citizen that he was trying to instill, and in the course of this, the materials that I saw he was using were mostly university-level materials. He himself was a very sophisticated and well-educated man.

I talked to another teacher who had been a psychology undergraduate at an ivy league college. His orientation to teaching was that he was teaching adolescents who were confronting very severe problems of developing a life philosophy, who were asking themselves questions such as "Do I really believe in God?" Now he was formally teaching history. Two things, though, excited him. He claimed that these students were bright enough and he was a good enough teacher —he could prep them to pass achievement tests in history, which are mostly factual, according to him, but using a limited period of time. What he really liked to use any marginal time for was discussions, exploration with them of these burning issues. And secondarily he was on *another* kind of kick, he was interested in teaching them to read, and was using special materials—designed to improve reading performance at the high school level. He was convinced that you get greater substantive gains in history or in anything else by teaching vocabulary and comprehension to these kids than you do by teaching history directly. He claimed to have been able to demonstrate this, but you see his approach was quite different from the chairman's.

The third man had an interesting background. He came from a working-class family. He received a football scholarship at a good private college. Now he is teaching in this upper-middle-class system. He had started off, he was telling me, deeply interested in history. But, as he had worked with these kids, he had gotten more and more concerned with the problems of the boys whose fathers were often away. These are the $60,000-a-year kind who travel a great deal. It was interesting to see the latent gratification that this teacher was receiving—a lower-class boy working in an upper-class school system had, in fact, become the father to many of these kids in a very direct and personal way—something like the second man I mentioned, but *he* stressed, rather, the extracurricular contacts that he had with them—the ski weekends, and so forth.

Now here are three men working in the same department, which has some kind of policy because the chairman kept talking about departmental policy. Yet, in this use of marginal time, they emphasize different ends. This raises a very basic question, I think, about how we ought to operate as schools. Would it be wiser for a group of persons concerned about curriculum to sit down and pick one limited set of objectives—the most effective means to achieve goals and thereby gain greater effectiveness in such a school? Or are there advantages in the pluralism represented by these three different teachers and their different emphases? Granted, such an operation has its inefficiency, but at least the students have the chance to be exposed to a diversity of minds. This, I think, ultimately rests upon some kind of value choice, and also upon an analytic choice. What is more important to our society today? Is it to have persons who have cognitive mastery over a given area? Or is it, in a society confronted with cold war pressures and the like, to keep alive some kind of value diversity, some sense of the options in life?

EPIE: How can a superintendent, or any official of his community be satisfied that he is keeping value diversity alive? Is it safe for him to say, "If I get the right people as my teachers, I can rest comfortably—the right things will happen"? Certainly he is observant, he is an insightful man, he is going to see some of the things that are going on; but is it safe for him and his staff to depend on casual observation? How might he use some of the research talents in the social sciences to further his vision—to further his reach into his community and his schools and to perceive the maintenance of value diversity?

Lortie: I think research can help in a narrowly technical sense to identify, say, the range of values that exists in the community or the society at large, and we can certainly interview people and find the extent to which there is diversity or narrowness in a given faculty and so forth. But I would think that if we were interested, say, in maximizing value diversity within the schools, we would have to become, in a sense, political advisors. The constraints that keep schools banal, conservative, and conforming derive from the way in which we have structured schools. We have vulnerable school boards. We have vulnerable superintendents. Our right-wing groups can make an awful lot of trouble, right now, in various parts of the country. Why are educators so conservative? One man at a teachers' college was telling me he's worried about placing a fellow with a beard. I think school officials take any sign of deviation on the part of a teacher as evidence that he is likely to produce trouble in the political sense.

So I think that much of the conservatism we have, much of the lack of diversity—and this happens to concern me—is a result of this kind of political vulnerability. How are we to increase American tolerance for diversity?

EPIE: What do you think can be the response of school administration to the flood of new curriculum materials and techniques that are helping to create more and more instructional options?

Lortie: In some cases schools will have to add evaluation specialists to deal with information about these materials. This will be particularly necessary when a school system undertakes wide-spread adoptions of a radical change such as Pittsburgh's recent commitment to create six educational parks. But many of these innovations will necessarily be extensive, and it should be possible for school systems to pool their experience with them. Sharing experiences and evaluations would reduce unnecessary duplication.

2

EVALUATION AND AN
ADMINISTRATOR'S AUTONOMY

David A. Erlandson

The school administrator is rare who would not build a strong case for the worth of evaluation in education. "Evaluation is necessary." "It's impossible to build an educational program without it." "The public demands it. People have a right to know what's going on in the schools."

The whole current notion of accountability in education is central in this. The public would like to know how good a return it is getting on its money. The superintendent wants to know how well each of his schools is being run. The principal wishes to distinguish accurately and defensibly between his strong and weak teachers. The teacher finds it necessary to rank and classify his students.

Yes, evaluation in education is a wonderful thing—at least from the viewpoint of the person doing the evaluating. From the viewpoint of the person being evaluated, it is another story. The superintendent is more than a little suspicious of the state agency or local citizens' watchdog group that proposes to evaluate his program. The principal bristles at the thought of a presumptuous superintendent who chooses to rate the productivity of a school from the safety of his office downtown. The teacher knows that the principal visits his classroom chiefly to determine grounds for his retention or dismissal. The student is convinced that the teacher is out to fail him or, at least, to discredit him in the eyes of his peers.

Evaluation will inevitably be carried on by many people in and around the school. Some of this evaluation will be formal, explicit, and overt; much will be informal, implicit, and covert. The administrator may be worried about a vocal minority group that is calling for his resignation; he perhaps should be more concerned about a general public dissatisfaction with the schools that has not yet attracted his attention. Evaluation, whether a particular administrator considers it acceptable or not, is a fact of life in the schools, and the wise administrator, concerned with his own future existence and usefulness, had better comprehend it and know how to use it.

From a more altruistic point of view, a working knowledge of evaluation purposes and procedures is essential for the administrator who wishes to provide positive direction for his school program. The evaluation process is powerful. Whoever evaluates a situation defines both the problem and the probable solutions. The power to collect, organize, assess, and control information, and the power to select evaluative instruments and criteria are essential elements of the power to run a school. The administrator can probably best judge the power of the evaluation tool by recalling his own apprehension and concern when he and/or his program were last evaluated.

Typically, as suggested by the examples given above, evaluation is something that someone does to someone else. The final product is seen as a rating of value. This view of evaluation is the pervasive one, and it has a limited utility. Concrete decisions, made on its categories of value, are usually based upon binary options: to hire or reject a teaching applicant, to fire or retain a principal, to pass or fail a student, to implement or discard a new program. It suggests little finite, systematic change and improvement.

A more useful view of evaluation is that it is a system responsible for both assessing the pertinent features in and around a school program and generating alternatives to improve that program. An adequate evaluation system should identify what needs to be examined and ask questions that will lead to something more than yes and no alternatives. The evaluation of a program should not merely tell potential users whether to accept or reject the program but also should tell them how to use the program, when to use it, and what parts of it to use. If the evaluation is to assess all the pertinent features of a school program, the administrator must keep in mind that he, and some of the program's features that he values most, may be fair game for the evaluation.

THE ADMINISTRATOR'S ROLE

If the administrator expects to maintain a central role in the school organization, he must maintain a central role in the evaluative process. He cannot let himself be frightened or intimidated. This does not mean that he must be a technical expert or get involved in all the details of evaluation; it does mean that he cannot totally delegate evaluation either to subordinates or to experts.

Many administrative and technical features of evaluation he will have to delegate, but he must retain real control of the process. Complete delegation means either that the subordinate has been given the power to run the school or, if the administrator chooses to disavow a distasteful report, that the evaluation has been emasculated.

The administrator can, and often should, call in outside experts to help him with his evaluation but, in doing so, cannot afford to abdicate his central role in the process. He needs to know specifically what he wants of the evaluation. He should realize that not all evaluation specialists are the same. His decision to call in a particular expert should be based upon that expert's particular competence. Evaluation, like other marketable educational services, has its share of "medicine men" who are all too willing to "tell ya what I'm gonna do." The administrator should tell the expert: "This is what I want. Can you get it for me? If you can, how do you propose to do it? If not, I'll shop around." Without having some specific questions he wants answered, he nearly guarantees that he will not be able to understand or use the evaluation, even if it is a professional one. He will be left with a bad taste in his mouth about esoteric professional evaluators; the evaluator will leave mumbling to himself about the simplemindedness of school administrators.

The administrator can best ensure his central role in the evaluative process by doggedly pursuing the answers to three basic questions: What do I need to evaluate? Why do I want to evaluate? What do I intend to do with the results of my evaluation?

"What Do I Need to Evaluate?"

In considering his answer to the question, "What do I need to evaluate?" the administrator should realize that poor decisions in education are not usually made because of inaccurate data, but chiefly because of a failure to consider adequately a sufficient range of data. This is not to imply that a school should attempt to evaluate everything. Because the range of potential objects for evaluation is nearly infinite and because resources are scarce, choices must be made and priorities must be assigned. Schools, however, tend to focus relatively narrowly, chiefly on observations of academic outcomes.

The items to be evaluated will not be the same for every district or school, but the screening process should be sufficiently broad to assess adequately the need for evaluation in a variety of areas. The cognitive and affective conditions of students before they are given a particular course of instruction, organizational communications, climate, environmental and community forces, and likely future program alternatives for the students—all might usefully be evaluated, although they are not usually included in the sphere of evaluation.

Administrators do not fail to consider a sufficient range of data because the data are not available but because they do not take the data into account. Data may be hard to obtain, or simply overlooked or ignored. Administrators themselves unconsciously build a bias into their systems. The administrator needs consciously to ensure an adequate flow of information from the system and to develop the sensitivity to recognize pertinent information when it comes to him. His particular system for obtaining information is likely to be idiosyncratic; it may be organized or personal, but it must furnish him with accurate feedback. If he fails to recognize and judge adequately emerging issues in the school and its environment, he may well forfeit his central role in running the school.

In determining what to evaluate the administrator should focus his evaluation on programs, not on people. He is not going to succeed entirely in convincing people that he is concerned with educational programs and not with their personalities; but any alleviation of pressure on individuals increases the likelihood that the evaluation will produce the intended results. Any move that reduces interpersonal tension and enlists support for the legitimate goals of the evaluation will be worth the administrator's effort.

"Why Do I Want to Evaluate?"

The second question, "Why do I want to evaluate?" may seem tautological until one considers that most evaluations in schools produce results that are never used. One of the clearest examples of this waste is to be seen in the use of standardized achievement tests, which, if the scores are bad enough, provoke some temporary resolutions but, typically, stimulate little real change in the teaching that produced poor scores. This is not what ought to be done, but it does illustrate the type of evaluation that is done, not because anybody is prepared to change the program if necessary, but because the materials—in this case the standardized tests—are readily available.

Evaluation efforts are often wasted primarily because the question "Why?" is not answered specifically enough. The question should help to clarify not only what the administrator is evaluating but also what he is not evaluating. Different answers will lead to vastly different types of evaluations.

For instance, suppose an administrator decides that he would like to evaluate his reading program and then asks himself the question, "Why?" Probably his immediate response would be: "Because reading is important, and we need to know where we stand." This is a justifiable reason for evaluation but one that, if it is to be taken seriously and comprehensively, calls for more resources than most school districts are willing or able to provide. The administrator probably needs to go back at this point and press his question a little more specifically. He might recall, for instance, that his junior high school teachers are complaining that the reading skills of students from the elementary grades are increasingly weak. He then must specify the particular reading skills that are lacking and the relationship of these skills to the tasks that the new students are expected to perform. He must determine whether this reading weakness applies to all new junior high students or only to some. He must also examine both the elementary and junior high reading programs to determine which skills can most effectively be taught at what levels, with what other materials. His answers will help him to specify what is to be evaluated, which evaluative instruments are to be used, and the overall structure of the evaluation.

He may conclude that he really wants to evaluate the reading program because minority groups are protesting that too many of their children are reading below their grade level. This answer, although it also needs to be refined, suggests an evaluation different from that suggested by the complaints of junior high school teachers and more manageable than that suggested by the global answer that "reading is important, and we need to know where we stand."

A particularly honest administrator might admit that the chief reason for evaluating his reading program is to impress the public that the school is doing a good job. Such a response would probably be fairly common if all school administrators were perfectly honest with themselves; and, unquestionably, it has some legitimacy. But, if it is assumed that the legitimate purpose of an evaluation is to ferret out weaknesses in a program and generate improvement, such self-advertisement is hardly justifiable as the sole purpose for evaluation. Indeed, much of what passes for evaluation in the schools probably has nothing at all to do with the legitimate purposes of evaluation.

"What Do I Do with the Results?"

Finally, the administrator needs to consider the question: "What do I intend to do with the results of my evaluation?" The successful evaluation of an educational program (not one intended strictly as a public relations device) will always detect failure, at least in certain aspects of the program. Let us begin with the assumption that no school is ever perfect. This being so, the job of an evaluation is to uncover weakness and specify improvement. An evaluation that fails to do this can hardly be termed successful. Typically, evaluation is considered a success only when it shows how good a job the school is doing. Evaluation instruments that will make a school program look good are chosen. Having assumed that no school is ever perfect, we must acknowledge that an evaluation that makes the school look good, but fails to show any direction for improvement, fails to fulfill its promise and hardly justifies the bother and expense.

In many quarters there seems to be an implicit faith that evaluation can, by itself, correct many evils in the schools. It is, apparently, assumed that, if we know how badly we are doing we will be better off. This is not necessarily so, any more than it is true that a chest x-ray will, by itself, cure the tuberculosis it reveals. The evaluation, like the x-ray, is useless unless specific action is taken to change the conditions that have been discovered. An evaluation is a waste of resources unless it leads to some action, or at least a conscious, explicit decision not to take any action. Yet, so often evaluations of school programs, like the achievement test described above, lead to no action at all.

COVERT EVALUATION

Left alone, evaluation will, more often than not, come at times the administrator would not choose. The administrator's performance, and that of his organization, will be evaluated by many other people: administrative superiors and subordinates, teachers, the public, parents, the press, and students. Some of this evaluation may be overt; most of it will be covert. Since he and his organization function largely in terms of the perceptions and expectations of others, these evaluations are extremely important for his operation.

The administrator needs to know about the value systems of each of his evaluators and the criteria being used in the evaluation. What do these persons and groups really value? How can he use their underlying value systems to resolve conflict before it is too late? How can he make sense out of their apparently inconsistent expectations? No surface analysis can yield him answers to such questions. The questions themselves suggest the framework for a particular kind of evaluation. In addition, the administrator needs to ascertain the practical potency of each of his evaluators in relation to the operation of his organization. He may totally reject the value system of a particular group evaluating his program, but, if the group is powerful, he can hardly ignore it.

Consider the situation of an administrator who wonders whether to introduce a sex education program in a community in which there are strong sentiments for and against such programs. If he decides that a sex education program should be introduced, he must still decide what type of program to introduce and at what grade levels. He must assess the degree to which he is responding to powerful pressures for and against such programs. He still wants to introduce the best possible sex education program, but what has the rating "best" come to mean in this context? A new element has been introduced into his evaluation. His evaluation can no longer focus only upon the needs of students for sex education; it must take into account what their parents and the community will demand and tolerate.

In dealing with the overt and covert evaluations, perceptions, and conflicts that surround him and his school program, the administrator should not ignore the potency of overt evaluation that he initiates himself. An evaluation, if it deals comprehensively with a problem, specifies and structures future approaches to that problem. The language and classifications of subsequent evaluations, even covert ones, tend to be limited by earlier evaluations. It is difficult for new evaluations to escape the necessity of responding to the original position. The initial overt evaluation spells out many of the ground rules for the evaluation game. The administrator, who would use evaluation, must seize and maintain the initiative.

Evaluation is going to take place whether the administrator likes it or not. His understanding of the nature and uses of evaluation will, in large measure, help determine both the length and comfort of his tenure and the positive educational impact that he is able to make. Evaluation can be a powerful tool for him, but only if he controls it and does not merely react to it. The administrator's control of an adequate evaluation process decreases that portion of his educational program that is determined by the particular forces, whims, and circumstances that are most spectacular at any given moment.

3

AN EVALUATION "NEEDS ASSESSMENT"

Gordon Hoke

The current surge of interest in evaluation and accountability, regardless of its varied causes, suggests that public education may be drastically changed in the 1970s. That conclusion is highly controversial, and there are numerous observers who staunchly believe that contemporary institutions of formal schooling have an infinite capacity for absorbing and nullifying reform. Nevertheless, in the late fall and winter of 1968/69, I was part of a field study on accountability in education that, viewed from today's perspective, was prophetic. The results of this pilot effort guided the development of a resource booklet in evaluation and accountability (Office of the Superintendent of Public Instruction 1969).

Although the participants were few—there were only sixteen—their responses underscored issues that are of even greater concern in 1973. Perhaps the diversity of respondents accounts for the broad span of pertinent topics. Classroom teachers, directors of demonstration centers, curriculum coordinators, building principals, superintendents (among whom were chief administrators of elementary districts and leaders of K-12 units operating in rural, urban, and suburban locales), top-level officials in a state department of education, and a county superintendent of schools all participated.

Each respondent submitted to a lengthy interview and completed a brief rating scale of attitudes toward evaluation. The project was divided into three stages and we obtained feedback from each phase.

The study was centered in Illinois, and limited efforts were conducted in Wisconsin and Indiana. The work was supported by a now defunct regional laboratory, the Cooperative Educational Research Laboratory, Inc. (CERLI), situated in the Chicago area, and the Center for Instructional Research and Curriculum Evaluation (CIRCE), at the University of Illinois at Urbana-Champaign. Designed as an attempt to assess the information that decision makers in educational administration were needing and to gather responses to an "evaluation kit" developed by CIRCE-CERLI personnel, the project failed in its original intent to capitalize on a demand for evaluation materials and services, because we had *presumed* the demand to exist. This attempt reflected the beliefs of university-affiliated research and development personnel that public school officials would respond to a need perceived from the outside in a manner deemed appropriate by those same outsiders. Historically, schools have adapted to changing pressures in a manner most congruent with the maintenance of institutional stability. Professional and lay critics have viewed such adaptation as an evasion of responsibility, but workers inside the system are, logically, more concerned with day-to-day survival in a sea of conflicting forces. Even today, when calls for accountability have reached a crescendo, the tendency to underestimate the sense of urgency, that is, the "now" atmosphere in which public schools function, pervades the writings of skeptics who live and operate in more leisurely fashion.

MAJOR ISSUES

The results of the field study pinpoint problems still confronting teachers and administrators on the one hand, and their adversaries on the other.

The Need for Translators

Demands for increased accountability may arise from a wide variety of sources; the rationale and models ultimately guiding data collection are usually fashioned by researchers. Our respondents cited the need for "translators" who could serve as middlemen between their institutional settings and new developments in other areas. (For an updated description of a role analogous to that of "translator," see the remarks of Sidney P. Marland, U.S. Commissioner of Education, on the "educational renewal extension agent" [1971].)

R. Schaefer, Dean of Teachers College, Columbia University, has outlined (1967) a place for "scholar-teachers" who could serve as local translators. Participants in the CIRCE-CERLI study were not enthusiastic about his idea. Schaefer's description, and the speculations of others about the establishment of specialized positions, places the translator somewhere outside the central administrative structure and could mean that his responsibility would lack adequate resources. In an era of serious funding difficulties for public education, it is very unlikely that any new role will become useful unless adequate resources—tangible and intangible—are allocated to it.

A curriculum coordinator in a prestigious suburban high school system in the Chicago area that relied on strong leadership by department chairmen expressed misgivings. If these instructional leaders are to act as local translators, he noted, they will require considerable training. Translators, it appears, would require excellent training programs and comprehensive support systems, for the problems confronting them would be formidable. (Wisconsin, for example, created a center for shared services, the Cooperative Education Services Agency (CESA), in 1968. The administrator of an elementary school district in Wisconsin expressed his approval of such centers, but thought that they needed general consultants who were familiar with the process approach to teaching and learning.) Our participants reported that teachers and administrators had distinctly different attitudes toward and needs for evaluation. Teachers are concerned mainly about accountability in the classroom. For them, evaluating is virtually synonymous with testing and grading, and few requested assistance with major components of program evaluation.

> Not only did administrators and teachers seem to have few mutual interests but each group related to the institute's content quite differently. Teachers experienced difficulty in relating to the material and recognizing its practical application to the local situation. Conversely, administrators found some of the material (statistics, for example) repetitious (Cooperative Educational Research Laboratory 1968, p. 42).

Evaluation as a Tool

A director of special programs for the Office of the Superintendent of Public Instruction (OSPI) reported that participating schools saw evaluation as another demand to justify what they were currently doing. He was supported by the director of a demonstration center, who stressed that visitors to his center regarded evaluation as a critical review of the past, an attempt to find out where mistakes had been made. Justification and criticism are part of accountability, but they are not the whole. There is no denying that formal evaluation reports have had little impact on program development. Yet, the primary responsibility of an evaluation effort, in the opinion of numerous evaluators, is to help improve the program being evaluated. Participants in the field study provided several illustrations of such a responsibility in situations that seemed applicable elsewhere.

According to the director of another demonstration center, program evaluation would foster improved articulation between the junior high and the senior high school. Teachers at the secondary level resented the way in which special projects were introduced into elementary grades and the junior high school. Program articulation continues to be a major problem for schools, and the increasing tempo of activity in early childhood education underscores the need to recognize that schools are parts of an interdependent system; interventions at one level should affect all others if program development is to have lasting results.

A third director visualized program improvement as being directly tied to in-service training. Both she and her superintendent saw the scarcity of effective supervisors as the chief obstacle in using evaluative feedback to improve practice. They mentioned the necessity for having someone inside the system act as a translator, a linkage person capable of expediting responses to demands for accountability. Skilled supervisors are still in short supply and their responsibilities have increased since 1968, partly because the New Careers Movement has been using schools as training grounds for paraprofessionals, instructional aides, and so forth. Many supervisors have been caught in the middle when the administrators were on one side of the bargaining table and the classroom teachers on the other.

Several participants in the study asked for instruments that would ascertain changes in students as individuals, not solely in their academic achievement. They were concerned about the influence of such intangibles as "school atmosphere," and charged that standardized measures are: culturally biased, to the disadvantage of the poor and various minority groups; misleading, when group tests are used to assess individual progress; measuring minor variables and failing to gauge the significance of elements outside the school. Such allegations are unlikely to cease; in fact, they may increase if teachers consider that demands for accountability seem unduly directed toward themselves.

Systematic Use of Feedback

Officials from OSPI predicted in 1968 that fiscal demands on the legislature would inevitably spawn pressure for more accountability at local levels. How right they were! Illinois is only one of many states to experience heated debates about the financing of public education. Arguments will certainly become even more intense, for legislatures and schools lack comprehensive procedures for using evaluative feedback.

One superintendent commented that a lack of communication among school administrators was preventing them from sharing information about their common problems and possible solutions. While his remarks reflected a criticism others have made of individuals who work in the broad realm of community development, many of education's difficulties are uniquely tied to local conditions. (An excellent treatment of the problems confronting proponents of educational and social change is to be found in Goodenough [1966], p. 15-34.)

OSPI personnel felt that information retrieval systems could not effectively interpret and synthesize data. Complex systems, such as NASA, MEDLARS, ERIC, were handicapped by their lack of working subsystems. Not one of the respondents in this study reported that he had used the national information systems in operation at the time and their remarks pinpointed two other defects of information systems for education. State offices hesitate to develop coordinated networks of data processing lest local endeavors foster a host of incompatible units. An inability to produce good quality information in easily assimilated form represented a fatal flaw in the eyes of legislators responsible for granting funds to finance the development of information systems and reinforced the reluctance of educators to rely on such services. We found, even in our limited study, that costly information systems have been launched on the basis of extremely sketchy assessments of the needs of those who will use them. Evaluation and accountability face the same hazard.

Two curriculum coordinators, one with a sophisticated background of training and work in a suburban school, the other an older, experienced person, with years of "school savvy" acquired while working in rural areas, agreed that schools required help in developing specific measures. "We need something, anything," the latter cried, "that can show that new programs, approaches, etc., are producing desirable changes with *our* students." He also wondered whether any improvement could be made in schools without making "structural changes," without modifying, for example, the school day, school week, or school year.

All of our respondents expressed the belief that both programs and evaluations were failing to deal with the major variables that affect student performance. Such misgivings will have increased since 1968.

Decision Makers

Superintendents of large city schools operate within a "political matrix," noted one of the participants, who himself spent most of his time as a power broker between community militants and the school board. In one context or another, all the chief administrators touched on the political dimensions of their roles.

Rural superintendents foresaw more school consolidation and reorganization, especially in high schools. These changes would be volatile, they feared, for their boards were still dominated by farmers.

Suburban officials reported that teachers were basically unaware of how much their role had been affected by new expectations on the part of an enlightened public. The art of discerning community opinion, a suburban elementary superintendent declared, "is politics in its purest form."

Rural and suburban administrators both considered that local residents placed an unrealistic value on district autonomy. At the same time, none of them minimized the emotion-laden issues embedded in mergers and consolidations. Their reservations were shared by OSPI staff, who insisted that major educational issues were certain to become political, and the "politics of education," in their opinion, demanded more knowledgeable responses from state and local school officials.

If knowledge and information are to stimulate a better understanding of what decision making requires, educators will need more time to reflect. They need assistance in conceptualizing problems, in devising strategies for attacking them—needs that were reported by respondents in 1968/69. There is no sign that they are less intense today. Indeed, fiscal pressures, at least, have increased.

SUMMARY

Evaluation accomplishes several aims, the report (1971) of a North Central Association study submits, adding: "it is somewhat less successful, however, in changing fixed practices within the school." Schmuck, a noted researcher in educational administration, cites (1968) the lack of knowledge utilization as an example of social psychological barriers. Admittedly, educators have, traditionally, made little use of the findings of behavioral science, but the barriers are more than inter- and intrapersonal.

Schools are vulnerable institutions. They operate constantly at the focal point of conflicts: responding to today's crisis, preparing for tomorrow's lessons, using the summer months to establish procedures for processing next year's students. As our respondents stressed, even with better communications, schools are likely to find their most difficult problems impervious to local resources and talents. Future evaluators must accept the fact that their information and their conclusions are only part of the picture. If evaluation is to affect practice, better methods will have to be developed for helping those individuals and groups who are responsible for the consequences of decisions that have been based on evaluative findings.

REFERENCES

Cooperative Educational Research Laboratory. *Report on the 1968 Summer Institute on Evaluation.* Northfield, Ill.: Cooperative Educational Research Laboratory Inc., (CERLI), 1968.

Goodenough, W. H. *Cooperation in Change: An Anthropological Approach to Community Development.* New York: John Wiley, 1966.

Marland, S. P. "Education U.S.A." *Washington Monitor* (6 December 1971): 83.

North Central Association. "Outcomes of School Evaluation." *North Central Association Quarterly* (Winter 1971): 303.

Office of the Superintendent of Public Instruction. "Evaluation and Accountability: A Resource Unit for Educators." Mimeographed. Springfield, Ill.: Superintendent of Public Instruction, Division of Research, Planning, and Development, 1969.

Schaefer, R. J. *The School as a Center of Inquiry.* New York: Harper and Row, 1967.

Schmuck, Richard "Social Psychological Barriers in Knowledge Utilization." In *Knowledge Production and Utilization in Educational Administration,* edited by T. Eidell and J. Kitchell. Eugene, Ore.: University of Oregon, Center for the Advanced Study of Educational Administration, 1968.

4

CAN EVALUATION BE USED
TO CUT COSTS?

Edward F. Kelly

"What does it profit a man if he evaluate his entire enterprise and suffer the loss of his mortal budget?" As accountability means increased public disclosure about educational programs, evaluation will be for some the process that leads to the unintended publication of negative or unfavorable information. Our biblical allusion reminds us that we may pay too great a price for evaluation. To choose, or, for that matter, to be required by law, to evaluate may mean that we must place limited resources in one enterprise rather than another. As most evaluations show little evidence of being effective, such allocations illustrate an abiding faith in some model of rational man or of obedience to a mandate rather than any esteem for the utility of evaluation.

If this is true, what shall we say about the relationship between evaluation and cost cutting? There appears to be no necessary relationship between the two, no more than there is between evaluation and any other specific criterion. In principle and, more often than not in practice, the two processes operate independently of each other. Nevertheless, the increasing clamor for accountability, the growing demands of students and the community, and decreasing funding and budgeting levels will no longer tolerate this separation of allocation, evaluation, and cost.

A COURSE DEVELOPMENT PROJECT

A project conducted by the Center for Instructional Development at Syracuse University provides us with an example of the difficulty and power of cost criteria as they relate to evaluation. Required courses in freshman composition had presented persistent problems; there was general dissatisfaction with their traditional format. The students were not happy with the lockstep lecture/discussion mode of instruction, and the faculty, faced with entering freshmen of disparate writing skills and with the double task of teaching both writing and introductory literary analysis, had tried various experimental approaches but with little success. The administration was concerned about the quality and efficiency of the large undergraduate classes in freshman composition and consequently placed a high priority on it.

The development team began redesigning the composition and literature course while working closely with faculty and with freshman students in English. The result was a three-level course in composition and literature that attempted to provide both flexibility and individualization. The course design (illustrated in figure 4:1) may be summarized:

After a battery of diagnostic tests in composition had been interpreted, students were assigned to one of the three course levels. Students clearly deficient in the mechanics of writing were assigned to the first level where they received intensive treatment for the specific deficiency: sentence structure, punctuation, agreement, or usage. Treatment consisted of commercially prepared programmed instructional materials and a weekly conference period that enabled students to seek private or group consultation. No credit was given for first-level work.

Students who scored above the first-level criterion in all four mechanical areas but who did not pass the written essay examination were assigned to the second level, which was designed to teach, review, and practice rhetorical principles. Organized as a writing clinic, the second-level instructors used tape recorded criticisms of the student essays as a feedback device instead of the traditional marginal notations. After writing two or three consecutive acceptable essays (all essays were graded pass/fail), students were passed out of the second level and given one credit.

Level III consisted of three major blocks of material. All students were required to complete the first block: two four-week programs in writing about fiction and writing about poetry. The completion of each of these units brought one credit respectively. In addition, Level III offered a wide range of optional additional credit available in the form of minicourses and independent studies. Minicourses of five weeks yielding one credit each were offered on a wide variety of topics that represented the diversity of faculty and student interests. Independent study formats required that the student compose a

FIGURE 4:1. INSTRUCTIONAL SEQUENCE FOR A FRESHMAN COURSE IN ENGLISH

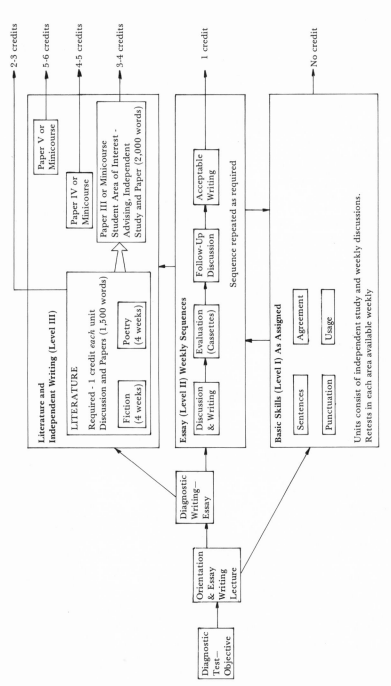

SOURCE: Student Manual - Freshman English (Experimental Section), Center for Instructional Development, Syracuse University, Fall 1971.

research paper on a topic of interest to him. If the topic fell outside the jurisdiction of the English department, it was graded for content on a pass/fail basis by a faculty member from the discipline concerned and, if judged passable, was graded for style by the English department. Each independent study paper judged acceptable on both criteria was worth one credit.

The evaluation that was conducted during the development and field testing of this project was designed to determine whether the intentions of the development staff and the English department were actually carried into practice.

INDICATORS OF COST

One of the English department's biggest problems had been its need for a large number of graduate assistants (usually more than seventy) to teach sections of freshman composition. It was important, therefore, that the redeveloped course be described in terms of its demand on faculty hours. This would make it possible to compare the redeveloped course with the traditional course and to estimate the altered need for faculty hours. Careful records were maintained of the students' progress through the three levels of the course at critical weeks during the semester. As a result of initial assignment, seventeen of the incoming students were assigned to Level III, twenty-nine to Level II, and fifty-four to Level I. By the sixth week of instruction, the pattern had altered to thirty-three, fifty-two, and fifteen; and, by the eleventh week, the final pattern was emerging: sixty-seven students had achieved Level III; twenty-six, Level II; and six were still at Level I.

We expected a logistical problem if the course were implemented later for a thousand or more students, so that our describing the flow of students through the course levels over the weeks of the semester was extremely useful. It enabled us to estimate staff requirements for a thousand students. We based this estimate on the answers to three questions:

1. How many students could a faculty member reasonably instruct on each of the three levels?
2. What was the flow pattern of students through the sequence and how did this pattern affect instructional load requirements?
3. Would there be any difference in faculty load when the new and the traditional patterns were compared?

Conversations and interviews with department faculty gave us the following estimates of traditional faculty teaching patterns:

1. Each full-time faculty member or graduate assistant in freshman composition normally instructed approximately forty students each semester.
2. We estimated that a single faculty member would be able to instruct up to sixty students in either of the required components of Level III.
3. At Level II, each faculty member would be able to instruct up to forty students. This figure represented the traditional teaching load.
4. Level I would require very few faculty because of its highly independent format. It was estimated that only one faculty member would be required for a hundred students, and he would be sufficient to accommodate students' requests for conferences and for clarification of individual problems.

The projection of staff requirements for one thousand students is presented in table 4:1. For each level of the course at the first, sixth, and eleventh week, the flow pattern observed during the field test was multiplied by ten in order to estimate the new pattern. Estimates of the number of graduate assistants were based on the judgment of the English faculty.

TABLE 4:1. REQUIREMENTS FOR GRADUATE ASSISTANTS (GAs), PROJECTED FOR 1000 STUDENTS

Course	1st week		6th week		11th week	
Level	Students	GAs	Students	GAs	Students	GAs
I	540	5½	150	1½	60	½
II	290	7	520	13	260	6½
III	170	3	330	5½	670	11
Total		15½		20		18

In the traditional mode, each faculty member taught up to forty students. For a student enrollment of one thousand, the traditional approach would require twenty-five instructors to maintain the 1:40 ratio. In the new course format, however, faculty time would be reduced by 20 to 40 percent for an enrollment of one thousand students. The new course format would free faculty at times to function at different levels of the course during the semester and would also enable them to attend to other concerns both inside and outside the freshman composition course. We made no effort whatsoever to translate the reduction of faculty time into dollars, but it was clear that the opportunity to reduce staff requirements was one of the advantages of the newly designed course.

We also examined the number of credits generated. With increasing attention to budget allocation, the number of credit hours generated for courses has been construed by some as an important indicator of product. Traditionally, approximately 6 percent of the students who enrolled in the freshman composition course each semester failed, and the typical enrollment pattern for 100 students would produce approximately 282 passing credits for this three-credit course. In the redesigned format, the field test population of one hundred students generated approximately 317 credits or an increase of more than 12 percent.

OTHER DATA COLLECTED

The faculty load and the credit hour generation were not the only parameters that had to be monitored. A brief summary of illustrative results may add pertinence to what is to follow. Faculty felt that, by the time students had completed Level III (one semester for most), their writing ability was at least equal to, if not better than, that traditionally achieved by the *end* of the *second* semester of freshman composition. Faculty also approved the varied teaching assignments that were available to them in the new format. The alternatives at Level III and the variety in assignments in Levels II and I increased the opportunity for specialization, for working with small groups of students, and for teaching brief courses (minicourses) on topics that were of interest to all. The redesigned format also seemed attractive to graduate assistants since it provided them with exposure to instruction in several different modes: writing laboratories, minicourses, and guided independent study.

Students' judgments of the course were also generally favorable, especially in the light of the traditionally poor reception given to freshman English courses. The students felt that they had learned; that the instructional sequence had used their time efficiently; and that the available options were beneficial and increased the relevance of the course to what they believed to be the important business of education.

The following representative student comments were taken from a summary questionnaire administered at the end of the field test:

> I enjoyed learning at my own rate more than listening to a boring lecture. I shall probably learn more this way.

> This tape helped me to see mistakes. I may have had troubles and didn't know why, but when they were pointed out, I could see they were wrong ... feel almost totally pleased with the second copy of my paper.

> It's not the typical dry stuff. You're working at your own rate, and your problems are pointed out to you. Because of the size of the school, ordinarily it would be almost impossible for the teacher to let the student know where the errors lie, and by this method you are able to hear directly from the teacher where the mistake is being made.

> I like it a lot because it allows you to work at your own pace and then it's possible for you to get through your freshman English requirement early, and I like the idea of having tapes instead of the comments on paper.

> I feel that this experimental course is excellent. Moving from Level II, I can assuredly say that I have learned so much, and for the first time I actually enjoy writing required papers and doing the assignments. The work is rewarding and the classes ... are definitely worthwhile.

The redesigned course received strong support from faculty in other disciplines as well. Many departments, having long requested that their students have an opportunity to write subject matter papers as part of the regular course requirements in English, cooperated in evaluating the specialized papers written at Level III.

What seems to emerge, even in this summary presentation of information, is that there is no single criterion for the judgment of effectiveness, even when that judgment is limited to a concern with changes in cost. The criterion of cost can be identified in more ways than simply in dollars and cents: the indices of comparisons and changes in instructional time, credit hour generation, the purchase and use of materials, faculty requirements, and data keeping and retrieval needs are in no way exhaustive of the broad range of cost factors that could be described in estimating the monetary impact of a development project.

It may be that some of the apparent cost reduction was actually absorbed by the students, who had to learn and practice new instructional patterns, and by faculty, who had to be willing and able to perform in specialized roles at several different levels of the course through the semester. The registrar's office *was* required to prepare a new system for tracking credit generation. Certainly these could also be counted as "costing" something: in the latter case, money; in the former two cases, possibly something more akin to custom, or patience, or style. There are many ways to determine cost.

Information collected during an evaluation can be used to examine costs. Some say that we need to emphasize cost more now than we have in the past. Particularly in the realm of the didactics of instruction or that part of human knowledge of facts, principles, and rules that can be transmitted easily through some technological device, there appears to be an opportunity to increase the efficiency of instruction and disencumber the lecture hall and classroom. It is probably on this basis that the programmed material of Level I and the use of tape recorded criticisms on Level II can be most easily justified.

II

POLITICS AS USUAL

Often evaluators believe that they are free of any concerns outside their "science." A cursory examination of any evaluation project will reveal this to be false. Evaluation affects the allocation of resources. As such it is an intensely political activity, and is affected by politics and in turn affects politics. That does not mean it is dishonest. Rather it is intimately involved with negotiations and relationships between people. It is the purpose of this section to try to untangle some of those complex relationships and explicate the role evaluation can play. A major theme of this book is that evaluation is one way a group justifies its behavior to other groups. In a pluralistic society that function is important.

Much ferment has been created by higher government units trying to evaluate the lower ones. Most states are developing their own assessment programs. Usually these are statewide testing programs with some provision for holding local districts accountable for the test scores. One of the most fully developed is the Michigan education assessment. The conflict between the state and local districts was dramatically emphasized in recent hearings before the U. S. Senate Select Committee on Equal Educational Opportunity. The issue at stake in the federal hearings was whether some federal programs should be subject to similar controls. It has been proposed that Title I of the Elementary and Secondary Education Act (ESEA) be funded according to test scores.

Kearney presents the argument for the Michigan Department of Education. He defines *assessment* as the determination over time of the outcomes of education in light of different contingencies. The Michigan approach makes five assumptions: first, that there are many influences on educational outcomes other than schooling, which suggests collecting many measures other than output; second, that in spite of different programs, there are goals common to all programs; third, that those goals can be accurately measured, if cautiously interpreted; fourth, that the resources are inequitably distributed; and fifth, that such information will be useful. Kearny concludes that the real utility of the assessment lay in highlighting the inequitable distribution of resources among districts.

The article on the Michigan assessment reveals in the clearest possible manner the political nature of evaluation. Kearney and Huyser recount blow for blow how the Michigan Department of Education was forced to reveal test scores for individual districts. At first local districts were promised that local scores would not be made public. Generally state officials were for such reporting and school people were opposed. However, once scores showing relative standings of districts were made available to local school people, a storm of demand came from legislators for the same data. At first, the state department resisted. The fiery exchange of letters between the state superintendent and one legislator is highly amusing and informative. Like all bureaucracies under political pressure, the department finally crumbled. Local test scores were made public. Local superintendents were incensed; one charged that, "the [program] is really politics, masquerading as research." As the authors note, assessment programs are political. As such they must serve the interests of competing groups. All in all, the Michigan assessment has been the center of more controversy than any other educational program in the state.

"The Michigan State Assessment program is reactionary, unprofessional, undemocratic, and if permitted to continue on its present course will cause irreparable damage to public education in this state." This is the indictment made by Lawrence Read, Superintendent of the Jackson, Michigan, Public Schools, also before the Senate Select Committee. While asserting that there is a place for evaluation and assessment, Read contends that the Michigan program simply amounts to comparative testing. That's all. As such it will ultimately be used to coerce people. Read objects to comparative testing on three grounds. The first argument is philosophical: such testing enforces the behaviorist view of the world, which says that an individual's learning must be entirely shaped by others and that the purpose of schooling is to prepare for life in a competitive world. Opposed to this is the humanist's view of learning, which says that learning is its own reward.

The second argument is based on research evidence, which, Read contends, is overwhelmingly opposed to the efficacy of such an approach. It is unrealistic to expect payoff from instruction to be registered in test scores. The tests do not measure very important factors and, in fact, their validity is questionable.

The third argument against testing is one of common sense. No matter how hard one tries, in comparative testing 50 percent will always be below average. The only alternative is for Michigan schools to practice large-scale deception. Public misunderstanding of test scores is likely to increase public dissension and be unfair to various individuals. Two principals have already been fired because of test results over which they had no control. The outcome will be a sterile unproductive system. Already state officials have commented that the locals have failed and the next step might be centralization. The ultimate purpose of the system, according to Read, is centralized control. This may be the result of charlatans offering panaceas.

Much of the pressure for evaluation has come from the federal government trying to account for money. The U. S. Office of Education is mandated by Congress to evaluate its programs. Ordinarily this requirement is passed on to the states. In turn the state departments of education put evaluation pressure on the local districts. Kerins describes in brutally realistic a fashion the current state of affairs: "Title I evaluations are a joke." A good part of the problem results from the state agencies confusing *monitoring*—being a watchdog for public funds—with *evaluation*—examining the effectiveness of programs for children. What happens is that auditors try to evaluate and evaluators end up auditing. The actual evaluation reports are miserable. And no one at the federal, state, or local level is happy. Kerins' solution is to split the monitoring and evaluation functions so that evaluators could help local people do real evaluations.

Besides being used by one group to coerce another, there is another way in which evaluation results are political—they are often used by the program only when they are favorable. Carter illustrates what often happens to evaluation findings. With numerous examples from both education and business, he contends that most findings contrary to the beliefs of the clients are too threatening. They are selectively ignored or refuted. Only those that agree with the preconceptions of the clients are acted upon. This is as true in business as in education, in universities as in elementary schools. Carter sees evaluation as essentially reinforcing the status quo.

Carter is certainly correct about the reluctance to immediately accept negative findings. This in itself is a finding of social science. Less certain is his contention that the client's self-image and ideology are always perpetuated. Even though immediately rejected, such findings may eventually affect the client's practice. Carter also underestimates the difficulty and importance of legitimizing programs to various publics, especially in institutions like the public schools. Nonetheless, he is correct in contending that evaluation that becomes "research for the sake of research" is debilitating in the long run.

The last two chapters in this section directly analyze the political nature of evaluation. Cohen argues that evaluation is political to the extent that information is a basis for changing power relationships. This is more likely to be true the larger the program because the political competition will be more intense. Concern is proportional to the political stakes involved. Evaluation is seen by the local and state people (correctly) as an attempt by the federal government to assert federal priorities.

However, when the evaluator tries to evaluate a program such as Title I, ESEA, he is often misdirected. Title I is in reality the educational equivalent of the harbors and rivers bill: there is no provision for withdrawal of funds; the distribution of money itself is considered a positive good. Any rational resource allocation scheme is seriously weakened by this formula granting of funds. This reflects the vested interests and decentralized power structure of the school system. Ordinarily evaluators do not recognize the diversity and conflict that such programs must naturally entail. Being fuzzy- and single-minded, they fail to grasp the diverse nature of such social action programs. Ultimately evaluators must attend more to program delivery than to traditional outcome measures.

Finally, since all evaluations are imbued with these political considerations, what good are they? House tries to show a way out of this dilemma. Arguing that all evaluations proceed from biased origins, usually either to attack or defend a particular program, he holds that that bias does not necessarily invalidate the study. All knowledge is biased but some of it is also true. He distinguishes between the circumstances of the origin of an idea and its justification. Ideas always arise from biased circumstances but in order publicly to probe or justify an idea we must move into the "context of justification."

It is the public justification of an idea or program that determines its worth. The evaluator may be for a program yet he must show, through the use of accepted techniques, the presumed benefits of the program. This often involves the use of "scientific" paraphernalia such as experimental design or statistics. Often it involves more common sense notions, such as testimonials from the people involved. Finally House adds that the evaluator must also take some responsibility for persuading people that the results are useful.

5

THE POLITICS OF
REPORTING RESULTS

C. Philip Kearney & Robert J. Huyser

> The [program] is really politics masquerading as
> research. Promise after promise has been broken.
> Plans have been dictated and changed by the Legisla-
> ture . . . . It is not an operational purpose of the as-
> sessment project to improve instruction by identify-
> ing promising practices . . . . The conclusions were
> written before the project was undertaken . . . . Edu-
> cators at the district level have not been included in
> designing the tests and are not included in plans for
> the development of future tests (Grosse Pointe Public
> Schools Administration 1970).

In such fashion did the central curriculum staff of one of Michigan's suburban school districts view the implementation of the
1969/70 Michigan Educational Assessment Program. Perhaps no program administered by the Michigan Department of Education has
received more publicity or been the center of as much political controversy.

The writers have been—and continue to be—involved in administering the Michigan Educational Assessment Program and, therefore,
cannot be considered as unbiased observers. No doubt we suffer from
the problem of personal bias, from the problem of paying heed to
convention and good taste, and from what Gottschalk (1963) has
termed "egocentrism"—namely, the tendency of even a modest participant observer to recount his words and actions as if they were the
most important things said and done.

Ours is an overview or "broad brushstroke" attempt to identify
and describe certain of the key administrative events and activities of
the program, not a systematic study of educational policymaking. A

great deal of the documentary evidence was available to us, but we made no systematic attempt to interview the many participants and, as Bailey has pointed out (1950), live sources should be used in a study of policymaking for "what is committed to writing represents only the seventh of the iceberg above water."

THE BACKGROUND

Late in 1968, three staff members of the Michigan Department of Education's Bureau of Research began to discuss the lack of reliable information about the level, distribution, and progress of education in the state. These discussions led to the proposal that the department undertake a pioneering effort in Michigan—a statewide educational assessment program. Although it would be a radical step for the department (and for Michigan), and was fraught with potential controversy, the proposal was received with considerable enthusiasm and supported by both the State Superintendent of Public Instruction and the State Board of Education. (For an overview of the 1969/70 effort, see Kearney, Crowson, and Wilbur 1970.) Perhaps because of the rising concern about accountability in education the idea received the support and endorsement of the state legislature and the governor.

It also had its share of opponents—and resultant political problems. The active political participants included the department, the legislature, the governor's office, the press, the schools, professional education groups, parent and citizen groups, and individuals, all of whom exerted considerable influence, both directly and indirectly, on the program. (For a description of their activities, see Kearney 1970.)

The Purposes of the 1969/70 Program

In the first public report (Michigan Department of Education 1969) the assumption was made that "the most important education-related problem facing the State—and indeed the nation—is the inequitable distribution of school district performance levels and their correlates." Several studies in Michigan indicate that some school systems provide a better education than others. The 1967 Michigan School Finance Study, proposed by the State Board of Education and supported by the state legislature, indicated that affluent school systems provide their students with more special classes, programs and curricula, better qualified instructional staff, and better facilities than the less affluent districts (Thomas 1968). Guthrie and others (1969) conclude that, in general, "high quality school services are provided to children from wealthy homes. Poor quality school services are provided to children from poor homes." Thus the basic purpose of the program was to provide members of the State Board of Education and the legislature with information needed for allocating the state's educational resources to equalize and improve the educational opportunities for all children. The 1969/70 assessment program was designed to answer four questions:

1. For the state as a whole, what are the present levels of educational performance and the levels of certain factors related to performance, such as staffing, expenditure, and economic status?
2. For Michigan's geographic regions and community types, what are the present levels of educational performance and the levels of certain factors related to performance?
3. Do schools that score high (or low or average) on certain factors related to performance also score similarly on the performance measures?
4. What changes over time may be noted in the answers to the previous three questions?

A parallel but subsidiary purpose was to assist local school districts to identify needs and priorities. The relative emphases on these two purposes were considerably reshuffled after the 1969/70 program.

REPORTING THE 1969/70 RESULTS

One of the major limitations in any statewide assessment arises from inherent political considerations. "Accountability" is essentially a political word; assessment programs are essentially political programs. By this we do not mean that they are essentially "evil" (as the authors of our opening quotation hold); we mean simply that they must serve competing groups to whom the persons or agency charged with developing, implementing, and reporting on the program must pay heed.

Whether or not to report publicly, by school district, the comparative results of the assessment was an issue that plagued the program from its inception. (It is also an issue that has plagued, and continues to plague, the national assessment effort.) On the one hand, there is the argument that such reporting serves no good purpose and, because of misinterpretation, leads to invidious comparisons. On the other hand, there is the argument that such data should be public

information and that the public—as well as the legislature—has a right
to know how its schools are doing. Legislators and state officials
seem to favor, and indeed expect, public disclosure of comparative
data. School superintendents, administrators, and teachers generally
oppose public disclosure. Parents and students—at least in Michigan—
have yet to come out strongly on either side of the issue, although
there is a growing indication that parents favor public disclosure once
they become aware that comparative data on performance are available. The press generally advocates public disclosure.

In the initial design of the 1969/70 assessment program, the department attempted to strike a compromise on the issue by establishing a three-part policy on reporting (Michigan Department of Education 1969). First, the assessment program was designed to gather
data, not only on performance or output measures, but also on the
conditions or circumstances under which each district operated.
These input factors included measures of each district's financial
resources, human resources (the teaching staff), the socioeconomic
level of the students, and their attitudes and aspirations. The design
was to provide data in such fashion that outputs would always be
interpreted in relation to inputs.

Second, the school districts of the state were categorized into five
community types and four geographic regions. Thus, comparisons
could be made among community types and among geographic regions, as well as among combinations of the two—for example, large
urban and suburban districts, or city school districts in northern and
southeastern Michigan. Under this arrangement no single school district would need to be identified publicly.

Third, the department stated publicly that it would neither prepare nor publish any ranking of Michigan school districts based on
1969/70 assessment results. In effect, the department had gone on
record as stating it would not release data on individual local school
districts to anyone but local school administrators—unless forced to
do so by external factors. This policy was made, not by formal
action of the State Board of Education, but by several senior administrators in the department, including the State Superintendent.
The State Board gave its tacit approval to this policy when it adopted
and disseminated its first assessment report. The staff recognized
that, if put to the test, they might well have to rescind this policy or,
at least, considerably modify it.

The first public report was distributed on 24 June 1970, an additional report was released in September, and a report, sent to each of
Michigan's public school districts during the latter part of August,

1970, included the local assessment scores, which the State Superintendent encouraged each superintendent to make public (Michigan Department of Education 1970, 1970a, 1970b).

The latter report provoked pressure, from several sources, for comparative data, in one document, on all the schools in the state or, at least, on the schools in any given region. Requests from the press were referred to local superintendents. Requests from the state government provided the strongest pressures.

Requests from the Governor's Office

The governor was interested in and supported the assessment. It was the governor who signed the budget bill that included $250,000 for the department's 1969/70 assessment program. (While the State Board of Education had the power to mandate a statewide assessment program, the program also required a relatively high level of funding. The only source of such funds was the legislature. Two possibilities existed: to seek new legislation that would not only mandate the program but also provide the necessary funds; or to establish the program and acquire the funds through the simple expedient of having a line item added to the department's annual budget for operations. Both alternatives required legislative approval, but the latter had the advantage of not treating the program as an entirely new and separate legislative issue. Thus, in seeking initial legislation, the decision was made to ask for an addition to the department's budget bill.) It was the governor who introduced, supported, and subsequently signed Act No. 38 of the Public Acts of 1970 which, while it changed the thrust of the program somewhat, gave the assessment effort its own basis in statute. How was a state agency —which, although independent of the governor, was a branch of the government—going to respond to the governor's legitimate request for comparative assessment data on all Michigan school districts when it was the agency's policy that no ranking of individual districts would be publicly available? And, if we acceded to the governor, how could we refuse legislative committees, individual legislators, or—for that matter—individual citizens?

Requests from the Legislature

Nor were legislators hesitant to throw forward their challenge. The local district report included tables of normative data and explanatory materials prepared to assist superintendents in interpreting their school district's scores, the actual scores on all assessment measures for the district and for each of the schools in the district, and data for a hypothetical district, Michville, to illustrate the scores. A copy of the local report, without any actual data on school districts, was sent to each member of the legislature. The two public reports on assessment results, which did not identify individual school districts, produced little reaction among legislators; the release of the local reports brought on a torrent of requests by legislators for actual data on "their" districts. The requests were made formally and informally, by letter, telephone, and word-of-mouth. The Chairman of the Senate Appropriations Committee, the House Appropriations Committee, the House Education Committee, the House Special Committee on the Quality of Elementary and Secondary Schools, the Legislative Fiscal Agency, and several individual legislators all wanted the data. A number of individual members of the State Board of Education felt quite strongly that public disclosure of the data should be made.

The department was caught squarely between legislators and other state officials who demanded the data, and local school personnel who felt they had been assured that no such disclosure would be made. Reluctant to reverse arbitrarily the original policy and in an attempt to gain time, the department undertook to review its reporting policies. Legislators were not content to wait. One particularly impatient member of the Michigan House of Representatives, upon receiving a copy of the local district report, wrote to the Director of the Bureau of Research:

> Regretfully I have not yet received the scores for my school districts.
>
> I am not concerned with Michville. Therefore at your earliest convenience please provide me with my local school districts' tables and scores. My districts are: ____ , ____ , and ____ .
>
> I regret the Department has not provided the Legislature with this relevant information. I am sure you would agree that there is nothing secretive about it, and this is merely an oversight on the part of the Department (Member, Michigan House of Representatives to Director, Bureau of Research, 4 September 1970).

The Director of the Bureau of Research replied:

> Thank you for your letter . . . regarding release of local district assessment scores. The Superintendent of

Public Instruction was recently authorized to explore the releasing of local results to legislators. Therefore, [he] is discussing the release of data from the local schools with the appropriate local administrators and will write you shortly regarding this matter (Director to Member, 30 September 1970).

The legislator would have none of this:

Thank you for your letter . . . in response to mine . . . in which I requested that you forward to me my local school district assessment scores. You indicated that [the State Superintendent] is discussing the release of this data with appropriate local school administrators and will communicate shortly regarding this matter.

. . . I cannot stress too strongly my shock and amazement at this tactic. Whether or not local school administrators wish to have this information released to legislators is no concern of mine nor should it be of the Department's. As a legislator, it is my position that I have an absolute right to the test data.

. . . Secrecy and the withholding of information is a classic bureaucratic technique which has no place in a free society. I am not unmindful of the reasons the Department will attempt to put forth as to why such scores should remain secret, and I am unconvinced by them.

Therefore I expect by return mail the test results of my school districts (Member to Director, 9 October 1970).

Facing the inevitable, the State Superintendent wrote to the legislator:

I received a carbon copy of your letter to [the Director]. Let me assure you our office does provide the test data to legislators. [The Director's] reference to our office establishing a procedure for releasing such data goes back to a previous commitment which indicated, in the initial assessment document, that this information would not be made available. The State Board of Education has since that time modified that position. (State Superintendent of Public Instruction to Member, 13 October 1970).

The legislator's response was brief:

> I am delighted with your response to my inquiry concerning test scores for my area schools. I am pleased that the Board has this kind of policy.
>
> P.S. When can I expect the test scores for my area schools? (Member to State Superintendent, 15 October 1970).

However, the legislator did see fit to drive home his point in a letter, written one day later, to the staff member concerned—and, of course, he sent a copy to the State Superintendent:

> Yesterday's [local newspaper] carried a most interesting story in which our Superintendent of Schools discussed at some length the test scores for [his] students. While this makes interesting reading, I would still prefer to have a report from your Department.
>
> I would greatly appreciate it if you could find time in your busy day to forward me this information, as per [the Superintendent's letter] . . . Perhaps if you communicated less with my local superintendent concerning this problem, you would be able to stuff an envelope with this information in thirty seconds.
>
> I intend to amend the law next year to make it mandatory that legislators receive this information prior to the Department of Education's releasing it to the superintendents. If you play the game that way, we'll just change the ground rules (Member to Director, 16 October 1970).

The final chapter in this episode was written by the State Superintendent in two letters to the legislator.

> As per your request, I am pleased to indicate that consistent with the State Board of Education's policy of September 8, and procedures which we are formulating, I have obtained a copy of the Michigan basic skills printout for [the school districts in the legislator's area].
>
> I also wish to inform you that staff has discussed the release of this data with [the local superin-

tendents concerned] and each of them has assured
staff that they would be most pleased to have their
representative staff sit down with you and discuss this
data in greater detail.

As you may know, the first document prepared on
the Assessment Program indicated to school districts
that this information would not be released to the
public. However, due to changes in Section 3, and to
the advice of the Attorney General's office, we are
now aware of the fact that such information cannot
be withheld, especially from public officials. I would,
however—and I need not share this with you—indicate
that we are moving cautiously in this area because of
the great deal of concern of local school officials regarding comparisons that might be made among districts without a full explanation (State Superintendent to Member, 16 October 1970).

The legislator, upon receiving that letter and the results for "his"
districts, acknowledged the department's efforts and thanked the
State Superintendent for his assistance. The State Superintendent
then wrote his final letter:

Thank you for your letter . . . indicating to me that
you received the test score results.

As you know, I made the recommendation to provide such information to public officials to the State
Board of Education . . . I have been criticized by
school officials as a result of taking this position.
Consequently there is no one who would be more
pleased with a legislative act authorizing the distribution of these scores, and thereby clarifying this issue,
than myself (State Superintendent to Member, 23
October 1970).

Copies of this letter were sent to members of the State Board of
Education, members of the House Education Committee, the Chair-
man and the leading minority member of the Senate Appropriations
Committee, the Chairman of the Senate Education Committee, the
Chairman and the leading minority representative of the House Ap-
propriations Committee, and the staff assistant to the Speaker of the
House.

The disclosure was greeted with mixed reactions from local school district administrators. Some saw it as inevitable and chose to remind the department staff that "we told you so." Others were greatly disturbed by this chameleon maneuver:

> The complete breaking of trust between the State Department of Education and the local districts in terms of releasing 1969/70 scores [on assessment] is extremely unethical (School District Superintendent to Department of Education, 25 October 1970).

It was this disclosure that provoked the accusations, quoted at the beginning of this chapter, made by the Grosse Pointe Public Schools Administration.

Section 3 of the State Aid School Act

The decision to release the results of the 1969/70 assessment publicly was reinforced by an additional turn of events. During the 1968 session of the legislature, there was added to the state School Aid Act a section that established an aid program for schools marked by a "high degree of economic and cultural deprivation." Approximately $6.3 million in additional aid was allocated to forty-seven Michigan schools during the 1968/69 academic year (Michigan Department of Education 1969a). The program, with the same criteria but more money was continued during the 1969/70 school year. In the 1970/71 School Aid Act, the legislature allocated $17.5 million and changed the criteria.

Section 3 of the 1970/71 School Aid Act requires that, to be eligible, individual schools have a high percentage of poor and underachieving students. The criteria were based on the results of the 1969/70 assessment of each school for grade 4. A school falling in the bottom quartile on composite achievement received points in relation to its rank within that quartile—one point if it were at the twenty-fifth percentile, twenty-five points if it fell at the first percentile. In addition, a school falling in the bottom quartile when judged on its relative socioeconomic level also received points—from one to ten points, depending upon its percentile ranking (Mich. Public Acts 100, ch. 1, § 3 [1970]).

The legislation, in effect, required that the department prepare a ranking of all schools in the state and be prepared to release the point scores (and thus the relative standing) of all schools falling in the bottom quartile on two of the assessment measures: composite achievement and relative socioeconomic level. Thus, for practical purposes, the Section 3 legislation removed from the department's jurisdiction the question of whether or not assessment results would be released publicly, and left it no alternative but to modify its policy—the entreaties of local school personnel notwithstanding. The scores of individual districts were made available to legislators and other public officials. The Department is now preparing for public release a district-by-district summary of the results of the 1969/70 assessment program.

As a final "hardening" of the new policy, the state Board of Education has stated that it intends to release local assessment results from the 1970/71 program:

> The controversial statewide "educational assessment" testing program is being revamped for next year to make the results more useful and more public.

> The State Board of Education intends to publicly release local assessment results, rather than relying on local districts to voluntarily publicize results for their schools.

> The State Board itself will release all local results this time because of new state . . . legislation requiring at least some of the data to be made public and apparently because of [the] feeling that some local school boards and superintendents weren't voluntarily releasing all the information.

> The State Board and some legislators have long wanted to ensure that all pertinent data would be released, to help parents and taxpayers get a better idea of how well their students are doing compared with other districts (Cote 1970).

REPORTING DESIGN FOR 1970/71

The manner in which the 1970/71 assessment results will be reported has been changed. The initial designers of the assessment program were concerned primarily with providing information for state-level decisions about the allocation or distribution of educational resources. The 1969/70 program was designed so that the basic—or smallest—unit of analysis was a school building. The measures of socioeconomic status, attitude, and performance were constructed to yield reliable scores for groups of pupils—not for individual pupils. Consequently, no reports of the results of individual pupils was or could be made.

Many persons—including local school district officials and the governor—were not satisfied with a program that did not deliver scores for individual pupils, nor furnish local school personnel with information needed to construct better programs or curricula. (See, for example, Grosse Pointe Public Schools Administration 1970.) While local educators generally agreed that the assessment program might furnish information about more equitable allocation of educational resources, they were more concerned with acquiring information that would help them to design or redesign programs for the children in their local schools. They felt strongly that the assessment program should give equal emphasis to providing useful data for local decisions; they felt a need to be able to report the results of individual pupils to teachers, parents, and the pupils themselves.

This concern was echoed—and given great prominence—by none other than the governor. As a result of the work of his Commission on Educational Reform (1970) (and see also H. B. 3886, Mich. Special Sess. [1969]), he wanted legislation that would not only give a solid statutory base to the assessment effort but also ensure that the program would be designed to identify *individual students* "who have extraordinary need for assistance to improve their competence in the basic skills (Michigan, House of Representatives 1969)." Remedial assistance programs, funded by the state, were then to be made available to local districts to raise the basic skills of the pupils identified. This legislation did become law and so the question of whether to continue with measures reliable only for groups or to move to measures reliable for individual pupils became moot (Mich. Public Acts 38 [1970]). Thus, the assessment effort was redesigned and its two basic purposes would receive equal emphasis. For an overview of the 1970/71 program see Michigan Department of Education 1970c.

REFERENCES

Bailey, S. K. *Congress Makes a Law*. New York: Columbia University Press, 1950.

Cote, W. E. "State School Test Being Revamped After Criticism." *Flint Journal* (16 December 1970), p. 10.

Gottschalk, Louis. *Understanding History*. New York: Alfred A. Knopf, 1963.

Grosse Pointe Public Schools Administration, Department of Instruction. "The Michigan Assessment of Basic Skills: A Summary of Concerns." October 1970.

Guthrie, J. W., Kelindorfer, G. B., Levin, H. M., and Stoot, R. T. *Schools and Inequality: A Study of Social Status, School Services, Student Performance, and Post School Opportunity in Michigan.* N. p., Urban Coalition, 1969.

Kearney, C. Philip. "The Politics of Educational Assessment in Michigan." *Planning and Changing* 1, no. 2 (July 1970): 71-82.

Kearney, C. Philip, Crowson, Robert L., and Wilbur, Thomas P. "Improved Information for Educational Decision-Making: The Michigan Assessment Program." *Administrator's Notebook* 18, no. 6 (February 1970).

Michigan, *Act 38, Public Acts 1970.*

Michigan, *Act 100, Public Acts 1970,* chap. 1, sec. 3.

Michigan Department of Education. "Purposes and Procedures of the Michigan Assessment of Education." Assessment Report no. 1. Lansing, Mich., 1969.

Michigan Department of Education. "A Description and Evaluation of Section 3 Projects in Michigan, 1968-69." Lansing, Mich., 1969(a).

Michigan Department of Education. "Levels of Educational Performance and Related Factors in Michigan." Assessment Report no. 4. Lansing, Mich., 1970.

Michigan Department of Education. "Distribution of Educational Performance and Related Factors in Michigan." Assessment Report no. 5. Lansing, Mich., 1970 (a).

Michigan Department of Education. "Local District Report." Assessment Report no. 6. Lansing, Mich., 1970 (b).

Michigan Department of Education. "Objectives and Procedures of the 1970-71 Michigan Educational Assessment Program." Assessment Report no. 7. Lansing, Mich., 1970 (c).

Michigan, House of Representatives. *H. B. 3886.* Special Session, 1969.

Michigan. *Report of the Governor's Commission on Educational Reform.* Lansing, Mich., 1970.

Thomas, A. J. *School Finance and Educational Opportunity in Michigan.* Lansing, Mich.: Michigan Department of Education, 1968.

6

AN ASSESSMENT OF THE
MICHIGAN ASSESSMENT

Lawrence F. Read

A comprehensive and continuing testing program is a
powerful educational instrument (Cook 1932).

The Michigan State Assessment Program is reactionary, unprofessional, undemocratic and, if permitted to continue on its present course, will cause irreparable damage to public education in this state.

The word *assessment* means evaluation and appraisal, and no rational person will deny the need to evaluate and appraise the progress of education. The truly professional educator has always been and will always be anxious and eager to assess educational progress.

It is exceedingly unfortunate, therefore, that the Michigan State Education Department confuses assessment and appraisal with comparative testing. Despite the department's protests to the contrary, the only significant component of the current Michigan assessment program is standardized testing.

To avoid confusion about terms, I will deal primarily with the comparative academic testing aspects of the Michigan State Assessment Program because this, in effect, is the program. The other components may have some minor academic significance but, for state officials, comparative academic testing is really synonymous with assessment. The use of normative and comparative test data to determine what children have learned and how we can help them learn more is not the real intent of the Michigan Assessment Program. Comparative testing in the hands of any authority, no matter how benign it may be, will ultimately be used to coerce. The threat of a test makes the student do his assignment; the results of the test enable the authority to reward those who do his bidding and punish those who will not conform. Left unchallenged, the state is likely to use this powerful instrument of testing to impose stringent, rigid, and unprofessional restraints on students, classroom teachers and local school districts. If the state assumes that tests can be valid assessment instruments, its returns will have to be used to force change. Perhaps this is necessary and it may be unavoidable. Before it comes to pass, however, the issues should be thoroughly defined, discussed, and analyzed.

STANDARDIZED TESTING

> I suspect that if we can deliver the basic skills, we will find that the attitudes, the self-esteem, the self-concept and all of these peripheral areas will fall into place. When you teach a black kid, or Spanish speaking kid or a poor white how to read and write, you are in effect teaching that kid a self-concept that is positive and I don't buy the argument that you have to spend a lot of time humanizing him (Porter 1971).

Philosophic Implications

Recently behaviorism has had an amazing revival. Relying largely on the writings of Skinner, Watson, and others, those who support this philosophy contend that education is simply one big Pavlovian process of conditioning. The behaviorist starts with the assumption that the individual is essentially not free and, as a consequence, his learning must be directed by those who are wise enough to know what he must learn and how he must learn it. Usually, children are conceived of in terms of pieces of clay that must be shaped and molded by the omniscient authority.

There is little place for emotions, feelings, attitudes, individuality or self-image in the behaviorist's plans for education. To him, these are peripheral, vague, and cannot be measured. Learning is largely directed to the basic academic skills of reading, writing, and number usage, which are deemed sufficient for a constructive and competitive role in the economy and society as a whole. The behaviorist is deeply concerned with developing a system of education that will produce an individual who can become an efficient and well-disciplined laborer in a technocratic and competitive world; hence, he refers frequently to the school as a microcosm of the society it serves.

His philosophy demands an educational system that resorts to external and competitive devices such as marks, honor societies, certificates, plaques and, most important, continuous and constant testing to keep the learner and the teacher in line. The behaviorist cannot conceive of learning as its own reward. He is prone to anxiety and does not believe that teachers and learners, if left to their own devices, can possibly succeed. Because he cannot trust, he must constantly use reward and punishment conditioning. Success, in terms of conforming to the authority's value system, is rewarded; creativity expressed through nonconformity is punished. The behaviorist views educational output only in terms of the acquisition of certain basic skills that are valued by the society. These skills are taught through a conditioning process that uses external competitive devices based on a reward and punishment psychology. Essential to this process is a system of testing that motivates better conditioning, limits the scope of the conditioning, and gives the authority information on how well or how poorly the conditioning is operating.

All of this can be appealing to the inexperienced or unsophisticated observer of the educational scene. It is a simple, precise, and easily understood process that manifests many of the common homilies and prejudices of the prior conditioning of most adults. Unfortunately, since adults have been programmed in this way, they can hardly be expected to fault it if they have been successful.

Erasmus was an early nonconformist who suggested that education was more than rote learning. In 1497, he wrote:

> I have no patience with the teacher who spends his time making students learn the rules of grammar while neglecting the beauty, power, and scope of language.

Since Erasmus, there have been numerous philosophers who have expressed the basic concept of humanism. In contrast to the behaviorist, the humanist is deeply concerned about individual man—his freedom and his destiny. He does not believe that education exists merely to perpetuate an existing social order. Instead, he sees education as a vehicle for improving man and his capacity to live and work with others. The humanist, in education, is willing to deal with facts and knowledge organized into systematic subject areas, not for their own sake, but only as they interrelate and contribute to individual learning. His only dogma is an unwavering belief in the worth, basic goodness, and dignity of each learner as a unique person with the capacity to grow and mature.

The humanist educator accepts the learner as he is rather than what it is thought he should be, acknowledging that what he is is neither to his credit nor his shame. The learner is never judged on how his talents compare with those of others, but on how well he uses his talents. For the humanist, the purpose of education is to help each learner know himself, respect himself, and become himself as he learns to work with and for others.

Humanistic philosophy regards the development of skill in the schools as incidental to broader humanistic goals. Learning experiences are geared to individual rather than group standards, in an environment in which learning and achievement are their own rewards. Skills are acquired from the individual's self-determined need and desire, without external devices that compare, reward, and punish. Individual feeling, emotion, attitude, self-concept, and self-image are the major concerns because they have a powerful influence on learning. The humanist is forced to reject all testing unless it is used to assist individual learning.

> There is no reason except to relieve our own anxieties and insecurity that we should constantly know what children are learning. What true education requires of us is faith and courage—faith that children want to make sense out of life and will work hard at it, courage to let them do it without continually poking, prodding and meddling (Holt 1969).

It should be recognized that, while American tradition supports the humanistic approach not only in education but for all major social problems, actual educational performance has been largely an expression of behaviorist philosophy. It is difficult indeed to find a truly humanistic educational model while behaviorism abounds in public school classrooms and is quite possibly the cause of much of the current unrest in the schools.

Legitimate reform of education will require a serious, dedicated effort by professionals, and the public, to establish a truly humanistic climate in the schools. This is nothing new and has characterized every reform movement in education for at least five centuries. But the winds of change have increased their velocity to the point where educators no longer have the luxury of wasting time pursuing improper goals.

At the very time when education seems poised for some significant progress in the right direction, uniform testing looms as not only a detriment to reform but as a measure that will further entrench a behaviorist system that has never worked and can never work unless educators are willing to repudiate the basic democratic tradition of the dignity and worth of the individual. This is the hypocrisy about which young people are so concerned today. This is the crux of the philosophic issue.

Implications from Educational Research

> It is always unrealistic to expect [that] the payoff
> from instruction will be apparent in the performance
> of learners at test time (Stake 1971).

The compilation of comparative data based on uniform testing has frequently intrigued professional educators. Mann suggested this possibility as far back as 1845. He rejected the idea because he soon perceived its dangerous consequences and later wrote:

> We cannot drive our people up a dark avenue, even
> though it be the right one, but we must hang the
> starry lights of knowledge about it, and show them
> not only the directness of its course but the beauty of
> the way that leads to it (1849).

Despite continuous rejection, the idea has persisted because it seems to satisfy the drive to excel, to win, to demonstrate superiority, to impose one's values on others. The efforts to garner comparative data from standardized testing reached their zenith in the mid-thirties.

Systematic research and study of these programs convinced most professional educators that normative data from standardized tests could never be used in making valid decisions because of their unreliability and misinterpretation. Douglass (1934) identified the following major consequences of uniform testing:
1. It artificially determined educational objectives and tended to freeze the curriculum.
2. It tended to dwarf the teacher, reducing him to the status of a tutor for examinations.
3. It motivated regimentation and mechanization of education.
4. It emphasized memorization as the major factor in learning.
5. It prevented adaptation of instruction to the needs of local school systems.
6. It stimulated standardization and an undesirable uniformity.
7. It emphasized only those educational outcomes that could be measured by objective tests.

8. It created a serious barrier to growth, evolution, and improvement of education.
9. It produced no evidence that greater educational efficiency resulted from its operation.

As a result of these studies, test writers have apparently turned their attention to the development of diagnostic tests and general achievement tests that measure correlates of learning rather than learning itself.

Most testing experts recognize that any general achievement test is essentially an authoritarian instrument based primarily on the author's idea of what should be learned and how it should be measured. They are all quick to point out that scores from such tests correlate only moderately with actual performance. Only the most blatantly commercial testing specialist would contend that a standardized test can accurately assess what a student is capable of doing. Research has universally disclosed an abundance of errors and hazards that preclude the use of these results for assessing either the quality or progress of systems, groups, or individuals. No one has yet been able to eliminate testing errors.

Objective research has identified these major weaknesses of standardized tests:

1. There is no such thing as the validity of a test. No test is valid for all purposes in all situations, or for all groups of students.
2. There is no standardized test that can be used to judge the educational level of a community, state, or nation, nor were any ever constructed to serve such a function.
3. Tests may measure individual differences among students, but cannot be used to assess the extent to which students have learned what the school attempted to teach.
4. Educational scholars, in seeking suitable instruments for appraising educational achievement, have examined and rejected all of the achievement tests commonly used in American schools.
5. Test scores of Negroes are poor predictors of their performance and the error in prediction slights their potential ability; hence, any standardized achievement test produces a grossly inappropriate assessment.
6. Uncritical acceptance of a test result is not justified by either the theory or research of testing and will result in unwise decisions.
7. There are no tests that can adequately measure listening comprehension, ability to analyze, or motivation—all important factors in the learning process.
8. Most human gifts and talents cannot be identified or measured in a standardized test.

9. Testing specialists have not developed scales that describe the similarity between teaching and testing; hence, we have no way to know how closely the tests match the instruction.

10. Interpretation of test results is frequently wrong.

11. Many tests do a poor job of predicting future performance.

In summary, research indicates that test results may be used as one tool in diagnosing individual student learning problems. Normative data from such tests are so error-laden and subject to so many variables that their use in assessment and decision making can be very dangerous.

Common Sense Perceptions

> The greater the threat posed by a test, the less it can measure and the less it can encourage learning (Holt 1969).

While humanist philosophy suggests that testing is a major tool of the educational autocrat and objective research clearly demonstrates the unreliability of test data, common sense and logic provide some devastating arguments against the Michigan State Assessment Program. The teachers and other professional educators who work regularly in local school districts may not be familiar with either the philosophic or research implications about standardized testing, but their perceptions about the effect of testing on the day-to-day educational operation will be much more accurate than the perceptions of theorists or school officials far removed from the classroom.

Regardless of how diligently teachers and administrators strive to raise student achievement scores, 50 percent of the students tested will still score below average on any test that is administered.

There has been much concern recently about students who score below the fifteenth percentile on the state achievement tests. Somehow the impression has been given that the achievement level of these students can be improved. We hope that real achievement for all students improves every year. For the sake of argument, however, assume that considerable effort is concentrated on just the students who score below the fifteenth percentile and that their average achievement score (not necessarily their achievement) is raised to the fortieth percentile. What has been gained? Since this is comparative data, someone will always score the highest and someone else will score the lowest with the balance of those tested falling in between.

Comparison based on test norms will inevitably motivate large-scale deception.

As the state continues to gather comparative information from its uniform testing program and publicly identifies the rank of individual schools and school districts, administrators, teachers, and students will join forces to outwit the state by any means possible. No one appreciates being compared unfavorably and unfairly with someone else. Those who are compared unfavorably will try to change their status or learn to hate themselves. Even if the group that is compared unfavorably accepts the validity of the test results and honestly tries to improve its status, there is no guarantee that its status will improve, particularly if everyone else puts forth an equal effort. Game playing and deception, which have characterized the past history of such situations, are much easier. In fact, deception is the only practical way to escape a degrading identification. Deception can work both ways. The security measures associated with the distribution of the Michigan state test booklets is evidence that the state Education Department does not really trust local educators. What guarantees do local educators have that the state Education Department will not manipulate the test scores? This is a grossly unhealthy situation.

Comparisons based on test norms will create injustices for many individuals.

Already the Michigan Assessment Program has affected adversely many competent educators. Recently two highly respected, experienced, and well-qualified black principals were placed on probation because the state test norms for their schools were in the lower percentiles. Originally, the local board of education proposed to dismiss these principals but public pressure forced a reconsideration.

Last spring one of Michigan's larger school districts was selecting a new superintendent. The board was considering two final candidates. Three members supported candidate A, three supported candidate B. The seventh member, in announcing his support for candidate A, gave as his reason the fact that state test norms from candidate A's school district were at the sixty-fifth percentile while norms from candidate B's district were only at the twentieth percentile.

In a middle-sized school district, a citizens' committee was organized to oust the school administration and board of education when it was learned that the state testing norms in that district were lower than in neighboring school districts.

These are isolated examples, but they will increase in frequency as the testing program becomes more firmly entrenched. It is not impossible to conceive of citizens awaiting as anxiously for the state test results as they do for the result of a football game with a traditional rival. And, if the district loses out in the competition, woe to the poor teacher or administrator who is finally identified as being responsible for the low scores.

Comparative test scores will motivate dissension and controversy at the very time the profession needs unity and cooperation.
It is unfortunate that many uninformed, naive, but well-meaning people will regard the state test scores as infallible criteria for judging the worth of a local school or school system. In those schools or districts where the norms are low, they will be accepted as absolute evidence that certain educators have performed poorly. Demands will be made for scapegoats; individuals and groups will become overly defensive, and the resulting dissension and controversy will divert energy and effort away from productive projects for improving the quality of education. Needless time and effort will be wasted in a fruitless, negative, and impossible attempt to fix blame.

It is tragic indeed that this must occur when many schools are finding it difficult just to keep operating because of the lack of adequate financing. Buffeted by inflation, taxpayer revolts, employee demands, student dissent, and genuine concern about the quality of its programs, Michigan education, more than ever before, needs professional unity if it is to survive. The testing program merely introduces unnecessary confusion and division, and prohibits an honest, sincere attempt to cope with the real problems of our schools.

The Michigan testing program wastes funds that are more urgently needed for other projects of greater importance.
When there are insufficient funds to support even basic educational programs, how can substantial expenditures be justified for a program so fraught with controversy, which really duplicates the efforts of many local school districts? Most school systems have financed and maintained a local testing program for many years. The imposition of a statewide uniform program is simply a duplication of local effort and is unwarranted, particularly during a period of acute financial deprivation.

The use of Michigan test scores as a basis for distributing compensatory education funds constitutes double jeopardy.

In medieval days, people were tried, for their alleged misdeeds, by ordeal. It was a common practice to bind the hands and feet of the accused and throw him in the water. If he floated, he was guilty and quickly hung. If he sank, he was innocent but left to drown. How little things have changed since the Dark Ages. In Michigan it is now necessary for a significant number of students to score below the fifteenth percentile on the State Achievement Tests before a school district can qualify for compensatory education funds.

After qualifying, the school district is expected, by using the money, to show substantial progress in raising its achievement norms. If it accomplishes this objective eventually it will lose the funds because it no longer has so-called disadvantaged students. If it fails to raise the achievement norms it will lose the additional money because it failed. The double jeopardy is obvious.

If the Michigan State Testing Program continues and expands, it will in time produce a sterile, unproductive, autocratic, and uniform state school system.

When opposition is silenced or eliminated, the deception exposed, and people grow weary of the continuous search for scapegoats, the state will finally be able to establish its absolute hegemony over Michigan schools. There will be no local decision making. No longer will individual Michigan school districts be characterized by their exciting, innovative, and creative programs. Teachers, principals, and superintendents will be mere civil servants operating as marionettes in a vast bureaucratic wasteland. Decisions will be made by the computers in Lansing and the curriculum will be based on behaviorist conditioning. Courses of study will be prepared in Lansing and state inspectors will visit local schools to make certain that the uniform program is being followed.

Inadequate financing, racism, poverty, student unrest, and irrelevant learning experiences will still plague the schools, but no local board or faculty will have the courage or desire to attack these problems with boldness, vigor, imagination, or creativity. Significant local needs will undoubtedly be ignored on most occasions because they will conflict with uniform state standards. Control, rather than democratic leadership, will be the order of the day.

The firm establishment of uniform state testing and the adoption of common goals will provide the state Board of Education with the major tools necessary to impose its control. Already the more forthright state Education Department officials are saying openly that "local leadership has failed in its efforts to solve crucial educational problems and it is now time for the state to take over."

Local educators are the only ones who live daily with major educational problems. They share with students and parents the grave concern about the defects of current educational programs. They have had many unfortunate experiences with faddism and are quite familiar with the nostrums being peddled by charlatans who trade on this concern by promising quick and simplistic cures for all educational ills. The experienced educator is painfully aware that there is no panacea for those ills. Legitimate progress is brutally slow and requires money, time, patience, understanding, professional unity, involvement, and cooperation. Knowing all of this, the professional educator senses immediately that a comparative state testing program works against all of the requisites for real educational reform and improvement.

The Michigan State Assessment Program in its current context can only be viewed as a reactionary fad of the kind that was tried and rejected fifty years ago. Unfortunately, while most educational fads are harmless, uniform state testing is a poison that will prolong the sickness in our midst and has the potential to kill.

REFERENCES

Adkins, Dorothy C. "Measurement in Relation to the Educational Process." *Educational and Psychological Measurement* 18 (1958): 221-240.

American Psychological Association. *Standards for Educational and Psychological Tests and Manuals.* Washington, D.C.: American Psychological Association, 1966.

Barnette, W. Leslie, Jr. "Advanced Credit for the Superior High School Student." *Journal of Higher Education* 28 (1957): 15-20.

Bloom, Benjamin S., ed. *Taxonomy of Educational Objectives: The Classification of Educational Goals.* "Handbook 1: Cognitive Domain." New York: McKay, 1956.

Brenner, Marshall H. "Test Difficulty, Reliability, and Discrimination as Functions of Item Difficulty Order." *Journal of Applied Psychology* 48 (1964): 98-100.

Broudy, Harry S. "Can Research Escape the Dogma of Behavioral Objectives?" *School Review* (November 1970): 43-56.

Buros, Oscar K., ed. *The Sixth Mental Measurements Yearbook.* Gryphon Press, 1965.

Caldwell, Otis W., and Courtis, S. A. *Then and Now in Education, 1845-1923.* New York: Harcourt, 1924.

Coffman, W. E. "Developing Tests for the Culturally Different." *School and Society* 93 (1965): 420-433.

Connolly, John A., and Wantman, M. J. "An Exploration of Oral Reasoning Processes in Responding to Objective Test Items." *Journal of Educational Measurement* 1 (1964): 59-64.

Cook, W. W. "The Measurement of General Spelling Ability Involving Controlled Comparisons between Techniques." *Studies in Education* 6, no. 6. University of Iowa, 1932.

Courtis, S. A. "Measurement of Growth and Efficiency in Arithmetic." *Elementary School Teacher* 10 (1909): 58.

Douglass, H. R. "The Effects of State and National Testing on the Secondary School." *School Review* 42 (1934): 497-509.

Dressel, Paul L., and Mayhew, Lewis B. *General Education: Explorations in Evaluation.* New York: American Council on Education, 1954.

Dyer, Henry S. "Educational Measurement—Its Nature and Its Problems." In *Evaluation in Social Studies,* edited by H. D. Berg. New York: National Council for Social Studies, 1965.

Dyer, Henry S., and Coffman, W. E. "The Tests of Developed Abilities." *College Board Review* 31 (1957): 5-10.

Ebel, Robert L. "The Social Consequences of Educational Testing." *School and Society* 92 (1964): 331-334.

____. "When Information Becomes Knowledge." *Science* (January 1971): 130-131.

Ebel, Robert L., and Damrin, Dora E. "Tests and Examinations." In *Encyclopedia of Educational Research,* edited by Chester W. Harris, 3d ed., pp. 1502-1517. New York: Macmillan, 1960.

Engel, Martin. "Assessing the Alternatives." *American Teacher* (April 1971): 24-27.

French, Will, et al. *Behavioral Outcomes of General Education in High School.* New York: Russell Sage, 1957.

Furst, Edward J. *Constructing Evaluation Instruments.* New York: McKay, 1958.

Goslin, David A. "Testing in Education." In *The Search for Ability: Standardized Testing in Social Perspective.* New York: Russell Sage, 1963.

____. "Ethical and Legal Aspects of the Collection and Use of Educational Information." A paper read at the Invitational Conference on Testing Problems, New York, October 1970.

Hoffman, Banesh. *The Tyranny of Testing.* New York: Collier, 1962.

Holt, John. *The Underachieving School.* New York: Pitman, 1969.

Jackson, Rex. *Developing Criterion-Referenced Tests.* Princeton, N.J.: Educational Testing Service, 1970.

Johnson, P. A. "Differential Functions of Examinations." In *Studies in College Examinations.* Minneapolis: University of Minnesota, Committee on Educational Research, 1934.

Kelley, T. L. "The Reliability of Test Scores." *Journal of Educational Research* 3 (1921): 370-379.

Learned, William S., and Wood, Ben D. *The Student and His Knowledge.* Chicago: Carnegie, 1938.

Lindquist, E. F., ed. *Educational Measurement.* New York: American Council on Education, 1951.

Long, J. A. "Improved Overlapping Methods for Determining Validities of Test Items." *Journal of Experimental Education* 1 (1934): 264-268.

Long, J. A., and Sandiford, Peter. "The Validation of Test Items." Bulletin no. 3. Toronto: University of Toronto, Department of Educational Research, 1935.

Malcolm, Donald J. "Content Validity of Achievement Tests as Judged by Teachers." In *ETS Annual Report, 1963-64.* Princeton, N.J.: Educational Testing Service, 1965.

McGhan, Barry R. "Accountability as a Negative Reinforcer." *American Teacher* (November 1970): 13.

Mann, Horace. *Twelfth Annual Report of the Secretary of the State Board of Education.* Massachusetts, 1849.

Michigan Department of Education. "Purposes and Procedures of the Michigan Assessment of Education." Assessment Report no. 1. Lansing, Mich., 1969.

_____. "Objectives and Procedures of the 1970-71 Michigan Educational Assessment Program." Assessment Report no. 7. Lansing, Mich., 1970.

Pearson, Richard. "The Test Fails as an Entrance Examination." *College Board Review* 25 (1955): 2-9.

Porter, John. "Teacher's Voice." *MEA* (March 1971).

Richardson, M. W. "The Relation Between the Difficulty and the Differential Validity of a Test." *Psychometrika* 1 (1936): 33-40.

Richardson, M. W., and Kuder, G. F. "The Calculation of Test Reliability Coefficients Based on the Method of National Equivalence." *Journal of Educational Psychology* 30 (1939): 681-687.

Sarason, S. B., et al. *Anxiety in Elementary School Children.* New York: Wiley, 1960.

Scates, Douglas E. "Fifty Years of Objective Measurement and Research in Education." *Journal of Educational Research* 41 (1947): 241-264.

Stake, Robert E. "Testing Hazards in Performance Contracting." *Phi Delta Kappan* (June 1971): 583-589.

Thorndike, E. L. *An Introduction to the Theory of Mental and Social Measurement.* Teachers Co., 1904 (rev. ed., 1913).

Thorndike, Robert L., and Hagen, Elizabeth. *Measurement and Evaluation in Psychology and Education,* 3d ed. New York: Wiley, 1969.

Tinkelman, S. N. "Regents Examinations in New York State after 100 Years." In *Invitational Conference on Testing Problems.* Princeton, N. J.: Educational Testing Service, 1966.

Tyler, R. W. *Constructing Achievement Tests.* Columbus, Ohio: Ohio State University Press, 1934.

Votaw, D. F. "Graphical Determination of Probable Error in Validation of Test Items." *Journal of Educational Psychology* 24 (1933): 682-686.
Wood, B. D. "Studies in Achievement Tests." *Journal of Educational Psychology* 17 (1926): 1.

7

ACCOUNTABILITY AND
THE STATE

C. Thomas Kerins

Accountability is an issue facing every living and breathing school administrator today. It is hardly a new issue, but its growing importance has tended to cloud the already murky relationships that exist between the State Education Agency (SEA) and the Local Education Agency (LEA).

Concurrent with an increase in state and federal monies has been the outcry for accountability from the public in general and the legislators in particular. They are demanding fiscal accountability. This requires the SEA to monitor, to be a watchdog for the public funds.

Usually state or federal programs require an evaluation at the local level, upon pain of disinheritance. Everyone knows that this evaluation threat has become more of a paper tiger than an ominous portent. Still, the SEA is put in the position of assisting the LEA to plan an evaluation, implement it, and then receive it for filing. Almost no one is seriously looking at the quality of the program that is being evaluated. Incredibly, what teachers "do" with children is quite secondary to the ability of the local administrator to observe guidelines and to write behavioral objectives.

This development has occurred in the same decade in which the quality of educational leadership provided by local administrators has come repeatedly under attack. When the Sputnik affair raised the issue of good education, Americans only knew how to answer the challenge in terms of quantity—more of the basic courses, more grants for college students, more of what existed.

However, over the intervening years, Illich (1970), Freire (1970), and their more popularized brethren, Postman and Weingartner (1970), Dennison (1969), Repo (1970), and Kohl (1969) have questioned the basic value underlying our educational system. Their challenge goes beyond the issue of whether trigonometry should be taught in the sophomore or junior year. Administrators were challenged with ideas that shattered their perceived image of "what should be." While some attempted to answer the challenge, most local administrators remained in a state of anomie—hanging between traditional beliefs and the radical new ideas of the aforementioned authors, between their own teachers and students.

Into this picture stepped the SEA with its own almost fatal case of anomie since it must both hold the LEA fiscally accountable for all funds given to it and participate in the evaluation of the programs being offered by local districts. The SEA usually asked the same representative in its employ to count the dollars used to buy materials and to evaluate the quality of the program in which the materials are used. The result was predictable: it is much easier to count dollars than to evaluate programs. The LEA teachers and administrators feel cheated because the state had promised evaluation help; the SEA, and especially its field staff, feels frustrated because it knows it is doing only half the job; and the general public is duped because it often equates monitoring of its district's program with evaluation—a distortion of reality.

LOCAL EVALUATION

The first step to resolve this conflict is for the state to clarify its image with local school administrators and teachers by distinguishing those employees who have fiscal responsibility from those who are program auditors and those who provide services, that is, assistance with evaluation and program development. This clarification of roles appears obvious but, in reality, a mixture of tradition and inconsistent leadership has led program auditors to be analyzing budgets while accountants evaluate classroom programs and service-oriented staff are rebuked as monitors.

The steps after this role clarification fall into a sequential range of activities that depend on an intensive retraining of state staff and LEA personnel. First, the SEA must go beyond the state of not only requiring specific behavioral objectives but also of giving the LEA program direction. For example, an SEA could state that, the philosophy of the state in compensatory education being preventive rather than remedial, all project efforts should be directed toward using Follow Through programs from kindergarten through grade three rather than remedial reading in high schools. After the directions have been indicated, the state should establish the minimum criteria it will accept before it will reimburse a local district.

Second, once the project has been written according to the specifications of state guidelines and accepted, it is open for a monitoring team from the state Office of Education to conduct a fiscal and a program audit. These audits will ask the questions: are the monies being spent according to federal and/or state fiscal guidelines and according to the project's budget, and do the interactions between the teachers and students actually reflect those described in the project proposal?

Third, and perhaps the most difficult, the state has to convince LEA administrators that evaluation is the key to the development of good programs. As long as school administrators view evaluation as an exercise in how to manufacture data creatively or how to shuffle papers, there is little the state staff can do but monitor. However, the state has also to regard evaluation as a means of providing service and exerting leadership rather than as fulfilling an ambiguous legislative requirement.

If the SEA has the courage to take such a leadership role, it is feasible that the state and local districts will change their relationship toward one another. Obviously, this change will be difficult.

HOW IT MIGHT WORK

Let us assume the existence of a hypothetical SEA and see how it would operate within the above recommendations. However, in order to focus attention on accountability and not on a particular SEA, let us take one small section of a state's operation: its Department for Exceptional Children, composed of three sections—for educationally disadvantaged, gifted, and handicapped children. Let us assume that, for the educationally disadvantaged, the SEA receives about $70 million a year from the federal government and for the gifted and handicapped it receives state funds of $4 and $60 million a year respectively. All three sections demand evaluation and fiscal accountability. Staff members from each section read local district proposals, help to plan programs, and then monitor them.

A separate fiscal unit, Division A, established for the three sections, would be accessible to administrators, not just during spring when the proposals are submitted, but throughout the year. Thus, it would not matter which of the three sections a superintendent were writing a budget for; he could call one number at the state office for help. Division A would also participate in workshops for local administrators so they could answer questions about guidelines and the writing of budgets. These sessions would not only provide the "ounce of prevention," but also could humanize the fiscal unit so that LEA administrators would be calling more than just a phone number. Obviously the staff would have to be more than bookkeepers or clerks; they would be people with some "feel" for education.

Division B would contain staff members who would constantly be in the field actively monitoring the treatments the school administrators planned for their pupils when they submitted their application to the state Office of Education for approval. While members of this division would selectively investigate critical areas of LEA fiscal responsibility, their primary task would be to audit programs. By visiting classes, using observation checks, and interviewing teachers, students, parents, and administrators, the state staff will be able to verify whether or not the LEAs are using the money in the way they had planned. (Obviously, flexibility is honored. A district should not be held in contempt if its goals change over time. However House, Kerins, and Steele[1971] illustrated that chaos is a more accurate term than flexibility when a district's programs are analyzed in detail.)

We would hope that these monitors will do more than complete their audit and leave; rather they will relate their findings to the LEA personnel. In this way they may be viewed as one part of the district's own evaluation team.

Division C would be a team responsible for assisting LEA personnel in incorporating their evaluation results and in developing their present evaluation designs as they write their proposals. This procedure in itself could serve as an education process in assisting administrators to think of evaluation as a built-in and continuous element of their proposal.

The evaluation unit's other main task would be to look at local evaluation from a statewide perspective, to see what materials, techniques, style of teaching, and so on made a difference in producing good quality programs for children. The evaluation personnel would be in an excellent position to discover the better programs and disseminate the results of local evaluations, along with state summaries, in a multimedia presentation illustrating the statewide evaluation, followed by a section analyzing the local district's results.

This procedure would go a long way to ensure that evaluation findings would be reflected in the programs to be written for the following year, and that there would be a broader base of participation by teachers in the writing of projects. Evaluations for federally funded programs usually do neither. The programs are often written and approved before the evaluation of the previous year's program is received or even completed. Teachers are sometimes unaware that they are participating in the required evaluation and are usually ignored by the state and local administrators even when results are available.

FIGURE 7:1. EVALUATION FUNCTIONS OF A
STATE EDUCATION AGENCY

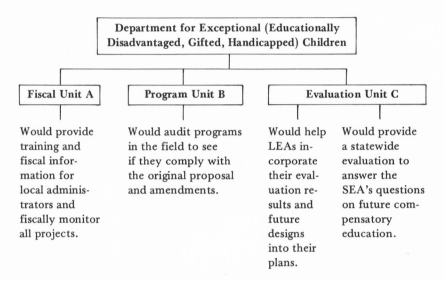

Such an organization can be only as good as the standards developed for each of the three sections. The standards may be as diverse as the target population each attempts to serve, but the ultimate criterion is whether they are meaningful and understandable to the local teachers and administrators. Included in a statement of philosophy, or a state plan, written standards would eliminate the conflicts that develop when state criteria change as often as state personnel.

However, the provision of incentives to encourage self-evaluation is sometimes necessary. A district could legally be meeting all the fiscal guidelines, receive a clean bill of health when visited, and still not pursue the issue of evaluation even if excellent assistance from the SEA were available. The only two means of positive reinforcement available to the state are additional money and favorable publicity, perhaps in the form of published rating scales. Only incentives will nudge some administrators over the line.

In any case, the ultimate basis of any good evaluation is cooperation. If the program auditors and evaluators were part of a decentralized unit, they would have a much better chance of understanding local problems, obtaining cooperation from district administrators, and eventually building the rapport that is necessary if the state is heading in a new direction in applying the concept of accountability.

As long as evaluation is viewed as an impersonal, useless edict from a state capital hundreds of miles away, it may take more than public relations incentives and ideals to sway pragmatic administrators. Personalized and consistent assistance in evaluation efforts is essential. However, this is almost impossible unless the state strongly considers decentralization of its staff to specified geographic areas of responsibility. A strong central authority located in the state capital may be necessary to collect massive amounts of data necessary to the lifeblood of any bureaucracy, but if the state Office of Education wishes to take leadership in this area it is going to have to individualize its approach. Although some cynics would view such a liaison as hidden potential for relaxation of standards, ultimately the fiscal unit in the state capital holds the purse strings.

The ideas presented here suggest a few considerations that could change the accountability relationship that often exists between local education administrators and state Office of Education personnel. The SEA would assume greater leadership but no greater control. Both agencies would be able to answer honestly the shouts for accountability, and the school districts would be able to use the state agency's leadership and knowledge about evaluation in responding positively to the critics' demands for good quality programs.

REFERENCES

Dennison, George. *The Lives of Children*. New York: Random House, 1969.
Freire, Paulo. *Pedagogy of the Oppressed*. New York: Hender and Hender, 1970.
House, E. R., Kerins, C. T., and Steele, J. M. "The Gifted Classroom." Mimeographed. Urbana, Ill.: University of Illinois, Center for Instructional Research and Curriculum Evaluation, 1971.
Illich, Ivan. *Deschooling of Society*. New York: Harper and Row, 1970.
Kohl, H. R., *The Open Classroom*. New York: Random House, 1969.
Postman, Neil, and Weingartner, Charles. *Teaching as a Subversive Activity*. New York: Delacorte Press, 1970.
Repo, Satu, ed. *This Book is About Schools*. New York: Random House, Parthenon Books, 1970.

8

CLIENTS' RESISTANCE TO NEGATIVE FINDINGS

Reginald K. Carter

Many social action programs such as the Peace Corps, Job Corps, Upward Bound, and Head Start have recently been assessed for their effectiveness through social science evaluation research. Educational and industrial innovations have been similarly evaluated to determine the degree of their success or failure. The need for systematic appraisals of these programs has come to be "accepted, even sought, as an accompaniment to rational action" (Hyman and Wright 1967, p. 742). Several recent writers have cited some of the difficulties encountered in the practical application of ideal research designs in evaluating social action programs (Leeds and Smith 1963; Riley 1967; Rossi 1966; Wright and Hyman 1964). Concomitant to such research is the resistance frequently encountered by social scientists when their findings do not positively reinforce the expectations and ideological value system of their client. This resistance unveils one of the primary latent functions of many evaluation studies, namely, a legitimization process for predetermined policies.

DEFINITION OF EVALUATION RESEARCH

While most applied social scientists agree on the need for program evaluation, in practice, there is little consensus as to the essential characteristics of such research. Although there has been a need for evaluation research within the educational institution, there is little

Reprinted from *The American Sociologist*, 1971, 6 (May): 118-124. Copyright 1971 by the American Sociological Association.

evidence that educational institutions have ever been systematically assessed. Miles (1967) notes that

> in the absence of evaluatory evidence, substitute bases of judgment are used, such as educational ideology, sentiment, or persuasive claims by advocates or salesmen. Most educational decisions appear to be made in an intuitive, prudential manner. Sometimes the merits of an innovation are said to be 'self-evident'; for example, the various positions on methods of teaching reading seem to have antedated the advent of research to test them. More frequently, the opinions of users and clients are invoked. Informal student reactions and teacher responses are assessed; perceived student boredom is taken as an indicator of lack of learning, and the extra enthusiasm [of] teachers and students usually found in a new program (with its additional encouragement, recognition, and shared wishes for goal accomplishment) is mistaken for the success of an innovation. *Yet, no hard data have been collected,* and decisions to terminate or continue the innovations are founded on sand (p. 658).

Suchman (1968) describes evaluation research studies as attempts

> to apply the methods of science to action programs in order to obtain objective and valid measures of what such programs are accomplishing. . . . Evaluation research asks about the *kinds* of change desired, the *means* by which this change is to be brought about, and the *signs* by which such changes can be recognized (pp. 2-3).

According to Suchman, evaluation research studies should raise not only the administrative question of whether the program was a success or failure but the research question of *why* it was or was not effective. To answer the question "why" requires an analysis of the dimensions of the program, the differential impact of the program on the populations exposed to it, the milieu within which the program takes place, and the multidimensional results of the program in terms of short- and long-term effects, attitudinal and behavioral changes, and so on.

There are many reasons why clients choose to accept the findings and recommendations of social science research. Several recent publications (Glock 1961; Lyons 1969; National Research Council 1968; National Science Foundation 1969) have reviewed some of the conditions where social science research has been useful for various private and public organizations. There are also many reasons clients choose *not* to accept the results of such research. These include the psychological characteristics of clients and/or researchers, the quality of the research, the feasibility of implementing the recommendations, past negative experiences with social science research, and inappropriateness of data and/or researcher to generate policy recommendations. Consequently, the situation has arisen that the results of a considerable portion of social science research should not be used as the primary basis for a client's making specific decisions. There are, at the same time, a number of case studies that indicate specific conditions where evaluation research findings have been selectively ignored. Thus, even if evaluation research is competently conducted, the fate of the results is often determined by another set of criteria.

My object is not to investigate the difficulties experienced by social scientists in conducting evaluation studies (for which, see Berry 1967; Gross and Fishman 1967; Leeds and Smith 1963), but to cite some of the special problems that evolve when the researcher's findings do not agree with the client's anticipated results. Most of the examples are drawn from industrial and educational organizations. It is assumed, however, that the basic characteristics of the client-researcher relationship and the fate of negative findings will also be found in other settings. By negative findings I mean research results and conclusions that are opposed to the expectations of the client for whom the research was conducted. The administrators or managers who are referred to are employed by the client and represent his interests. They also have their own personal political investments within the organization.

THE COMMITTED PLANT MANAGER

In June 1968, the management of the central distribution warehouse of a national manufacturer introduced an employee motivation program for hourly rated workers. The plant manager was ideologically committed to the underlying principles of the motivation program and was active in introducing it into the plant's operations. He early reported its success to his immediate superior and other plant representatives. In short, he invested considerable time and effort in implementing the innovation and had a big stake in its success.

In the fall of 1968 I was requested by the director of the employee motivation program to assess the effectiveness of the program as it was then operating. The director of the program was not affiliated with the manufacturing firm. Using data released by the committed manager, I drew a comparison between employee motivation during the first six months of 1968 (before the program) and the last six months of the same year (with the program). The comparison indicated that the motivation program had *not* produced the expected results. My findings contradicted those found earlier by the plant manager. A copy of my findings was forwarded to the plant manager along with a request for further information to clarify my contradictory findings. His reply was that no more data would be made available to this researcher. Furthermore, he wanted assurance that no one else would see my report. Since that time, our relationship has been cool and impersonal and there have been no further evaluations. The program is still being used, unaltered by the findings.

My analysis of this experience is that the manager was ideologically committed to the success of the innovation. He had publicly announced its initial success, and a release of contradictory findings would not only threaten the existence of the program but, more important, would probably mean loss of face for the manager. The findings had no effect on the organization because the perceived psychological cost to the plant manager's self-concept prevented their being released.

This example demonstrates that it is naive to assume that research findings that recommend the introduction or elimination of an innovation to a program will automatically be implemented. Often initiators of new programs are so convinced of the success of a program that they find evaluation research unnecessary. Kendall (1967) found that

> the creators of experimental programs often impress one as being men of conviction who have little question about the efficacy of the changes they have introduced. They know that the courses they have developed are the best possible under existing conditions; and in the light of this assumed fact, systematic evaluation seems superfluous (p. 344).

In support of this same caricature of program initiators Miles (1967) contends that their personality is a major factor in explaining the infrequency of evaluation studies within educational organizations.

> The innovative enthusiasm and messianic zeal often noted in experimental enterprises may come to have a self-justifying strength: systematic evaluation might prove risk takers wrong and dampen the satisfying ardor of the mutually converted. And the imperatives of organizational survival inevitably enter the evaluation of any particular innovation (p. 659).

Gouldner (1965) has also observed that administrators selectively perceive the results of evaluation projects in the light of their own self-concept:

> Men in power are not merely technicians, concerned solely about the effective means of their ends; they are also politicians, committed to morally tinged precepts and symbols, and striving like all other men to maintain a decent self-concept. Truths which are inconsistent with their own self-images are demoralizing and thus, in this very real sense, by no means useful to them (p. 20).

Each client, moreover, has his own theory or explanation of human behavior, which may differ from that of the social scientist. Consequently, when the findings of the latter conflict with those of the former, the research results of the scientist may not be enough to convince the manager that he should alter his assumptions about the way people behave. The client may feel, on the basis of his own experience, that the data being presented by the social scientist are in some way inaccurate. Berry (1967) reviewed the research process in personnel research departments in a number of major United States industrial corporations. The directors of such research departments reported that in order for their findings to have an altering impact on the organization they had to be dramatic, clear-cut, startling, nonthreatening, and not disagreeable. Furthermore, they must not lay blame, contradict decisions, or be politically distasteful. At times they had to agree with the preconceptions of the user. One director reported in an interview that "managers here tend to feel that, because of their experience, they know as much as there is to know about managing people and they resent and resist a psychologist telling them how to run things better (p. 89)."

The committed manager's response to the negative findings suggests the following two propositions, that:

1. The greater the perceived threat to the client's or manager's positive self-concept, the greater will be his resistance to negative research findings.
2. The greater the difference between the client's or manager's concept of the social reality being studied and the research findings, the greater will be his resistance to the results.

THE COMMITTED EXECUTIVE

The following case study tends to support the position that research findings are selectively ignored or refuted by the promoters of an innovative program. An international corporation initially developed the motivation program mentioned earlier. One of its eastern plants had been performing consistently below the mean production levels of comparable plants. Top management, seriously considering closing the plant, sent the corporation's director of training and development programs to the plant to try to improve production. This top executive soon introduced a number of alterations in operating procedures and management-employee relationships. For example, jobs were rotated, employees participated in decision making, there were employee-supervisor interviews and up-dated job descriptions, and audio-visual presentations of plant operations were developed and shown to all employees. Results were dramatic. Units of production increased, machines operated more efficiently, grievances decreased, and other improvements followed. This striking change encouraged the top executive to crystallize the combination of alterations he had introduced into the eastern plant into a packaged "program" that was presented to the five other plants in the corporate structure.

Two years later, in 1965, the same program was introduced commercially to outside industrial firms, although by then the program was no longer being implemented in the original eastern plant. Moreover, in each of the other five plants it had failed to be installed for various reasons. For example, individual plant managers had not become committed to the program or union officials had objected strongly. The top executive, however, was still asserting the program's remarkable success in its first six months at the eastern plant.

In short, the initial results indicated remarkable success for the program, but in the long run it was eliminated in the first plant and rejected in the others.

The top executive may have selectively ignored the long-term negative results because they were basically at variance with his personal commitment to the success of the program. It has now been almost seven years since the program was initially developed, and there are still no data that indicate its long-term success. The executive continues to disregard the fact that none of the plants introduced to the program installed it permanently.

THE TERMINATED RELATIONSHIP

Some clients react strongly to research findings that do not support their expectations. Often they either ignore or rationalize negative results. Rossi (1966), formerly a member of the National Opinion Research Center (NORC), has reported a number of client reactions to negative evaluation findings. The NORC is one of the most highly respected social survey organizations in the United States and uses very sophisticated methodological technology to gather highly valid and reliable data for its clients. After a long history of evaluation studies, however, NORC has become fully aware of the reality that "evaluation studies usually make the client look bad" (Davis 1964, p. 217).

A few years ago NORC conducted a study on the effects of fellowships and scholarships on graduate students for the academic societies that sponsor such awards. The clients had supposed that the awards were tremendously important to the recipients and that the disciplines that were granted the most graduate fellowships were able to attract the better students. The results of the survey indicated that the financial support of these sponsors did not greatly influence a student's choice of discipline for graduate study. Moreover, the committed Ph.D. candidate eventually found some means to complete his formal education and was not seriously restricted in pursuing his studies because of lack of a fellowship or scholarship.

These findings, of course, contradicted the clients' expectations. While the sponsors inaugurated no changes in their policies regarding awards, a change did occur in their dealings with NORC. Rossi reported (1966) that the relationship between the sponsoring societies and the researchers had become cool, if not distant. Moreover, after ignoring the negative results of the survey,

> the sponsoring groups are still adamantly claiming
> more and more in the way of financial support for
> graduate students from the federal government on the
> grounds that such support materially affects the num-
> bers of talented students who will go on to graduate
> study beyond the B.A., and, furthermore, materially
> affects the distribution of talent among various fields
> of study (p. 129).

In this same article Rossi gave another example of social science evaluation research that has been selectively ignored. It centers around the impact of class size on learning. He summarized his analysis in the following fashion:

> By and large, class size has no effect on the learning
> of students with the possible exception of classes in
> the language arts. But, the net results of more than
> two hundred researchers on educational ideology and
> policy has been virtually nil. Every proposal for the
> betterment of education calls for reductions in the
> size of classes, despite the fact that there is no evi-
> dence that class size affects anything except possibly
> the job satisfaction of the teachers (p. 129).

The case studies of the committed top executive and the NORC suggest the following proposition, that:

3. The greater the importance or salience to the client or manager of the function being evaluated, the greater the perceived threat to his positive self-image and the greater his resistance to the negative findings.

THE MIDDLE MANAGERS

The following case history illustrates the formal legitimization function that many evaluation studies perform. If the role of evaluation research is basically to reinforce the status quo, it will have little opportunity to generate change within an organization. Moreover, once this latent function becomes obvious to past respondents, there is a strong probability that the quality of data collected in future social science research projects will decrease. I shall return to some of these consequences presently.

A few years ago, sociologist Richard Hall was asked to conduct a survey for the division of student personnel in a large state university. He was to study the division's communication and coordination processes and submit recommendations to improve these processes. The student personnel division had the responsibility of administering residence halls, handling problems of student discipline, and helping to manage the program of student activities. The division was divided into subdivisions, each under the direction of a manager. These middle managers were the ones who felt they might lose face from the report, since top management was removed from the scene and the personnel under them were students who did not have any real responsibility. Hall (1966) notes of these middle managers:

> In addition to this anxiety [that the research might show their ineffectiveness], they also had their own pet ideas concerning appropriate means of improving the Division's operations as a whole. They were, therefore, anxious for our suggestions to support their own preconceptions of appropriate means of improving operations (p. 34).

After completing the analysis of the data, Hall reported his findings and proposed several changes in the communication and coordination processes. His summary highlights the criteria that brought change:

> The most evident problem in this kind of applied research described previously revolves around the implementations of the findings. In our situation, despite words to the contrary, the organization primarily wanted verification of its own prior conclusions regarding trouble spots. Where our findings coincided, action was taken. When we pointed to other trouble spots than those initially perceived, the organization tended to ignore them. For whatever reason, action research in this type of setting may prove simply a way of legitimating the preconception of organizational leaders (p. 38).

This case history reinforces proposition three that, the greater the importance to the client or manager of the function being evaluated, the greater the perceived threat to his self-concept and the greater his resistance to the unexpected negative or different findings. It also adds support to proposition two that, the greater the difference between the client's or manager's concept of social reality and the research findings, the greater the resistance to the results of an evaluation study.

MANAGERIAL BIAS

The foregoing case studies of resistance to negative evaluation research findings concern high or middle managerial levels, a source of resistance not usually cited in research literature as a primary inhibitor of change. When several key articles in this area were reviewed (Argyle 1967; Coch and French 1948; Lawrence 1954; Zander 1961) it became evident that most of the analyses were in terms of employee resistance to change. Bias toward management (Carey 1967; Krupp 1964) has led to the selective avoidance of investigating the amount of resistance to change exhibited by top executives or administrators.

A theory frequently used to explain planned change within a complex organization is the "power-equalization theory" (Leavitt 1965). This stresses the importance of sharing the decision-making process with the members of the organization who will be implementing the desired change. Once they have participated in formulating the proposed innovation, these members, in theory, should be committed to its successful fulfillment.

However, such emphasis on overcoming employees' initial resistance to change ignores many other conditions that may be equally responsible for the success or failure of a new or established program. Gross, Giacquinta, and Bernstein (1968) cite a number of critical managerial and administrative reactions that led to the failure of a specific educational innovation. These researchers investigated the failure of an experiment in an elementary school to redefine the role of teacher and student according to a Summerhillian (Neill 1960) concept of learning (that is, unstructured classroom environment, emphasis on the student's interests, concentration on the learning process rather than course content, and so forth). The program was directed and staffed by professionals who were committed to the change, so there was little employee or managerial resistance. Moreover, the project was adequately funded by Title III, which enabled the experiment to have above-average financial and personnel resources. In addition to the regular teaching faculty, there were three subject specialists, student teachers, and teacher aides.

Six months after the program was begun, the researchers were called upon to evaluate it. They found that it had failed to be implemented. In this case the basic causes could not be traced to the *initial employee* resistance to change since they all had favored the introduction of the experiment. However, as the program was being implemented, many of the teachers became disenchanted or experienced such frustration in coping with the many changes that they invested decreasing amounts of time and energy in meeting the objectives of the experiment.

Gross and his associates explained the main reasons for the program's collapse as the top administrators' failure to take the steps necessary to provide the teachers with a clear concept of their new role definition, adjust organizational structures to make them compatible with proposed changes (that is, students were still required to participate in recess from 10:30 to 11:00 and lunch from 12:00 to 12:30, and they were required to participate in certain academic areas regardless of their interests), provide teachers with resocialization experiences to develop the capabilities of implementing innovation, provide resources (that is, equipment, educational toys) to carry out the goals of self-learning, and provide the necessary reinforcing psychological support and rewards to continually encourage the teachers to make renewed efforts (that is, feedback to administrators and other teachers regarding unresolved problems).

Gross and his colleagues have essentially noted that administrative characteristics were the primary factors in the success or failure of this educational experiment. This finding is supported by the research of Brickell (1967) who reviewed 2,906 innovations that were introduced into the New York State school system from 1953 to 1961. Brickell found that the great bulk of schools as structured institutions remained stable during this period. The most successful innovations were accompanied by the most elaborate help to teachers as they began to install the new program. In summarizing his findings, Brickell deemphasized initial faculty disposition and emphasized the need for adequate material and personnel resources:

> Whereas initial faculty reaction to the proposed change is not critical in determining its success, the amount of help provided is critical. New instructional programs can be successfully introduced despite initial apathy—or even opposition—on the part of a number of teachers. . . . An innovation which falters is more likely to be suffering from simple staff inability than from conscious or unconscious sabotage (p. 505).

CONSEQUENCES OF RESISTANCE

The examples cited so far have illustrated what happened when research findings were inconsistent with the beliefs and values of the clients whose programs were being evaluated. The net result in each case was the perpetuation of the client's ideology, self-image, and concept of social reality.

Once subordinates within an organization or researchers become aware of the granitelike rigidity of top management, they may choose to distort and/or selectively report only that information that supports the status quo. Likert (1967), director of the Institute for Social Research, has encountered this phenomenon within industrial organizations that have attempted to introduce new systems of management (that is, participative democratic, or Likert's System 4) in a corporation in which the top executive staff had a different concept of the correct style of managing (that is, benevolent authoritative, or Likert's Systems 1 or 2):

> We have seen corporate staffs and divisional presidents in more than one firm withhold from their top corporate officers results of measurements which would correct the false impressions held by these top officers. These measurements of the causal and intervening variables were obtained either for, or by, the corporate staff and accurately revealed the system of management of the corporation's most productive departments. But, these data conflicted with the convictions held by top corporate officers about the kind of management system which is most productive. These officers believe System 2 or 2.5 is best, but the data showed that their highest-producing managers are using something close to System 4. . . . It is hazardous to feed important, but unsolicited information upward, especially, when such information is contrary to views that are strongly held by the higher echelons and which, to no small degree, proves them wrong. As a consequence, these senior corporate officers have not seen the measurements and are unaware of how seriously wrong they are in their impressions of the management system which yields the best results in their own corporation, as demonstrated by the behavior and results of their highest-producing man-

agers. Until these officers actively seek such data,
they are not likely to have the results presented to
them (p. 110).

Another result of clients' resistance to change is that social science
evaluation studies may simply become a ritualistic ceremony to reinforce the image that top management actively supports scientific
evaluations. Thus a latent function of research projects conducted by
social scientists may be an exercise in scientism: research for the sake
of research. Such endeavors have historically contributed little toward introducing changes within organizations. This brings up specific implications about the future of traditional social science research
techniques, that is, the questionnaire and interview process. Once
future questionnaire respondents and interviewees recognize the ritualistic nature of social science research in general and evaluation
studies in particular the quality of our data may be seriously reduced.

In recent interviews with the Michigan Employment Security
Commission and the Department of Social Services I encountered
varying degrees of cooperation and willingness to answer questions
because of the explicit recognition by members of these organizations of the low utility value of such research in introducing change.
This perceived futility of social science research may have a serious
effect on both the validity and reliability of future data. What is even
more alarming is that we do not have a present measure of the extent
of this bias. We have tended to aggregate respondents' data irrespective of their perceived utility. We should at once develop instruments
to enable us to measure this bias and consider it systematically in our
analyses. So far, there are few critiques (Form 1970) or empirical
studies in the sociology of social research that have attempted to
develop the means of assessing the varying degrees of such responses.

SUMMARY

Although there are a number of examples within the industrial and
educational settings that demonstrate the effects of social science
research on implementing successful organizational change (Likert
1967; Myers 1970), they are exceptions rather than the rule. Innovations introduced may simply reinforce the ideology of top management. There are many suggestions in sociological literature as to
effective means of introducing organizational change (Bennis 1966),

but there are few reports on how to overcome resistance at the top management level to the findings of social science research evaluations. A collection of case histories where management resistance was successfully overcome would be of great benefit to future researchers, and a study of organizational and interpersonal conditions would be an important initial step toward changing the dominant latent function of evaluation research from mere ritualism to a rationale for change.

Rossi (1966) offers the following insight into the main reasons that negative results have so little impact on an organization.

> The main reason lies in the fact that the practitioners, first of all (and sometimes the researchers), never seriously entertain the possibility that results would come out negative or insignificant. Without commitment to the bet, one or both of the gamblers usually welshs (p. 129).

A researcher should confront the client with as many alternative potential findings as possible before he begins his study so that tentative organizational adaptions can be anticipated for each possible result. One industrial psychologist resolves the problem by varying his fee for a study according to the number of his recommendations adopted. The larger the number and relative importance of the recommendations introduced, the lower the fee. A similar format could be used in contracting for evaluation research. If the wager is high enough, the probability of a client's welshing may be reduced.

REFERENCES

Argyle, Michael. "The Social Psychology of Social Change." In *Social Theory and Economic Change,* edited by T. Burns and S. B. Saul, pp. 87-101. London: Tavistock, 1967.

Bennis, Warren G. *Changing Organizations.* New York: McGraw-Hill, 1966.

Berry, Dean. "The Politics of Personnel Research." Ann Arbor, Mich.: University of Michigan Graduate School of Business Administration, Bureau of Industrial Relations, 1967.

Brickell, H. "State Organization for Education Change: A Case Study and a Proposal." In *Innovations in Education,* edited by Matthew Miles, pp. 493-533. New York: Columbia University, Teachers College Press, 1967.

Carey, Alex. "Hawthorne Studies: A Radical Criticism." *American Sociological Review* 32 (June 1967): 403-416.

Coch, L., and French, J., Jr. "Overcoming Resistance to Change." *Human Relations* 1 (Winter 1948): 512-532.

Davis, J. A. "Great Books and Small Groups: An Informal History of a National Survey." In *Sociologists at Work*, edited by Philip E. Hammond, pp. 212-234. New York: Basic Books, 1964.

Form, W. H. "The Sociology of Social Research." In *Organization, Management and Tactics of Social Research*, edited by Richard O'Toole, pp. 3-42. Cambridge, Mass.: Schenkman, 1971.

Glock, C. Y. "Applied Social Research: Some Conditions Affecting its Utilization." In *Case Studies in Bringing Behavioral Science Into Use*, edited by Charles Y. Glock et al. Stanford, Calif.: Stanford University, Institute for Communications Research, 1961.

Gouldner, Alvin. "Explorations in Applied Social Science." In *Applied Sociology*, edited by Alvin Gouldner and A. M. Miller, pp. 5-23. New York: Free Press, 1965.

Gross, Neal, and Fishman, J. "The Management of Educational Establishments." In *Uses of Sociology*, edited by P. F. Lazarsfeld, W. H. Sewell, and Harold Wilensky, pp. 304-358. New York: Basic Books, 1967.

Gross, Neal, Giacquinta, J., and Bernstein, M. "Complex Organization: The Implementation of Major Organizational Innovations." Paper presented at the annual meeting of the American Sociological Association, 1968.

Hall, Richard. "The Applied Sociologist and Organizational Sociology." In *Sociology in Action*, edited by A. B. Shostak, pp. 33-38. Homewood, Ill.: Dorsey Press, 1966.

Hyman, Herbert and Wright, Charles. "Evaluating Social Action Programs." In *Uses of Sociology*, edited by P. F. Lazarsfeld, W. H. Sewell, and Harold Wilensky, pp. 741-782. New York: Basic Books, 1967.

Kendall, Patricia. "Evaluating an Experimental Program in Medical Evaluation." In *Innovations in Education*, edited by Matthew Miles, pp. 340-360. New York: Columbia University, Teachers College Press, 1967.

Krupp, Sherman. *Pattern In Organizational Analysis: A Critical Examination*. New York: Holt, Rinehart and Winston, 1964.

Lawrence, P. R. "How to Deal with Resistance to Change." *Harvard Business Review* 32 (May-June 1954): 49-57.

Leavitt, H. J. "Applied Organizational Change in Industry: Structural, Technological, and Humanistic Approaches." In *Handbook of Organizations*, edited by James G. March, pp. 1140-1170. New York: Rand McNally, 1965.

Leeds, Ruth, and Smith, Thomasina. *Using Social Science Knowledge in Business and Industry*. Homewood, Ill.: Richard Irwin, 1963.

Likert, Rensis. *The Human Organization*. New York: McGraw-Hill, 1967.

Lyons, Gene. *The Uneasy Partnership: Social Science and the Federal Government in the Twentieth Century*. New York: Russell Sage, 1969.

Miles, Matthew. "Innovations in Education: Some Generalizations." In *Innovations in Education*, edited by Matthew Miles, pp. 631-662. New York: Columbia University, Teachers College Press, 1967.

Myers, Scott. *Every Employee a Manager*. New York: McGraw-Hill, 1970.

National Academy of Sciences, National Research Council. *Behavioral Sciences and the Federal Government.* A report of the Advisory Committee on Government Programs in the Behavioral Sciences. Washington, D.C.: National Research Council, 1968.

National Science Foundation. *Knowledge Into Action: Improving the Nation's Use of the Social Sciences.* A report of the Special Commission on the Social Sciences of the National Science Board. Washington, D.C.: Government Printing Office, 1969.

Neill, A. S. *Summerhill.* New York: Hart, 1960.

Riley, W. "The Sociologist in the Non-Academic Setting." In *The Uses of Sociology,* edited by P. F. Lazarsfeld, W. H. Sewell, and Harold Wilensky, pp. 798-805. New York: Basic Books, 1967.

Rossi, P. "Boobytraps and Pitfalls in the Evaluation of Social Action Programs." In *Proceedings* of the Social Statistics Section of the Annual Meeting of the American Statistical Association, Washington, D.C., 1966.

Suchman, Edward. "Action for What? A Methodological Critique of Evaluation Studies." Paper presented at the annual meeting of the American Sociological Association, 1968.

Wright, Charles, and Hyman, Herbert. "Evaluators." In *Sociologists at Work,* edited by Phillip E. Hammond, pp. 121-141. New York: Basic Books, 1964.

Zander, R. "Resistance to Change: Its Analysis and Prevention." In *The Planning of Change,* edited by W. G. Bennis, K. D. Benne, and Robert Chin, pp. 543-548. New York: Holt, Rinehart and Winston, 1961.

9

POLITICS AND RESEARCH

David K. Cohen

Although program evaluation is no novelty in education, its objects have changed radically. The national thrust against poverty and discrimination introduced a new phenomenon with which evaluators must deal: large-scale programs of social action in education. In addition to generating much activity in city schools, these programs produced considerable confusion whenever efforts were made to find out whether they were "working." The sources of the confusion are not hard to identify. Prior to 1964, the objects of evaluation in education consisted almost exclusively of small programs concerned with such things as curriculum development or teacher training; they generally occurred in a single school or school district, they sought to produce educational change on a limited scale, and typically they involved modest budgets and small research staffs.

This all began to change in the mid-sixties, when the federal government and some states established broad educational improvement programs. The programs—such as Project Head Start, Title I of the 1965 Elementary and Secondary Education Act (ESEA), and Project Follow Through—differ from the traditional objects of educational evaluation in several important respects: they are social action programs, and as such are not focused narrowly on teachers' in-service training or on a science curriculum, but aim broadly at improving education for the disadvantaged; the new programs are directed, not at a school or a school district, but at millions of children, in thousands of schools in hundreds of school jurisdictions

Reprinted from *Review of Educational Research* 40, no. 2 (1970): 213-238. Copyright 1970 by American Educational Research Association, Washington, D.C.

in all the states; they are not conceived and executed by a teacher, a principal, a superintendent, or a researcher—they were created by Congress and are administered by federal agencies far from the school districts that actually design and conduct the individual projects.

Simply to recite these differences is to suggest major new evaluation problems. How does one know when a program that reaches more than eight million children "works"? How does one even decide what "working" means in the context of such large-scale social action ventures? Difficulties also arise from efforts to apply the inherited stock-in-trade evaluation techniques to the new phenomena. If the programs seek broad social change, is it sensible to evaluate them mainly in terms of achievement? If they are national action programs, should evaluation be decentralized?

POLITICS AND EVALUATION

There is one sense in which any educational evaluation ought to be regarded as political. Evaluation is a mechanism with which the character of an educational enterprise can be explored and expressed. These enterprises are managed by people, and they take place in institutions; therefore, any judgment on their nature or results has at least a potential political impact—it can contribute to changing power relationships. This is true whether the evaluation concerns a small curriculum reform program in a rural school (if the program is judged ineffective the director might lose influence or be demoted), or a teacher training program in a university (if it is judged a success its sponsors might get greater authority). Evaluation, as some recent commentators have pointed out, produces information that is at least potentially relevant to decision making (Stufflebeam 1967; Guba 1968). Decision making, of course, is a euphemism for the allocation of resources—money, position, authority, and so on. Thus, to the extent that information is an instrument, basis, or excuse for changing power relationships within or among institutions, evaluation is a political activity.

These political aspects of evaluation are not peculiar to social action programs. They do, however, assume more obvious importance as an educational program grows in size and number of jurisdictions covered: the bigger it is, the greater the likelihood for the overt appearance of political competition.

There is another sense in which evaluation is political, for some programs explicitly aim to redistribute resources or power; although this includes such things as school consolidation, social action programs are the best recent example. They were established by a political institution (Congress) as part of an effort to change the operating priorities of state and local governments and thus to change not only the balance of power within American education but also the relative status of economic and racial groups within the society. One important feature of the new social action programs, then, is their political origin; another is their embodiment of social and political priorities, which reach beyond the schools; a third is that their success would have many far-reaching political consequences.

One political dimension of evaluation is universal, for it involves the uses of information in changing power relationships; the other is peculiar only to those programs in which education is used to rearrange the body politic. Although one can never ignore the former dimension, *its salience in any given situation is directly proportional to the overt political stakes involved;* they are small in curriculum reform in a suburban high school, somewhat larger in a statewide effort to consolidate schools, and very great in national efforts to eliminate poverty. The power at stake in the first effort is small, and its importance slight. In the social action programs, however, the political importance of information is raised to a high level by the broader political character of the programs themselves.

This should be no surprise. Information assumes political importance within local school jurisdictions, but political competition *among* school jurisdictions usually involves higher stakes—and the social action programs promote competition among levels of government. These programs are almost always sponsored by state or federal government, with at least the implicit or partial intent of setting new priorities for state and local governments. In this situation evaluation becomes a political instrument, a means to determine whether the new priorities are being met and to assess the differential effectiveness of jurisdictions or schools in meeting them. As a result, evaluation is affected by the prior character of intergovernmental relations. State resistance to federal involvement, for example, predates recent efforts to evaluate and assess federal social action programs. The history colors the evaluation issue and the state response reflects the prior pattern of relations, for evaluation is correctly seen as an effort to assert federal priorities. Evaluation also can affect patterns of intergovernmental relations for it can help consolidate new authority for the superordinate government. In general, however, evaluation seems to reflect the established pattern of intergovernmental relations.

Of course, not all the novelties in evaluating large-scale social action programs are political. There are serious logistic difficulties—the programs are bigger than anything ever evaluated in education, which poses unique problems—and there is no dearth of methodological issues. These mostly center around making satisfactory comparisons between "treated" subjects and some criterion presumed to measure an otherwise comparable condition of nontreatment. These are difficult in any program with multiple criterion variables, and when the program is spread over the entire country the problems multiply enormously. But difficult though these issues may be, they are in all formal respects the same, irrespective of the size, age, aim, or outcome of the program in question. The large-scale programs do not differ in some formal property of the control-comparison problem, but only in its size. The bigger and more complicated the programs, the bigger the associated methodological headaches. What distinguishes the new programs are not the formal problems of knowing their effects, but the character of their aims and their organization. These are essentially political.

The politics of social action programs produce two sorts of evaluation problems. One is conceptual—the programs' nature and aims have not been well understood or adequately expressed in evaluation design. The other is practical—the interested parties do not agree on the ordering of priorities that the programs embody. As a result of the first, evaluation is misconceived; as a result of the second, evaluation becomes a focus for expressing conflicting political interests.

CONCEPTUAL PROBLEMS

The central conceptual difficulty can be simply summarized: while the new programs seek to bring about political and social change, evaluators generally approach them as though they were standard efforts to produce educational change. This results in no small part from ambiguity of the programs—since they are political endeavors in education, the program content and much of the surrounding rhetoric is educational. It also occurs because evaluation researchers identify professionally and intellectually with their disciplines of origin (mostly education and psychology), and thus would rather not study politics. They prefer education and psychology, since that is what they know, what their colleagues understand, and—if done well—what will bring them distinction and prestige (Dentler 1969).

But whatever the sources of the incongruence, it produces inappropriate evaluation. The aims and character of the programs are misconceived, and as a result evaluation design and execution are of limited value. Title I of ESEA (U.S. Congress 1965a) is a good example with which to begin.

In the four years ESEA has been in existence, the federal government completed several special evaluation studies, undertaken either by the Office of the Secretary for Health, Education, and Welfare or the Office of Education. (The National evaluations of Title I are little more than annual reports based on the state evaluation reports, which are little more than compilations of LEA reports. This is not to say that the reports are useless—but simply that they are not evaluations. The Office of the HEW Secretary was responsible for a study by Tempo [1968]. Also, see Piccariello [n. d.].) They concentrated mainly on one question—has the program improved achievement over what otherwise might have been expected? The answer in each case was almost entirely negative and, not surprisingly, this led many to conclude that the Title I program was not "working." This, in turn, raised or supported doubts about the efficacy of the legislation or the utility of compensatory education. Yet such inferences are sensible only if two crucial assumptions are accepted:

1. That children's achievement test scores are a sufficient criterion of the program's aims—the consequences intended by the government—to stand as an adequate summary measure of its success; and

2. That the Title I program is sufficiently coherent and unified to warrant the application of *any* summary criterion of success, be it achievement or something else.

Both assumptions merit inspection.

It does not seem unreasonable to assume that improving the achievement of disadvantaged children is a crucial aim of the Title I program. Much of the program's rhetoric suggests that it seeks to reduce the high probability of school failure associated with poverty. Many educators and laymen regard achievement test scores as a suitable measure of school success, on the theory that children with higher achievement will have higher grades, happier teachers, more positive attitudes toward school, and therefore a better chance of remaining and succeeding.

There are, however, two difficulties with this view. One is that achievement scores are not an adequate summary of the legislation's diverse aims. The other is that hardly anyone cares about the test scores themselves—they are regarded as a suitable measure of program success only because they are believed to stand for other things.

The second point can easily be illustrated. Aside from a few intellectuals who think that schooling is a good thing in itself, people think test scores are important because they are thought to signify more knowledge, which will lead to more years in school, better job opportunities, more money, and more of the ensuing social and economic status Americans seem to enjoy. Poor people, they reason, have little money, undesirable jobs (if any), and, by definition, the lowest social and economic status presently available. The poor also have less education than most of their countrymen. On the popular assumptions just described, it is easy to argue that "poverty can be eliminated" by increasing the efficiency of education for the poor.

Although much abbreviated, this chain of reasoning is not a bad statement of the reasons why improved achievement is an aim of Title I. Improved schooling was a major antipoverty strategy, and higher school achievement simply a proxy for one of the program's main aims—improving adults' social and economic status. The principal problem this raises for evaluation is that the criterion of program effectiveness is actually only a surrogate for the true criterion. This would pose no difficulty if reliable estimates of the causal relationship between schoolchildren's achievement and their later social and economic status existed. Unfortunately, no information of this sort seems to be available. There is one major study relating years of school completed and occupational status; it shows that, once inherited status is controlled, years of school completed are moderately related to adult occupational status (Blau and Duncan 1968). Other studies reveal no direct relationship between intelligence and occupational status, but they do show that the education-occupation relationship is much weaker for Negroes than for whites (Duncan 1968). The first of these findings should not encourage advocates of improved achievement, and the second is hardly encouraging to those who perceive blacks as a major target group for antipoverty programs.

There are studies that show that more intelligent people stay in school longer (Duncan 1968), but it is hardly clear a priori that raising achievement for disadvantaged children will keep them in school, nor is it self-evident that keeping poor children in school longer will get them better jobs. (By *achievement,* I mean measures of reading or general verbal ability; I do not include therein more specialized measures of achievement such as math., social studies, science, or driver education.) It is, for example, not difficult to imagine that the more intelligent children who stay in school longer do so because they also have learned different behavior patterns, which include greater tolerance for delayed gratification, more docility, less overt aggression, and greater persistence. Several compensatory programs are premised on these notions, rather than on the achievement-production idea. Without any direct evidence on the consequence of either approach, however, it is difficult to find a rational basis for choice.

This does not mean that compensatory education programs founded on either view are a mistake—absent any data one could hardly take that position. It does suggest, however, that using achievement—or any other form of school behavior—as a proxy for the actual long-range purpose of compensatory education is probably ill founded. The chief difficulty with this variety of agnosticism, of course, is that the only alternative is evaluation studies whose duration would make them of interest only to the next generation. What is more, they would be extremely expensive. The current proportion of program budgets devoted to evaluation indicates that the probability of undertaking such studies is nil.

Even if this scientific embarrassment were put aside, there is the other major difficulty with using achievement as an evaluation criterion. Schoolmen must be expected to assume that the greater application of their efforts will improve students' later lives, but there is no evidence that Congress subscribed to that view by passing Title I of the 1965 ESEA. Although the title did contain an unprecedented mandate for program evaluation—and even specified success in school as a criterion—this is scant evidence that the sole program aim was school achievement. The mandate for evaluation—like many congressional authorizations—lacked any enabling mechanism: responsibility for carrying out the evaluation was specifically delegated to the state and local education authorities who operated the programs. It was not hard to see, in 1965, that this was equivalent to abandoning much hope of useful program evaluation.

The main point, however, is that the purposes of the legislation were much more complex; most of them could be satisfied without any evidence about children's achievement. Certainly this was true for aid to parochial school students, and most likely it was also true for many of the poorer school districts: for them (as for many of the congressmen who voted for the act) more money was good in itself. Moreover, Congress is typically of two minds on the matter of program evaluation in education—it subscribes to efficiency, but it does not believe in federal control of the schools. National evaluations are regarded as a major step toward federal control by many people, including some members of Congress.

Although the purposes of Congress may be too complicated to be summarized in studies of test scores, they are not, by that token, mysterious. The relevant committee hearings and debates suggest that the legislative intent included several elements other than those already mentioned. (Bailey and Mosher [1968] provide a good general treatment. See also: U.S. Congress 1965*b*, U.S. House of Representatives Education and Labor Committee 1965*a* and *b*, U.S. Senate Appropriations Committee 1965, and U.S. Senate Labor and Public Welfare Committee 1965.) One involved the rising political conflict over city schools in the early 1960s; many legislators felt that spreading money on troubled waters might bring peace. Another concerned an older effort to provide federal financial assistance for public education: the motives for this were mainly political and ideological, and were not intimately tied to achievement. A third involved the larger cities; although not poor when compared to the national average expenditure, they were increasingly hard-pressed to maintain educational services that were competitive with other districts in their areas as property values declined, population changed, and costs and taxes rose. Educators and other municipal officials were among the warmest friends of the new aid scheme, because it promised to relieve some of the pressure on their revenues.

Indeed, many purposes of the legislation—and Congress's implicit attitude toward evaluation—can be summarized in the form which it gave to fund apportionment. Title I is a formula grant, in which the amount of money flowing to any educational agency is a function of how many poor children it has, not of how well it educates them. In a sense, Title I is the educational equivalent of a rivers and harbors bill. There is no provision for withdrawing funds for nonperformance, nor is there much suggestion of such intent in the original committee hearings or floor debates. Given the formula grant system, neither the federal funding agency or the states have much political room to maneuver, even if they have the results of superb evaluation in hand. Without the authority to manipulate funds, achievement evaluation results could only be used to coax and cajole localities: the one major implicit purpose of program evaluation— more rational resource allocation—is seriously weakened by the Title I formula grant system.

It is, therefore, difficult to conclude that improving schools' production of poor children's achievement was the legislation's major purpose. The legislative intent embraced many other elements: improving educational services in school districts with many poor children, providing fiscal relief for the central cities and parochial schools, reducing discontent and conflict about race and poverty, and establishing the principal of federal responsibility for local school problems. The fact that these were embodied in a single piece of legislation contributed heavily to its passage, but it also meant that the resulting program was not single-purpose or homogeneous. If any supposition is in order, it is precisely the opposite. Title I is typical of reform legislation in a large and diverse society with a federal political system: it reflected various interests, decentralized power, and for these reasons a variety of programmatic and political priorities.

CONSEQUENCES FOR EVALUATION

Misconceptions about program aims result in omissions in evaluations and in distortions of the relationship among various aspects of evaluation. The first problem is mainly confined to program delivery. For Title I, for example, there are several criteria of program success that appear never to have been scrutinized. One involves the impact of Title I on the fiscal position of the parochial schools: as nearly as I can tell, this purpose of the act has never been explored. (The most recent report of the National Advisory Council on the Education of Disadvantaged Children [1969] contains a brief section on this issue. It does not deal with program impact, but with private-parochial school relations.) Another involves the impact of Title I upon the fiscal situation of the central cities and their position *vis-à-vis* adjacent districts. Although the redistributive intent of the title was clear, there is little evidence of much effort to find out whether it has had this effect. With the exception of one internal Office of Education paper—which showed that Title I had reduced the per pupil expenditure disparity between eleven central cities and their suburbs by about half (Jackson 1969)—this subject appears to have received no attention. (Hartman [n. d.] concluded that the aims of Title I are so vague as to make the act little more than a general [i.e., noncategorical] vehicle for redistributing educational revenues.) A third involves the quality of education in target as compared with non-target schools. Thus far no data have been collected that would permit an assessment of Title I's effectiveness in reducing intradistrict school resource disparities, although this was one of the most patent purposes of the act. There has been an extended effort, covering 465 school districts (Project 465) to gather information on resource delivery to Title I target schools. This might turn up interesting data on differences in Title I services among schools, districts, or regions, but comparison with schools that do not receive Title I aid is not provided. Since Title I seeks to provide better-than-equal education for the disadvantaged, measuring its impact upon resource disparities between Title I and non-Title I schools within districts would be crucial. This is recognized in the Office of Education regulations governing the Title, which provide that Title I funds must add to existing fiscal and resource equality between Title I and non-Title I schools. (The requirement is found in U. S. Department of Health, Education, and Welfare [1968a]. There also is a special memorandum [Howe 1968] covering this issue.) Important as this purpose of the legislation is, only a few federal audits have been conducted; for the most part, states satisfy the federal requirements simply by passing on data provided by the local education agencies, most of which are so general they are useless.

Such things do not result simply from administrative lapses. Evidence on whether Title I provides better-than-equal schooling would permit a clear judgment on the extent to which federal priorities were being met. But the legislation allocates money to jurisdictions on a strict formula, and it delegates the responsibility for monitoring performance to those same jurisdictions: this reflects both the decentralization of power in the national school system and the sense of Congress that it should remain just so. An important source of inadequate program delivery studies is inadequate federal power or will to impose its priorities on states and localities; the priorities are enunciated in the statute, but the responsibility for determining whether they are being met is left with the states and localities.

The distribution of power is not the sole source of such problems in evaluating program delivery; the sheer size and heterogeneity of the society, and the unfamiliarity of the problems are also important. Project Head Start is illustrative. This program was not initially established within the existing framework of education. It existed mostly outside the system of public schools; its clients were below the age of compulsory education, and its local operating agencies often were independent of the official school agencies. Since the program came into existence, several million dollars have been spent on evaluation, and not a few of them on studies of program delivery. Yet it is still impossible to obtain systematic information on this subject. Several annual national evaluations and U. S. Census studies of program delivery are unpublished. But even if these studies had all been long since committed to print, they would only allow comparisons within the Head Start program. They would provide no basis for comparing how the services delivered to children under this program compare with those available to more advantaged children. That is no easy question to answer, but it is hardly trivial: without an estimate of this program's efficacy in delivering services to children, its efficacy as an antipoverty program could hardly be evaluated.

There have been some recent efforts to remedy the relative absence of information on Title I program delivery, through an extensive management information program under development in twenty-one states. Data are to be collected from a sample of schools that receive federal aid under several programs; it is estimated that the universe of schools and districts from which the sample will be drawn includes roughly 90 percent of all public school students in those states. Extensive information on teachers, on district and school attributes, and funding will be collected from self-administered questionnaires. Principals and teachers will provide information on school and classroom characteristics and programs, including compensatory efforts. In elementary schools the teachers will provide information on student background, but in secondary schools these data may be taken from the students themselves. Some effort also will be made to measure the extent of individual student's exposure to programs. In addition, common testing (using the same instruments in all schools) is planned, beginning with grades four and eleven. If this ambitious effort becomes operational in anything approaching the time planned, in a few years extensive data will be available with which to assess program delivery for Title I.

In summary, then, an underlying purpose of social action programs is to deliver more resources to the poor, whether they are districts, schools, children, or states. It is therefore essential to know how much more and for whom. It is important both because citizens should know the extent to which official intentions have been realized, and because, without much knowledge on that score, it is hard to decide what more should be done. Satisfying these evaluative needs implies measurement that is both historical (keyed to the target population before the program began) and comparative (keyed to the non-target population). (Not all the purposes of social action programs are so neat or abstract, nor can they all be evaluated by counting dollars, teachers, or special programs. One of the aims of large-scale social action programs is to produce peace, or at least to reduce conflict. Whether or not they serve these ends is well worth investigating. Similarly, little is known about the ways in which educational institutions change. This has been highlighted by the ability of many big-city school systems to absorb large amounts of activity and money designed to change them, and emerge apparently unchanged. If any question about the efficacy of social action programs is crucial, it is how such efforts at change succeed or fail. The requirement here may not be quantitative research, but political and social analysis, which follows the political and administrative history of social change programs. It may be possible to learn as much about the sources of programs' success from studying the politics of their intent and execution as from analyzing the quantitative relationships between program components and some summary measure of target group performance. Although such studies would be inapplicable in traditional educational evaluation, they are crucial in the evaluation of social action programs. These programs represent an effort to rearrange political relationships, and the sources of variation in their success are therefore bound to have as much to do with political and administrative matters as with how efficiently program inputs are translated into outcomes.)

Studies of program delivery also serve a building-block function with respect to evaluating program outcomes. Whatever criterion of program effect one might imagine, it could not intelligibly be evaluated in the absence of data that describe the character of the program. Improved health, for example, is a possible outcome of the health care components of Title I and Head Start: one could not usefully collect evidence on changes in students' health without evidence on the character and intensity of the care they received from the program. And, if one were interested in the impact of health care on school performance, it would be necessary to add some measure of students' achievement, classroom behavior, or attitudes. In the case of achievement outcomes, of course, evaluators commonly try to associate information about the type and intensity of academic programs with students' scores on some later test.

Despite the logical simplicity of these relationships, it is not easy to find large-scale social action programs in which outcome evaluation is linked to appropriate program delivery data. Without any direct evidence on program delivery, the only "input" that can be evaluated for a local program is its inclusion in a program. But an acquaintance with national social action ventures leads quickly to the conclusion that an important aspect of such endeavors is the "nontreatment project." There is no reason to believe that mere inclusion necessarily leads to change either in the substance of education or in the level of resources. This phenomenon takes many forms: it may consist of teachers or specialists who never see the target children; it may involve supplies and materials never unpacked, or educational goods and services that reach students other than those for whom they were intended; in still other cases it may consist of using program monies to pay for goods and services already in use. Whatever the specific form the nontreatment project takes, however, recognizing it requires extensive program delivery data. In a decentralized educational system the probability of such occurrences must be fairly high, and the obstacles to discovering them are considerable.

Even if the nontreatment project problem could be ignored, inadequate evidence on program delivery has other consequences for the evaluation of program outcomes. One of them is illustrated by the following excerpt from one Office of Education study of pre- and posttest scores in thirty-three big city Title I programs:

> For the total 189 observations [each observation was one classroom in a Title I program], there were 108 significant changes (exceed 2 s.e.). Of these 58 were gains and 50 were losses. In 81 cases the change did not appear to be significant.
>
> As the data in Appendix D show, success and failure seem to be random outcomes, determined neither clearly nor consistently by the factors of program design, city or state, area or grade level (Piccariello [n. d.] p. 4).

When one reads Appendix D, however, he finds that the categorization by program design rests exclusively on one paragraph program descriptions of the sort often furnished by the local project directors in grant applications. This makes it difficult to grasp the meaning of the study's conclusions. Perhaps success and failure were random with respect to program content, but, given the evidence at hand, it is just as sensible to argue that program content is unrelated to project descriptions, and that some underlying pattern of causation exists. (Actually, the evaluation found that gains were more common among classrooms that had low scores on the pretests and that losses were more common among those classrooms that had higher pretests. The most economical hypothesis, then, is a regression effect.). Without evidence on program delivery, it is not easy to see what can be learned from evaluations of this sort.

There is, however, an important counter-argument on this point. The recent Westinghouse evaluation of Project Head Start, for example, took as its chief independent variable *inclusion in Head Start projects*. The premise for this was that the government has a legitimate interest in determining whether a program produces the expected results. On this view, arguments about program delivery are irrelevant since, from the sponsoring agency's perspective, inclusion in the program is of overriding interest. (See Evans 1969.)

There certainly is no question that in principle overall program evaluation is justified. But the principle need not lead to a single summary evaluation in practice. Judgments about a program's overall impact can just as well be derived from an evaluation that distinguishes program types or differentiates program delivery as from one that ignores them. From this perspective, rather than reporting whether the "average" Head Start project raised achievement, it would be more meaningful to identify the several program types and determine whether each improved achievement.

This may seem sensible, but it is not easy to put into practice. How does one collect data on program types or distinguish program characteristics? Assume a hypothetical program in which the outcome variable is school achievement. The first step would be to drop all projects whose purpose is not to improve achievement. But, if one reads any compilation of project aims in Title I, he finds that only a minority aims to improve only achievement. Another minority aims to improve something else, and a majority aims to do both, or more. Given this heterogeneity of aims and the nontreatment project problem, one could not proceed on the basis of project descriptions—the stated purpose of improving achievement would have to be validated by looking at programs. The second step would be to distinguish the main approaches (the program types) from all those that actually sought to raise achievement. The main purpose of the evaluation is to distinguish the relative effectiveness of several approaches to this goal.

But if the logic seems clear, the procedure does not. To distinguish empirically the class of projects aimed at raising achievement, one must first know what it is about schooling that affects achievement. Only on the basis of such information would it be possible to sort out those projects whose execution was consistent with their aims from those that were not. But when the new programs were established very little was known on this point: prior compensatory education efforts were few, far between, and mostly failures. The legislation was not the fruit of systematic experimentation and program development, but the expression of a paroxysm of concern. Although a good deal has been learned in the last four or five years, researchers are still a good way from an inventory of techniques known to improve school achievement. The only way one can tell if a project is of the sort that improves achievement, then, is not to inspect the treatment but to inspect the results.

This creates an awkward situation. If there is no empirical typology of compensatory or remedial programs, what basis is there for distinguishing among programs? What basis is there for deciding which program characteristics to measure—if one does not know what improves achievement, how does one select the program attributes to measure? Some choice is essential, for evaluations cannot measure everything.

These questions focus attention on one important attribute of the new programs. To the extent that they seek to affect some outcome of schooling, such as attitudes or achievement, they represent a sort of muddling-through—an attempt at research and development on a national scale. This is not a comment on the legislative intent, but simply a description of existing knowledge. If program managers and evaluators do not know what strategies will affect school outcomes, it is not sensible to carry out overall, one-shot evaluations of entire national programs: the results of strategies that improved achievement might be canceled out by the effects of those that did not. If the point is to find what "works," the emphasis should be on defining distinct strategies, trying them out, and evaluating the results. The highest priority should be maximum definition and differentiation among particular approaches. Program managers and evaluators must therefore devise educational treatments based on relatively little prior research and experience, carry them out under natural conditions, evaluate the results, and compare them with those from other similarly developed programs. Insofar as school outcomes are the object of evaluation, the work must take place in the context of program development and comparative evaluation. This requirement raises a host of new problems related to the intentional manipulation of school programs and organization within the American polity.

EXPERIMENTAL APPROACHES

The problem, then, is not only to identify what the programs deliver, but also to experiment systematically with strategies for affecting school outcomes. This idea has been growing in the federal bureaucracy as experience with the social action programs reveals that the system of natural experiments (every local project does what it likes on the theory that good results would arise, be identified, and disseminated) has not worked. The movement toward experimentation presumes that the most efficient way to proceed is by systematic trial and discard, discovering and replicating effective strategies.

Under what conditions might social action programs assume a partly experimental character? For Title I this would not be easy, because the legislation did not envisage it. It is a major operating program, and several of its purposes have nothing to do with achievement. Activities in Washington designed to carry out systematic research and development would generate considerable opposition among recipient state and local educational agencies, and in Congress. Experimentation requires a good deal of bureaucratic and political control, and there is little evidence of that. The Office of Education, for example, does not require that the same tests be used in all Title I projects—indeed, it does not require that *any* tests be used. The Title I program's managers have neither the power nor the inclination to assign educational strategies to local educational agencies. Even if they did, the legislation would be at cross-purposes with such efforts. It aims to improve resource delivery—to ease the fiscal hardships of city and parochial schools, and to equalize educational resource disparities. Although the formula grant system is quite consistent with these aims, it is not consistent with experimentation. The two aims imply different administrative arrangements, reporting systems, and patterns of federal-state-local relations. The experimental approach requires a degree of control over school program that seems incompatible with the other purposes of Title I.

The question is whether other programs offer a better prospect for experimentation in compensatory education. In mid-1968, the White House Task Force on Child Development recommended that federal education programs adopt a policy of "planned variation"; the Task Force report argued that no learning from efforts to improve education was occurring with existing programs, and that it would result only from systematic efforts to try out different strategies under a variety of school and community conditions (U.S. Department of Health, Education, and Welfare 1968*b*).

The Task Force report focused its attention on Project Follow Through. Follow Through was originally intended to extend Head Start services from preschool to the primary grades, but severe first year budgetary constraints had greatly reduced its scope. Largely for this reason, the program seemed a natural candidate for experimentation. The Task Force recommended that federal officials select a variety of educational strategies and develop evaluation plans using common measures of school outcomes in all cases.

> The administration should explicitly provide budget and personnel allowances for a Follow Through staff to stimulate and develop projects consistent with these plans . . .

> The Office of Education should select all new Follow Through projects in accordance with these plans for major variation and evaluation.

After three years, can the effort be termed a success? Since the program is still under development it would be unwise to deal with the strategies or their impact upon achievement. My concern is only with the quality of the evaluation scheme and the discussion is meant to be illustrative; the evaluation design may change, but the underlying problems are not likely to evaporate.

The Follow Through program of experimentation is designed to determine which educational strategies improve achievement over what might otherwise be expected, and what the relative efficiency of the strategies is. The program began with little knowledge about the determinants of academic achievement and, as a consequence, equating schools and programs becomes much more difficult. Assume, for example, that all the Follow Through projects sought to change student achievement by changing teachers' classroom behavior, but no two projects used the same treatment or attacked the same dimension of behavior. Suppose further that in half the projects achievement gains for students resulted. How could one be sure that the gains derived from the Follow Through strategies, and not from selection or other teacher attributes than those manipulated by the program? The obvious answer is to measure teacher attributes and use the data to "control" the differences. But, since the program begins with little knowledge of what it is about teachers and teaching that affects achievement, evaluators must either measure *all* the teacher attributes that might affect achievement or closely approximate an experimental design. The first alternative is logically impossible, for the phenomena are literally unknown. The second alternative poses no logical problems; it requires only that the federal experimenter have extensive control over the assignment of subjects (schools, school systems, and teachers) to treatment. The problems it raises are administrative and political.

The Follow Through program has not been able to surmount them. Neither the districts nor the schools appear to have been selected in a manner consistent with experimental design. The districts were nominated by state officials; those nominated could accept or decline, and those who accepted could pretty much choose the strategy they desired from several alternatives. There was, then, room for self-selection. In addition, the purveyors of the strategies— the consultants who conceived, designed, and implemented or trained others to implement the strategies—seem also to have been recruited exclusively by self-selection. The usual ways of dealing with selection problems (never entirely satisfactory) seem even less helpful here. Although experimental and nonexperimental schools could be compared to see if they differed in any important respects, the relevance of this procedure is unclear when little is known about what those "important respects" (vis-à-vis improving education for disadvantaged children) happen to be.

The weight of the evaluation strategy seems to fall on comparison or control groups. The present plan calls for selecting a sample of treatment and control classrooms, carrying out classroom observation, measuring teachers' background and attitudes, and using variables derived from these measurements in multivariate analyses of student achievement. Most of the instruments are still under development. But, since there is neither a compulsion nor an incentive for principals in non-Follow Through schools to participate as controls, how representative will the control classrooms be? What is more, these control or comparison groups cannot serve as much of a check on selectivity among the participants. Many of the comparison schools are in the same districts that selected themselves into the program and chose particular treatments; even those that are not are bound to be somewhat selected, because of the voluntary character of participation. Even if no "significant differences" are found between experimental and control schools, this would only prove that selected experimental schools are not very different from selected control schools.

There also may be some confounding of Follow Through with related programs. Follow Through operates in schools that are likely to receive other federal (and perhaps state and local) aid to improve education for disadvantaged children. Students will have the benefit of more than one compensatory program, either directly or through generally improved services and program in their school. There is little evidence at the moment of any effort to deal with this potential source of confounding.

In addition to selection, there are problems related to sample size.

The design assumes that classrooms are the unit of analysis; this is appropriate, since they are the unit of treatment. Almost all measurements of program impact are classroom aggregates—that is, they measure a classroom's teacher, its climate, its teaching strategy, and so on. But it seems that relatively few classrooms will be selected from each project for evaluation (the 1969/70 plans called for an average of almost five per project, distributed over grades K-2). Since there are only a few classrooms per grade per project, it appears that in the larger projects there might be a dozen experimental units (classrooms) per grade. That is a very small number, especially when it is reasonable to expect some variation among classrooms on such things as teacher and student attributes, classroom styles, and so on. In fact, since only six or eight of the strategies that are being tried involve large numbers of projects, the remaining strategies (more than half the total) probably will not have sufficient cases for much of an evaluation.

There has been some effort to deal with this problem by expanding the student achievement testing to cover almost all classrooms in Follow Through. This has not, however, been paralleled by expanded measurement of what actually is done in classrooms, a procedure that is helpful only on the assumption that there is no significant variation among classrooms within projects or strategies on variables related to the treatment or the effect. If this is true, of course, then measuring *anything* about the content, staff, or style of the classroom is superfluous—one need only designate whether or not it is an experimental or control unit. Despite the evaluators' view that this approach is warranted, the inclusion of some classrooms for which the only independent variable is a dummy variable (treatment-nontreatment) seems dubious. This will inflate the case base and therefore produce more statistical "confidence" in the results, but it may so sharply reduce the nonstatistical confidence that the exercise will be useless. The evaluators argue that, given the fixed sum for evaluation, they cannot extend measurement of classroom content.

Sample size problems are compounded because the evaluation is longitudinal. Since there is interclassroom mobility in promotion (all classes are not passed on from teacher to teacher *en bloc*), following children for more than one year will sharply reduce the number of subjects for which two- or three-year treatment and effect measures can be computed. Add to this the rather high interschool pupil mobility that seems to be characteristic of slum schools, and nightmarish anxieties about sample attrition result. Although nothing is certain at this point, there will be considerable obstacles to tracing program effects over time.

A fourth problem relates to student background measures. Apparently these data are being collected only for a relatively small sample of families. The evaluators are not sure that it will be large enough to allow consideration of both project impact and family background variables at once, but budget constraints preclude expanding the sample.

There are a few additional difficulties that merit mention, though they do not arise from the evaluation strategy, but from the nature of social action programs. There are reports of "leakage" of treatments from Follow Through to comparison schools in some communities; there also seem to have been shifts in program goals in some projects, and apparently there has been conflict in definition of aims between the Follow Through administration and some projects. In fact, there appears to be an element of noncomparability emerging among the strategies. Some involve very broad approaches, whose aims center around such things as parent involvement in or control of schools; others are more narrowly defined and research-based strategies for improving cognitive growth. As long as traditional evaluation questions are asked (did treatment produce results different from an otherwise comparable nontreatment?), this poses no problem, but comparing treatments is close to the heart of Follow Through. It is difficult to see how such comparative questions can be answered when the programs are so diverse. The general change programs, for example, appear to be hostile to the idea of evaluations based on achievement. They seem to be moving toward establishing other outcomes—"structural change" in schools for example—as the program aim of primary concern. This heterogeneity of aims may well restrict the scope of comparative analysis for Follow Through.

The common element in all these difficulties is that the Office of Education is largely powerless to remedy them. Random assignment of schools to treatments and securing proper control groups are the most obvious cases; lack of funds to generate adequate samples of experimental classrooms or parents are other manifestations of the same phenomenon. Although there is no doubt that some problems could have been eased by improved management, no amount of forethought or efficiency can produce money or power where there is none. Nor is it easy to see how the Office of Education could effectively compel project sponsors not to change some aspects of their strategies or not to alter their motion of program aims.

The experience thus far with Follow Through suggests, then, that the serious obstacles to experimentation are political: first, power in the educational system is almost completely decentralized (at least from a national perspective), and federal experimentation must conform to this pattern; second, the resources allocated to eliminating educational disadvantage are small when compared to other federal priorities, which indicates the government's relatively low political investment in such efforts. Consequently, federal efforts to experiment begin with a grave deficit in the political and fiscal resources required to mount them, and there is little likelihood of much new money or more power with which to redress this imbalance. These difficulties are not peculiar to evaluation: they result from the same conditions that make it difficult to mount and operate effective reform programs. The barriers to evaluation are simply another manifestation of the obstacles to federally-initiated reform when most power is local and when reform is a relatively low national priority.

Several dimensions of social action program evaluation emerge from this analysis. My purpose here is not to provide a final typology of evaluation activities, but simply to suggest the salient elements. First among these is the identification of program aims; this ordinarily will involve the recognition of diversity, obscurity, and conflict within programs, and greater attention to program delivery. Evaluators of social action programs often complain that the programs lack any clear and concise statement of aims, a condition that they deplore because it muddies up evaluations. Their response generally has been to bemoan the imprecision and fuzzy-mindedness of the politicians and administrators who establish the programs, and then to choose a summary measure of program accomplishment that satisfies their more precise approach. I propose to stand this on its head and question the intellectually fuzzy single-mindedness of much educational evaluation. It generally has not grasped the diverse and conflicting nature of social action programs, and therefore produces unrealistically constrained views of program aims.

The second dimension is clarity about the social and political framework of measurement. In traditional evaluation the ideal standard of comparison (the control group or premeasure) is one that is just like the treatment group in all respects except the treatment. But in social action programs the really important standard of comparison is the nontreatment group—what one is really interested in is how much improvement the program produces *relative to those who do not need it*. As a result the evaluation of social action programs is essentially comparative and historical, despite its often quantitative character: it seeks to determine whether a target population has changed, relative both to the same population before the program began and to the non-target population.

Finally, the evaluation of social action programs in education is political. Evaluation is a technique for measuring the satisfaction of public priorities; to evaluate a social action program is to establish an information system in which the main questions involve the allocation of power, status, and other public goods. There is conflict within the educational system concerning which priorities should be satisfied, and it is transmitted, willy-nilly, to evaluation. This puzzles and irritates many researchers; they regard it as extrinsic and an unnecessary bother. While this attitude is understandable, it is mistaken. The evaluation of social action programs is nothing if not an effort to measure social and political change. That is a difficult task under any circumstance, but it is impossible when the activity is not seen for what it is.

SUGGESTIONS FOR AN EVALUATION STRATEGY

What might be the elements of a more suitable evaluation strategy? The answer depends not only on what one thinks should be done, but on certain external political constraints. There is, for example, good reason to believe that federal education aid will be shifted into the framework of revenue sharing or block grants in the near future, and this is unlikely to strengthen the government's position as a social or educational experimenter. The only apparent alternative is to continue with roughly the present balance of power in education as categorical aid slowly increases the federal share of local expenditures. This seems unlikely to improve the government's position in the evaluation of large-scale social action programs. In addition, there seems to be a growing division over the criteria of program success. Researchers are increasingly aware that little evidence connects the typical criteria of program success (high achievement and good deportment), with their presumed adult consequences (better job, higher income, and so on). More important, in the cities—particularly in the Negro community—there is rising opposition to the view that achievement and good behavior are legitimate criteria of success. Instead, political legitimacy—in the form of parent involvement or community control—is advanced as a proper aim for school change programs. It is ironic that the recent interest in assessing schools' efficiency—which gained much of its impetus from black discontent with white-dominated ghetto schools—now meets with rising opposition in the Negro community as blacks seek control over ghetto education. Nonetheless, this opposition is likely to increase, and the evaluation of social action programs in city schools is sure to be affected.

There is, then, little reason to expect much relaxation of the political constraints on social action program evaluation. This suggests two principles that might guide future evaluation: experiment only when the substantive issues of policy are considerable and reasonably well defined, and reorient evaluation of the nonexperimental operating programs to a broad system of measuring status and change in schools and schooling.

The first principle requires distinctions among potential experiments in terms of the political constraints they imply. One would like to know, for example, which preschool and primary programs increase cognitive growth for disadvantaged children; whether giving parents money to educate their children (as opposed to giving it to schools) would improve the children's education; whether students' college entrance would suffer if high school curriculum and attendance requirements were sharply reduced or eliminated; whether school decentralization would improve achievement; or whether it would raise it as much as doubling expenditures.

These are among the most important issues in American education, but they are not equally difficult when it comes to arranging experiments to determine the answers. In most cases, large-scale experimentation would be impossible. Experiments with decentralization, tuition vouchers, doubling expenditures per pupil, and radical changes in secondary education have two salient attributes in common: to have meaning they would have to be carried out in the existing schools, and few schools would be likely to oblige. If experimentation occurs on such issues it would be limited—a tentative exploration of new ideas involving small numbers of students and schools. While this is highly desirable, it is not the same thing as mounting an experimental social action program in education.

This may not be the case with one issue, however—increasing cognitive growth for disadvantaged children. It already is the object of several social action programs and would not be a radical political departure. As a result of prior efforts, enough may be known to permit comparative experimental studies of different strategies for changing early intelligence. Several alternative approaches can be identified: rigid classroom drill, parent training, individual tutoring at early ages, and language training. Relatively little is known about the processes underlying these approaches, but there may be enough practical experience to support systematic comparative study. Since all the strategies have a common object, researchers probably could agree on common criterion measures. Since cognitive growth is widely believed to be crucial, investment in comparative studies seems worthwhile. But if such studies were undertaken, they should determine whether the treatment effect itself (higher IQ) is only a proxy for other things learned during the experiment, such as academic persistence, good behavior, and whether cognitive change produces any change on other measures of educational success, such as grades or years of school completed.

In effect, the chances for success of experimental approaches to social action will be directly related to a program's political independence, its specificity of aim, and its fiscal strength. The less it resembles the sort of broad-aim social action programs discussed here, the more appropriate is an experimental approach and the more the evaluation looks like pure research. Of course, the further one moves down this continuum the less the program's impact is, and the less relevant the appellation *social action*.

The second principle suggested above implies that the central purpose of evaluating most social action programs is the broad measurement of change. Evaluation is a comparative and historical enterprise, which can best be carried out as part of a general effort to measure educational status and change. The aims of social action programs are diverse, and their purpose is to shift the position of specified target populations relative to the rest of society; their evaluation cannot be accomplished by isolated studies of particular aims with inappropriate standards of comparison. Evaluating broad social action programs requires comparably broad systems of social measurement.

A measurement system of this sort would be a census or system of social indicators of schools and schooling (not education). It would cover three realms: student, personnel, program, and fiscal inputs to schools; several outcomes of schooling, including achievement; and temporal, geographic, political, and demographic variation in both categories. If data of these sorts were collected on a regular and recurring basis, they would serve the main evaluation needs for such operating programs as Title I. They would, for example, allow measurement of fiscal and resource delivery and of their variations over time, region, community, and school type. They would permit measurement of differences in school outcomes, as well as their changes over time. If the measurement of school outcomes were common over all schools, their variations could be associated with variations in other school attributes, including those of students, school resources, and the content and character of federal programs. Finally, if the measurement of outcomes and resources were particular to individual students, many of these comparisons could be extended from schools to individuals.

One advantage of such a measurement system would be its greater congruence with the structure and aims of large-scale multipurpose programs. Another is that it would be more likely to provide data that could be useful in governmental decision making—which, after all, is what evaluation is for. Most evaluation research in programs such as Title I is decentralized, nonrecurring, and unrelated to either program planning or budgeting; as a result of the first attribute it is not comparable from community to community; as a result of the second it is not comparable from year to year; and as a result of the third it is politically and administratively irrelevant. Since the main governmental decisions about education involve allocating money and setting standards for goods, services, and performance, evaluation should provide comparable, continuing, and cumulative information in these areas. That would only be possible under a regular census of schools and schooling.

This is not to say there would be no deficiencies; there would be several, all of which are pretty well given in the nature of a census. By definition a census measures stasis, it quantifies how things stand. If done well, it can reveal a good deal about the interconnection of social structure; if it recurs, it can throw much light on how things change. But no census can reveal much about change other than its patterns—probing its causes and dynamics requires rather a different research orientation. And no census can produce qualitative data, especially on such complicated organizations as schools. There is, however, no reason why qualitative evaluation could not be systematically related to a census. Such evidence is much more useful when it recurs and is connected with the results of quantitative studies. The same is true of research on the political dynamics and consequences of social action programs. Although valuable in itself, its worth would be substantially increased by relating it to other evidence on the same program.

The central problem, however, is experimentation. Using a census as the central evaluation device for large-scale multipurpose programs assumes that systematic experimentation is very nearly impossible within the large operating programs and can best be carried on by clearly distinguishing census from experimental functions. It would be foolish to ignore experimentation—it should be increased—but it would be illusory to try to carry it out within programs that have other purposes. A clear view of the importance of both activities is unlikely to emerge until they have been distinguished conceptually and pulled apart administratively.

These suggestions are sketchy, and they leave some important issues open. Chief among them are the institutional and political arrangements required to mount both an effective census of schools and schooling and a long-term effort in experimentation. (Creating the capacity for experimentation would involve a few major decisions. One probably would be to separate the activity from the Office of Education, retaining its connection with HEW at the assistant secretary level. Another would be to create greater institutional capacity for support and evaluation in the private (or quasi-public) sector; at the moment, this important resource is not well enough developed to bear the load. A third would be to arrange its management so that the decisions about what experiments to fund resulted from systematic and sustained interaction between the political governors of such an institution, its scientific staffers and constituents, and the educational practitioners. Without this, it would probably do interesting but politically unimportant work.) Nonetheless, my suggestions do express a *strategy* of evaluation, something absent in most large-scale educational evaluation efforts. The strategy assumes that government has two distinct needs, which thus far have been confounded in the evaluation of large-scale action programs. One is to measure status and change in the distribution of educational resources and outcomes; the other is to explore the impact and effectiveness of novel approaches to schooling. If the first were undertaken on a regular basis the resulting time-series data would provide much greater insight into the actual distribution of education in America. It would thus build an information base for more informed decisions about allocation of resources, at both the state and federal level. If the second effort were undertaken on a serious basis, it should be possible to learn more systematically from research and development. Perhaps the best way to distinguish this strategy from existing efforts is this: were the present approach to evaluating social action programs brought to perfection, it would not be adequate—it would not tell us what we need to know about the programs.

My suggestions also assume that the evaluation of social action programs is a political enterprise. This underlies the idea of separating experimentation from large-scale operating programs. It also underlies the notion of a census of schools and schooling, which would almost compel attention to the proper standards of comparison and would emphasize the importance of change. In addition, only a broad system of measurement can capture the political variety that social action programs embody. Perhaps most important, measuring the impact of social change programs in this way is not tied to a particular program or pattern of federal aid.

Such a strategy could be implemented within the existing political constraints. That is not a scientific argument, but that is the real point: evaluating social action programs is only secondarily a scientific enterprise. First and foremost it is an effort to gain politically significant information on the consequences of political acts. To confuse the technology of measurement with the real nature and broad purposes of evaluation will be fatal. It can only produce increasing quantities of information in answer to unimportant questions.

FOOTNOTE

Research for this paper was supported by a grant from the Carnegie Corporation of New York to the Center for Educational Policy Research, Harvard University. Henry Dyer, Frederick Mosteller, and Martin Rein served as consultants to Dr. Cohen on the preparation of this chapter.

REFERENCES

Bailey, S., and Mosher, E. *ESEA: The Office of Education Administers a Law.* Syracuse, N.Y.: Syracuse University Press, 1968.

Blau, P., and Duncan, O. *The American Occupational Structure.* New York: Wiley, 1968.

Dentler, R. "The Phenomenology of the Evaluation Researcher." Paper read at the Conference on Evaluating Social Action Programs, American Academy of Arts and Sciences, New York, May 1969.

Duncan, O. *Socioeconomic Background and Occupational Achievement.* Ann Arbor: University of Michigan Press, 1968.

Guba, E. "Development, Diffusion, and Evaluation." In *Knowledge Production and Utilization in Educational Administration,* edited by T. Eidell and J. Kitchel, pp. 37-63. Eugene, Ore.: University Council for Educational Administration and Center for the Study of Educational Administration, 1968.

Hartman, R. "Evaluation in Multi-Purpose Grant-in-Aid Programs." Typewritten. Washington, D.C.: The Brookings Institution, n.d.

Howe, Harold. "Special Memorandum." Washington, D.C.: U.S. Department of Health, Education, and Welfare, Office of Education, 1968.

Jackson, P. B. "Trends in Elementary and Secondary Education Expenditures: Central City and Suburban Comparisons, 1965-1968." Mimeographed. Washington, D.C.: U.S. Department of Health, Education, and Welfare, Office of Education, Office of Program Planning and Evaluation, 1969.

National Advisory Council on the Education of Disadvantaged Children. *Title I ESEA: A Review and a Forward Look.* Washington, D.C.: 1969.

Piccariello, H. "Evaluation of Title I." Typewritten. Paper presented to the Department of Health, Education, and Welfare, Office of Education, Washington, D.C., n.d.

Stufflebeam, D. "The Use and Abuse of Evaluation in Title III." *Theory into Practice* 6 (1967): 126-133.

Tempo, G. *Survey and Analysis of Title I Funding for Compensatory Education.* Washington, D.C.: U.S. Department of Health, Education, and Welfare, Office of the Secretary, 1968.

U.S. Congress. Title I, *Elementary and Secondary Education Act of 1965*, Public Law 89-10. U.S. Statutes at Large, 89th Congress, First Session, 1965.(a)

_____. *Report of the Committee on Education and Labor, on the Elementary and Secondary Education Act of 1965.* House Report no. 143. 1965. (b)

U.S. Department of Health, Education, and Welfare. *Criteria for Applications Grants to Local Educational Agencies Under Title I, ESEA.* Washington, D.C.: 1968. (a)

_____. *Summary Report of 1968 White House Task Force on Child Development.* Washington, D.C.: Government Printing Office, 1968. (b)

U.S. House of Representatives Education and Labor Committee. *Hearings before General Subcommittee on Education, Eighty-Ninth Congress, First Session, on Aid to Elementary and Secondary Education.* 1965. (a)

_____. *Hearings before General Subcommittee on Education, Eighty-Ninth Congress, First Session, on the Elementary and Secondary School Act Formulas.* 1965. (b)

U.S. Senate Appropriations Committee. *Hearings before Subcommittee on Departments of Labor and HEW Appropriations for 1966, Department of Labor and HEW Supplemental Appropriations for 1966, Eighty-Ninth Congress, First Session.* 1965.

U.S. Senate Labor and Public Welfare Committee. *Hearings before Subcommittee on Education, Eighty-Ninth Congress, First Session, on the Elementary and Secondary Education Act of 1965.* 1965.

ADDITIONAL REFERENCES

Aldrich, Nelson. *The Urban Review* 2, no. 6, 7, 1968.

Bateman, W. "An Experimental Approach to Program Analysis: Stepchild in the Social Sciences." Paper read to the Operations Research Society of America, Denver, 1969.

Campbell, D. "Reforms as Experiments." *American Psychologist* 24 (1969): 409-429.

Campbell, D., and Stanley, J. *Experimental and Quasi-Experimental Designs for Research.* Chicago: Rand McNally, 1966.

Dyer, H. "Some Thoughts about Future Studies." In *Equal Educational Opportunity*, edited by D. Moynihan and F. Mosteller. New York: Random House, Vintage Books, 1972.

Evans, J. "Evaluating Social Action Programs." Typewritten. Washington, D.C.: Office of Economic Opportunity, 1969.

Hyman, H., and Wright, C. "Evaluating Social Action Programs." In *The Uses of Sociology*, edited by P. Lazarsfeld, W. Sewall, and H. Wilensky, pp. 741-782. New York: Basic Books, 1966.

Marris, P., and Rein, M. *Dilemmas of Social Reform*. Atherton, N.Y.: Atherton Press, 1967.

McDill, E.; McDill, M.; and Sprehe, T. "An Analysis of Evaluation of Selected Compensatory Education Programs." Paper read at the American Academy of Arts and Science Conference, Baltimore, May 1969.

Rivlin, A. "PPBS in HEW: Some Lessons from Experience." Paper prepared for the Joint Economic Committee, Brookings Institution, Washington, D.C., March 1969.

Rivlin, A., and Wholey, J. "Education of Disadvantaged Children." Paper read at the Symposium on Operations Analysis of Education, The Brookings Institution, Washington, D.C., 1967.

Rothenberg, J. "Cost Benefit Analysis: A Methodological Exposition." Paper read at the American Academy of Arts and Sciences Conference, Cambridge, Mass., May 1969.

Schwartz, R. "Experimentation in Social Research." *Journal of Legal Education* 13 (1961): 401-410.

Weiss, R., and Rein, M. "Evaluation of Broad-Aim Social Programs." Paper read at the American Academy of Arts and Sciences Conference, May 1969.

Wholey, J. "Federal Evaluation Practices." Typewritten. Washington, D.C.: The Urban Institute, 1969. (a)

_____. "Program Evaluation in the Department of Health, Education, and Welfare." In *Federal Program Evaluation Practices*, Appendix I. Washington, D.C.: The Urban Institute, 1969. (b)

Williams, W., and Evans, J. "The Politics of Evaluation: The Case of Headstart." *Annals* 385 (1969): 118-132.

10

THE CONSCIENCE OF
EDUCATIONAL EVALUATION

Ernest R. House

> Those persons who talk most about human freedom
> are those who are actually most blindly subject to
> social determination, inasmuch as they do not in
> most cases suspect the profound degree to which
> their conduct is determined by their interests. In con-
> trast with this, it should be noted that it is precisely
> those who insist on the unconscious influence of the
> social determinants in conduct, who strive to over-
> come these determinants as much as possible. They
> uncover unconscious motivations in order to make
> those forces which formerly ruled them more and
> more into objects of conscious rational decision
> (Mannheim [1936]).

In recent years many good papers have been written on educational evaluation. In one of the best, Robert E. Stake (1967) outlined the many kinds of data useful for evaluation and suggested
ways of processing those data. The liberating impact of his paper is
demonstrated by the reaction of a fellow evaluator who, in a frenzy
of orgiastic excess, exclaimed, "Stake has opened the data matrices!"
—a real highpoint in the evaluation world.

The title of Stake's paper was "The Countenance of Educational
Evaluation." The title of this chapter, "The Conscience of Educational Evaluation," reflects a somewhat different perspective. I wish
to look at some unpleasant facts, to examine evaluation from a different focus.

Reprinted from *Teachers College Record* 73, no. 3 (February 1972): 405-414.
Copyright 1972 by Teachers College Record.

UNCONSCIOUS MOTIVATION

The first observation I want to make is that there is no real demand among teachers and administrators for evaluating their own programs. To evaluate kids, yes, we cannot live without that; but to evaluate ourselves and our own programs—no. At times, in that strange ideology with which we disguise our motives and cover our tracks, we educators convince ourselves that we would be overjoyed to receive data about our teaching and educational programs. Well, try it sometime. Try evaluating a program. On simply asking teachers their goals, we have had them break into tears and throw chalk across the room. Rare events, but not unrepresentative of teachers' attitudes towards evaluation.

After all, what does a teacher have to gain from having his work examined? As he sees it, absolutely nothing. He is exposing himself to administrators and parents. He risks damage to his ego by finding out he is not doing his job as well as he thinks he is. Perhaps worst of all he risks discovering that his students do not really care for him, something a teacher would rather not know. The culture of the school offers no rewards for examining one's behavior—only penalties. Since there are no punishments for not exposing one's behavior and many dangers in so doing, the prudent teacher gives lip service to the idea and drags both feet.

And this is not so strange, is it? Do we have any serious evaluations of lawyers, or doctors, or cabdrivers? That there is no such demand is a corollary of a broader principle: no one wants to be evaluated by anybody at any time. Evaluate an evaluator's work and see how he reacts.

As recently as 1970 I believed in what might be called the "good instrument" assumption. If one could develop an instrument that was easy to administer, nonthreatening to the teacher, that spoke in terms meaningful in the teacher's world (unlike most psychometric instruments, which measure things like "convoluted neurasthenia"), and was cheap enough for even an administrator to purchase, the knot of evaluation would be partly unraveled. In fact, the Center for Instructional Research and Curriculum Evaluation (CIRCE) developed two such instruments. One could be administered in twenty minutes, measured things that teachers at least talk about, and cost about six dollars per class. The other was so nonthreatening that the teacher filled it out herself and sent it home with her students— simply a description of what was going on in class. The response to these instruments was considerably less than overwhelming. Teachers reacted as I've indicated: What have I to gain? Why do this extra work? Why set myself up for someone to shoot at? Why supply material for somebody's book?

Nonetheless, the instruments have been used somewhat. Although there is no demand for evaluation, there is a demand for personal attention and for someone to talk to. Teaching is a lonely profession and, if the instruments (or any innovations) are propagated by personal contact, some people will use them, at least as long as the personal contact lasts.

Budgets indicate the low priority administrators assign to evaluation. School districts spend no money for evaluation. State and federal programs typically allocate very little, usually a small percentage of the total budget. When budgets are cut (as they always are), evaluation funds are the first to go. Even when as much as 10 percent of the budget has been set aside for evaluation, it is difficult to get districts to spend the money for the purpose designated. The anti-evaluation attitude is deeply embedded in the school structure.

At the higher governmental levels the situation is only slightly different. Once when I was harping about the United States Office of Education evaluating some of its programs, a high OE official told me, "Look. In order to sell these programs to the Congress we have to promise them everything good that can possibly occur for the next ten years. What's an evaluation going to do? No matter how good the program, it's going to show that we are not delivering on all we promised." Generally speaking, in this country the claims for education have been so extravagant that there is no hope of living up to the promise. But without evaluation who's going to know the difference?

Why then have I been directing a large evaluation project over the last few years? There are, I think, a few important exceptions to the general rule. Evaluation becomes desirable when you think you are doing well but feel unappreciated; when you are in serious trouble; or when someone with authority over you insists that you be evaluated. For example, the large-scale evaluation of the Illinois Gifted Program got underway only when it was clear that the program was in deep trouble with the state legislature and even then only when higher authorities strongly pressured us to have it evaluated. State officials will confess that this evaluation was a novel and anxious event.

Under such pressures the personnel initially submitted with the enthusiasm of a chloroformed moth being pinned to a mounting board. They later warmed up when it appeared the evaluation might have some value for them. As it turned out, the evaluation has played an instrumental role in saving the program, but at the beginning no one knew that. By no means did the Illinois people volunteer themselves for examination.

As everyone knows, the troubles that beset most programs are economic: they need money. The contest for funds at the national level and the rising tax rates at the state level insure that educational enterprises are going to come under increased scrutiny. Accountability is one means of lassoing the wild stallion of educational spending.

A related set of forces are the interest groups who want one thing or another within the school. For instance, one of the Illinois independent study programs was under attack from conservative elements on the local board of education. Forces in favor of the program launched a counterattack. Right now there is an uneasy stalemate. The board has removed the school principal, but the independent study program is still operating. Since neither side has decisive political strength, words of evaluation are in the air. Conceivably either side may use data to bolster its case. A real resolution will come only when one side gains the upper hand politically.

Often evaluation activities are spurred by groups who feel they have been short-changed by the schools. Today this could be almost anybody. We have, for example, the NAACP audit of Title I, ESEA funds that revealed interesting irregularities in their disbursal. My point is that evaluations are not inspired by the heartfelt need of professionals to try to do a better job (frequent though that rhetoric is); rather, the impetus is usually traceable to a pressure group with a specific aim.

EVALUATIONS FOR DEFENSE AND FOR ATTACK

From such dynamics result evaluations for defense and for attack. Most Office of Education evaluations are a good example of the former. Under pressure the OE officials tell congressional aides, "Yes, we will evaluate this program if we get the money." So into the OE guidelines goes a requirement for evaluation. It is a symbolic gesture and is interpreted as such by the fund recipients. They respond with a token evaluation that says their project is doing fine. Everyone is happy. Paper begets paper.

These evaluations are faulted for their poor scientific methodology. But that is not the primary problem. One might get valuable information by asking one's cousin, or by other "unscientific" means. The problem is in the intent: the evaluations were never *intended* to produce relevant information. Rather, they were meant to protect the Office of Education from hostile forces in the Congress and the Bureau of the Budget. Occasionally the Office is surprised, as it was with the 1970 Title I evaluation.

The evaluations for attack are generally more carefully done since they are trying to change things, rather than defending an entrenched position. A recent example is the Carnegie report by Charles Silberman, *Crisis in the Classroom* (1970), which obviously laid the groundwork for a liberal assault upon the educational establishment. It attacks the "mindlessness" and restrictiveness of the public schools and takes as its positive model the "open classroom" as exemplified by the English infant schools.

Occasionally we also get evaluations that are simultaneously defensive and attacking. The following is an excerpt from the University of Illinois student paper:

> POLI SCI INVESTIGATIONS START
>
> The University political science department will be undergoing an evaluative investigation this week as initiated by the College of Liberal Arts. . . . The investigation is the first of its kind, although the political science department evaluation will not be the only one conducted this year in the college. . . . Sources in the political science department maintain, however, that the investigation was initiated by Chancellor J. V. Peltason. . . . Peltason initiated the evaluation, according to sources within the department, because certain department members' political activities have been "a thorn in his side" for at least two years (*Daily Illini*, 10 December 1970).

What might be interpreted as an evaluative attack on the political science department on one level, could be construed as an evaluation for defense of the University on another. Some very angry state legislators are breathing hard down the neck of the University over the strike activities of spring 1970, which featured prominent performances by members of the political science department.

Who sponsors and pays for the evaluation makes a critical difference in the eventual findings. Who conducts the evaluation is equally important. For example, knowing that the evaluation of the

University of Illinois political science department is to be conducted by a committee of three political scientists from other campuses might give one a clue to the outcome of the evaluation. Certainly the outcome will be different if the committee were comprised of three legislators. Even finer predictions could be made if we knew the relationships among these three professors and the principals in the case, for example how the evaluators were chosen. This is a gross example, but so are the differences that can result.

THE CONTEXT OF VALUATION AND OF JUSTIFICATION

Now this is quite a mess, is it not? If you have been following my argument, you should by now believe that evaluation is a branch of sophistry. And, judging from the number of times I've heard comments such as, "Well, you can prove anything with statistics," the feeling is fairly widespread. Formal evaluations do arise from political motivations and reflect the biases of their origins. Whom can you trust if you can't trust an evaluator?

However, this is not an entirely new problem in human knowledge. Thoughts always arise from obscure and suspect origins: from metaphors, from dreams, from all forms of illogic, quite often from the most perverse attempts at self-serving. Yet, whatever the genesis of these thoughts, it is often possible to determine the worth of an idea.

Philosophers of science have found it useful to distinguish between an idea's "context of discovery"—the psychological background from which the idea arose—and its "context of justification"—the publicly determined worth of the idea (Scheffler 1967). Even though we do not think in syllogisms or use formal logic, it is often desirable, perhaps necessary, to construct a logically idealized version of an idea so that it may be critically examined.

Analogously, in formal evaluation it may be useful to distinguish between the "context of valuation" and the "context of justification." The "context of valuation" involves the basic value slant derived from the genesis of the evaluation, and includes all those motivations, biases, values, attitudes, and pressures from which the evaluation arose. The "context of justification" involves our attempt to justify our findings. There are many means of justifying findings, but in formal educational evaluation it usually means using the logic and methodology of the social sciences (predominantly psychology) to collect and analyze data. In fact, Scriven (1967) defines evaluation as a methodological activity that consists of gathering and combining performance data to yield ratings, and in justifying the data collection procedures, the weighings of data, and the goals themselves. (Most operating definitions of evaluation set it down squarely within the "context of justification.")

Such "scientific" procedures do not *guarantee* that the findings are "true," but they do promise that biases originating from the "context of valuation" will be greatly reduced. Hence we get concepts such as "control group" and "random sampling" that are common sense attempts to eliminate one bias or another. It should be noted that, in addition to the nonargumentative logic of science, argumentative forms of logic are available for justifying findings, for example, the methodology of our court system to which we entrust our property and our lives. This raises the possibility of other legitimate forms of justification. In the main, however, we rely on the institutionalized methods of science to exorcise the demons of subjectivity.

Thus utilizing scientific methodology in the "context of justification" enables us to justify findings arising from the "context of evaluation." But, as much as evaluators love to appear in white lab coats and tell their clients that this brand of individualized instruction will decrease tooth decay (and as much as it comforts clients to have them do so), life is not so simple. Many leading scientists tell us that even our scientific approaches are ultimately biased. After all, the communities of men who establish scientific canons are subject to the same pressures as the rest of us. In fact, there can be no value-free social research. All research must proceed from initial valuations of some kind. So, if being "objective" means being totally free from bias, there can be no "objective" research. Try as we will, there is no escape from the "context of valuation."

Myrdal, the Swedish social scientist, contends (1969) that it is not necessary for social research to meet the impossible condition of being value-free in order to be useful to us. All that is important is that the scientist reveal the values on which his research is based. It is the hidden, unseen valuation that is damaging and that leads to opportunistically distorted research findings, for covert valuations allow us to pursue our base interests at the expense of proper justification. We trick ourselves as well as others.

Making valuations explicit demonstrates the evaluator's awareness of them, forces him to account for them, and exposes them for what they are. Ideally one would use alternative sets of values to judge a program. Resources are seldom available to do so. Practically one usually chooses one set of valuations and puts one's meager resources into that. But one can try to see that the valuations are neither hidden nor arbitrary. They should be relevant and significant to the audiences involved. According to Myrdal, only in this way can the evaluation be as *fair* and *honest* as possible.

For example, when I began to evaluate the Illinois Gifted Program I was not a neutral observer. I was not about (nor is anyone likely) to invest much time and effort in a project about which I had no feelings. Early in the project it was suggested by several people that we set up a massive testing design using standardized achievement tests to measure the outcomes of the state program. That was the "normal" thing to do and in fact would have been done by a "neutral" evaluator who was unwilling to spend much time. I knew in advance that the nature of achievement tests plus technical problems such as regression effects would combine to show no significant difference in favor of gifted programs.

Most importantly, by familiarity with the program, I knew that increasing achievement was not the state's main intent, and that the major efforts of the program had been to promote certain kinds of classroom achievements, namely higher thought processes and student involvement. So we looked into the area of environmental press measures and eventually developed an instrument to measure those factors. We measured the program at perhaps its point of greatest strength—that's what I mean by being fair.

At the same time in the "context of justification" we developed our instrument in a rigorous fashion and employed as good a sampling design as we were able. We in no way "set-up" the gifted people. Where the program did turn out badly we reported it. Through familiarity with the program we also knew where the weakest points lay. We knew that many districts were taking state funds for the program and doing absolutely nothing for the gifted. So we developed instruments to measure that too. That's what I mean by being honest.

We reported both favorable and unfavorable data to people in the program, to people with control over the program, and to state legislators, saying that in our opinion the good outweighed the bad. Although we were conscious of "context of valuation" problems at the time, even stating in the original rationale the intention of making all value assumptions explicit, in retrospect I see places where we did slipshod work because we were influenced by our prior valuations. For example, we intended to collect some achievement scores as well as the other types of data, yet succumbed to our own prior valuations by placing such data so low on our priority list that we never did so.

In looking at our earlier work I can also see all sorts of hidden valuations and implicit assumptions that resulted in systematic errors. Perhaps most important, we put many more resources into collecting data that might be positive rather than negative. For example, we never investigated the elitism that might arise from gifted programs. As Myrdal suggests, ignorance, like knowledge, is not random but opportunistically contrived. We don't know what we don't want to know. All these problems notwithstanding, I think we were as fair and honest as one is likely to be, though our work can certainly be criticized on these grounds.

THE CONTEXT OF PERSUASION

There is one final check on our own valuations and biases—the biases and interests of other people. I might note that, although the state legislature, influenced by our evaluation data, maintained the funding of the Illinois program at its previous level, it did not significantly increase funding in certain areas we suggested. Much to the chagrin of both evaluators and parents, people do not always do what you tell them to do. This final argument I will pursue under the label the "context of persuasion." Producing data is one thing: getting it used is quite another.

In fact, evaluation data will be utilized or ignored mainly to the extent that they are of advantage to the interpreting group. For example, the findings of the Kerner Commission on Civil Disorders, which said that the United States has a system of institutionalized racism, were never put into effect. More recently the Scranton Report claimed that a major reason for campus unrest was a lack of moral leadership from the White House. President Nixon replied that there are lots of people responsible for moral leadership, such as teachers and preachers. He did not even wait to read the commission report on obscenity and pornography, but rejected the findings out of hand without contaminating himself with the data. (Evidently not everyone felt as the President did. An illustrated copy of the Pornography Report was a bestseller at $12.50.) Along with these examples, all hot political issues, I submit the following from the *Chicago Daily News:*

WHITE HOUSE STALLS DATA
ON CONSUMER PRODUCT TESTS
The White House is delaying release of an order to
government agencies to publish data on the thousands
of products they test . . . including brand names of
everything from computers to toilet paper. The order
is based on a year-long study recommending that
[government agencies] publish for the first time results of tests they make on products for government
purchase. . . . White House sources say that pressures
from business groups . . . have postponed its release
indefinitely. The report, prepared by representatives
of twenty-one agencies under Mrs. Knauer's direction,
is weaker than consumer groups had hoped because it
concentrated on positive data. Groups such as Consumers Union had sought release of all information,
including negative facts on which products failed tests
and why. But the White House report . . . states "the
release of . . . adverse test data . . . would not contribute much in the way of useful data to consumers"

I submit that toilet paper is not a hot political issue, but evaluation is. Evaluation is political because it involves allocation of resources, which means that some people gain and some lose. Little
wonder that evaluation data are strongly slanted in the light of what
the results mean for the interpreting group. Early in the Illinois
evaluation we were amazed and confounded by the way our findings
were used. One group would pick up one finding and use it to press
its own position, ignoring the rest of the findings. Another would
take the same finding to justify maintaining the status quo. In the
legislature the part of the program—training—we found most effective for changing teacher behavior was severely cut because it was
labeled "fellowships" and fell under the ire of legislators during the
spring riots.

Later on we began to understand this phenomenon and use it to
our advantage, which brings me to my last point, the "context of
persuasion." We all live in a concrete world, in a world of metaphors
and anecdotes, of strong feelings and personal relationships. Even
evaluators live in that world. When I make decisions for myself it is
on the basis of this concrete world, not an abstract one. The kind of
information a person can act on must be meaningful in terms of
personal experience. And that means appeals to metaphors, anecdotes, and self-interests.

Evaluators are not very good at translating abstract data, such as correlation coefficients, into concrete experience for their audience. The more formalized the operations in the "context of justification," the more difficult it is to make the findings meaningful in personal terms. In fact, the very methods that increase our generalizing powers lead us away from concrete meanings into abstract relationships. There is a natural antipathy between personal meaning, which leads us to action, and abstract data. Communicating scientific findings is not a matter of understanding research terminology; it is a matter of translating the findings to fit the audience's personal experience. Every person has a vocabulary of action within his mind; only when evaluation data roughly correspond to his internal vocabulary does he respond to them.

Political lobbyists have been most effective in understanding and using the vocabulary of legislators. As one state legislator told me, "Man, I don't need another report. I've got sixty of those in my office. Don't tell me about statistics and all that stuff. I believe you. Tell me what you found out." In this case, personal credibility was his guide to action. On another level, the Silberman report is a good example of persuasive writing. In 525 pages there are only two lines explaining how data were collected. Though Silberman does refer to research studies, the bulk of the report is composed of anecdotes. And it is persuasive. Ordinarily evaluators greatly neglect the "context of persuasion." However, it seems to me that the producers of the data *must* assume some burden in seeing their information is properly understood. Simply wrapping the baby up warmly and leaving him on the doorstep at midnight does not absolve one of responsibility.

So there it is—a thumbnail sketch of the problems of trying to determine the social worth of educational programs: valuation, justification, persuasion; values, thought, action; morality, knowledge, power. New problems for education perhaps, but perennial problems for society.

REFERENCES

Mannheim, Karl. *Ideology and Utopia.* New York: Harcourt, Brace and World, 1936.
Myrdal, Gunnar. *Objectivity in Social Research.* New York: Random House, 1969.
Scheffler, Israel. *Science and Subjectivity.* Indianapolis, Ind.: Bobbs-Merrill, 1967.
Scriven, Michael. "The Methodology of Evaluation." In *Perspectives of*

Curriculum Evaluation. American Educational Research Association Monograph Series on Curriculum Evaluation, no. 1, edited by R. E. Stake, pp. 39-83. Chicago: Rand McNally, 1967.

Silberman, Charles E. *Crisis in the Classroom.* New York: Random House, 1970.

Stake, Robert E. "The Countenance of Educational Evaluation." *Teachers College Record* 68 (1967): 523-540.

III

EVALUATING TEACHERS

Does Anyone Really Want to be Evaluated?

Educators often feel that they are being unfairly singled out when asked to demonstrate the effectiveness of their programs. After all, there are no evaluations of lawyers or cabdrivers. People usually want to be evaluated when they feel they are unfairly treated or, less frequently, when they see the evaluation as being helpful to them. This section deals with the evaluation of teachers and of instruction.

Hastings makes a critical distinction in seeing the motivation for evaluations coming from two main sources: from outside pressures and from an internal desire to improve. Congruent with this dichotomy, there are two types of evaluation. *Summative* evaluation is designed to report to external audiences on the effectiveness and nature of the program. It is best done by external evaluators. *Formative* evaluation is intended to improve the program itself. It is directed internally and requires different types of data and design. Most of this book is devoted to information made available to public groups—the summative kind. But it is important when dealing with evaluations of teachers to distinguish between the two.

Rosenshine and McGaw attack head on the problem of holding teachers responsible for student growth. They contend that the paucity of knowledge about the processes of teaching and learning should give anyone pause. For example, even about basic skills there is no consensus and the most valid tests do not measure important skills. Most accountability schemes assume relationships between teaching behavior and educational outcomes that have never been proven. Sometimes it is possible to make judgments on the moral nature of classroom transactions. For example, few people would tolerate excessive corporal punishment, whatever the outcome. Such judgments may lead to abuses. The creator of the "new math." was

137

once denied a teaching job because the administrator did not like his appearance and dialect.

Wolf examines, in some detail, teachers' attitudes toward evaluation. Traditionally evaluation has meant the grading and classification of students, usually by standardized tests. It is clear that teachers are very reluctant to evaluate themselves. Most consider the primary audience of any evaluation to be not themselves but their administrators. Wolf explicates the insecure position teachers find themselves in.

The atmosphere in which they operate often prohibits them from seeing how classroom evaluation could possibly be in their own interest. Almost 60 percent are either not encouraged or are actively discouraged by administrators from doing evaluations. The feeling is very strong that they will be blamed for something whether or not such blame is deserved. This kind of blame-ridden atmosphere is obviously not conducive to open discussion, examination, or evaluation. These results should be compared to the needs assessment of administrators described in the first chapter. Like administrators, virtually all teachers see evaluation as quite important. Like administrators, teachers see it as quite threatening. Both groups see themselves as probable losers. It is clear that working solely with teachers on evaluation is entirely inadequate. Somehow the total atmosphere of threat must be reduced.

Bodine suggests a way of approaching evaluation that is consistent with teachers' attitudes. All improvement in education must ultimately result in the teacher's doing something different in the classroom. Hence it is reasonable that evaluation be primarily a self-assessment. The teacher learns to use the researcher's instruments, applies the measures to his own teaching performance, checks the discrepancy between his real performance as measured and his ideal performance, tries out new behavior, and checks again. Keeping the data in the teacher's hand dramatically reduces the threat of the evaluation and increases the chances that the findings will be used. Self-assessment thus becomes a mirror of existing behavior.

MacDonald describes his deliberations in conducting the evaluation of England's largest curriculum innovation project. The project itself was developed by specifying the course content and then formulating the course aims. From the beginning MacDonald saw that evaluating solely on the basis of short-term gains would be inappropriate. His basic aim was to present the project work in such a way that it would be accessible to both public and professional judgment. The curriculum project was found to be similar to all others—

confused and facing a series of unexpected problems. The evaluators chose to examine what was happening in order to explain some of the great differences among various schools. Several conclusions were drawn from this in-depth examination:

1. Human behavior in educational institutions varies widely because of the large number of variables included. Yet curriculum evaluation often assumes congruence between intents and practices.
2. The impact of a new program is not a discrete effect but related to everything else. A single act must be interpreted in overall patterns. There are many unexpected consequences.
3. No two schools are sufficiently alike that universal prescriptions can supplant local judgment.
4. The goals and purposes of the program developers are often not shared by the users. The curriculum takes on political meaning.

It was clear to MacDonald that he could not confine evaluation to measuring whether intents were achieved. Neither did he find evaluating for decision makers satisfactory. That assumes the decision makers know in advance the appropriate questions to ask. He finally saw evaluation as feeding the judgment of decision makers by promoting an understanding of considerations that affect action. His conclusion is that any attempt to reduce complexity to singularistic perspectives distorts reality.

The lesson from this section is that the direct evaluation of teachers has little probability of success. Both technically and politically the ground is shaky. In spite of this, several states are contemplating such action. California has actually passed a bill requiring that teachers be evaluated in terms of student performance. The wise administrator will approach this problem through negotiations, total program evaluation, or in-service training.

11

EVALUATION OF INSTRUCTION

J. Thomas Hastings

Evaluation of instruction is an expression that we are hearing more and more frequently and for which the pressures have been growing through multiple channels: students, the public, and funding agencies, including legislative bodies. The instruction in our schools and colleges will be evaluated with more seriousness than in most instances it has been. It may be evaluated—that is, some degree of worth placed on it—incorrectly or correctly by others in and out of the system. It therefore seems wise for those charged with administration of the systems to do some serious planning for some of the evaluation to be controlled from within.

There is another real stimulus to evaluation of instruction besides outside and inside pressures for accountability. Those of us within the schools or colleges *are* primarily interested in improving instruction—the content and the process, the relevance and the meaning. Evaluation is not the entire answer. Research on and development of techniques, goals, new settings, and new demands are a necessary part of improvement. But it remains that, without evaluation (a judgment of worth) in particular settings, the idea that we have improvement is apt to be fuzzy at best.

I set forth these two motivations from different sources—outside pressures and internal desire for improvement—in order to consider two related but somewhat separate purposes of evaluation. The first is spoken of as summative evaluation. It is primarily aimed at locating the worth of a completed (or perhaps there is no such thing) course, or curriculum, or text, or program. The purpose is usually that of "selling" the package to someone beyond the developer. Educational agencies may choose new curriculum materials or methods developed by some funded group of specialists; we hope the selection will depend in part on summative evaluation. Are we not

140

doing something similar to the curriculum developers when we tell the students, parents, legislators that X is a meaningful course or program of courses—that the instruction does have worth?

The second major and somewhat different purpose of evaluation has been labeled formative evaluation. It deals much more with the development or improvement of courses or curriculum materials. A curriculum developer engages in formative evaluation while the materials, presentations, and methods are being formulated. He uses field tests, obtains judgments about goals and objectives, procures statements about the attractiveness and validity of the subject matter. The counterpart for a given course or a set of departmental offerings would be to obtain various types of information to improve the instruction.

Sometimes evaluation attempts have failed because those directing the effort have failed to discriminate between formative—largely for inside, revision purposes—and summative—directed at an outside audience—evaluation. A well-developed system of formative evaluation may lead to many descriptions and judgments that will be useful later for an outside audience. A purely summative evaluation is seldom useful for revision, that is, reformation. This is so in part because summative evaluation is usually of necessity more general and less concerned with the smaller units of the instructional program.

I carry some strong biases from experience. If you care to know my special brand of truth, you had better know my biases. When people speak of evaluation of instruction, I hope that they are heading for formative evaluation and that the main audience and user is to be the individual instructor or, at most, the department. Most of us do not want to be evaluated for an outside audience. When we find that we must be, we try to give you *gwr*—a Welsh word meaning *garbage with rationale*. If we mean to do a summative evaluation of instruction—having an outside audience—we should do it with external evaluators (such as the North Central Association, the National Council on Accreditation of Teacher Education, The Bible Institute, recognized evaluators); and we should set up the ground rules and purposes in a clear-cut, understandable way. Some people have been hurt and others have been duped by a confusion of the two purposes, formative and summative.

TYPES OF INFORMATION

If an individual instructor is looking at his course—or a department is looking at several courses—there are at least three separable things that should be examined and three types of questions about the things. First, there is the question of entry behavior or antecedents. What are the entry skills of students and of instructors? Second, we must ask about the activities, assignments, transactions during the teaching. Third, we do need to know something about the outcomes (the learning) of students and of instructors.

In each of the foregoing cases, we want to know the intentions (or expectations), the actual scene (descriptively), and the judgments of experts concerning the value of each. That is a large order. To carry the case further, we need to know what the expectations or intents are for prior preparation of the students entering the course or set of courses. If we expect to have youngsters in college algebra who really know the concepts of arithmetic operation, that will be different from an expectation that the students will know little of the ideas of quantification. The judgment of experts as to whether the expectation matches the reality and whether this is good is a real part of the evaluation.

Obviously, it seems to me, outcomes of a given course—or set of courses—in terms of student performance are important considerations. We must look at expected performances and the actual performances as measures of worth. Instructors must state a number of their main aims or expectations of outcomes. There is now a fair body of literature on the techniques of going from the statements of goals and objectives to situations of stimulus and response that may be test items, or may take place in natural settings, or may lead to interviews or laboratory attacks.

Again my bias: if you stay with behavioral objectives that deal, as most of them do, with cognitive aspects (that is, knowledge of content, general ability in processing data), if you stick with these alone, you miss a number of important educational outcomes. Elliot Eisner, Professor of Art Education at Stanford University, has stated it best. He speaks of *expressive objectives* as separate from *instructional objectives*. The latter have been pushed most frequently by many evaluators. They are stated as observable outcome behavior, for example, the student can list certain events, or he can distinguish between this and that principle. An expressive objective does not specify the exact behavior that the student is to acquire. It does describe an educational encounter. For example, in a literature course an expressive objective might be "to examine and discuss the significances of a given novel." In an art course an expressive objective could be "to develop a three-dimensional art form through the use of beads and papier-mâché." The expressive objective is intended to improve understanding and skills in idiosyncratic ways. The goal is not to develop homogeneity in learning but rather to involve the student in expanding his own horizons.

If I were responsible for training navigators for air lines, I would want to use instructional objectives and have them stated in terms of precise, observable behavior. I would like my navigators to be "universal parts"—that is, any one could be substituted for any other one. If I were educating students in poetry writing, the "universal part" would be antithetical to my intent. If I were developing educational evaluators, I would use some instructional objectives and some expressive objectives—because my intent would be to have some behavior universal (for example, the treatment of statistical handling of data) and some quite idiosyncratic.

Particularly when we think of expressive objectives, we need information concerning the quality of the encounters. For that matter, we should acquire data on perceptions of a course or program in such terms as *interest, relevance, clarity* whether or not it is using expressive objectives.

I have mentioned several types of information needed: antecedents, transactions, outcomes, and, in some cases, expressive objectives. In each case we need some description of the intentions or expectations of each of these domains as well as data on actual events.

There is one final type of information we should attempt to sample: judgments concerning the worth of various aspects. For example, we have frequently been too easily satisfied with a set of objectives developed by a specialist or group of specialists without outside judgments of the relative worth of these objectives. Experienced educators do attach values to behavior and content outside their special expertise. Students and lay personnel attach values. We need some sampling of these if we are to evaluate our educational programs.

SOURCES OF INFORMATION

The types of data required call for several different sources and methods of data collection. Because we want to know something descriptive about the instructor's intentions or expectations about antecedents, transactions, and outcomes, the instructor or the department is a necessary source. I am convinced, however, that merely asking him (or them) to make a list of aims is less than adequate. What you are apt to get is the current prattle of a particular discipline. What you want is his (or their) most rational, specific thoughts. This probably means that discussions and interviews are necessary. It might be useful to tape some discussions with colleagues.

Certainly one source of prime data is a record of class activities. In some cases a videotape will be possible; in other situations the most we can expect is a weekly log of activities written by the instructor. Students may be a source of information about what went on in class, but such information must be checked against observations or the instructor's descriptions.

Students can be an excellent source of data about perceptions of structure, relevance of material presented, adequacy of reference material, and tests. If students are used as a source of information, something of their expectations for a given course or program should be learned. We do know that sometimes courses fall down not in what they offer but in how they meet the expectations of the audience.

At the University of Illinois we are obtaining evaluations of teaching effectiveness from peers. None of us is sure of the methodologies, but we believe that it may take some class observation by peers and some carefully designed interviews. It does remain, however, that excellent sources of information about instruction are the peers of the instructor—sources we have failed to tap in our usual evaluations. There are problems, of course—the main one being the competition for promotion in rank and in pay. There are also problems with any other source of data in the evaluation of instruction. We need a multifocus approach in order to balance the effects of various problems.

The act or process of evaluation—of students' learning or of courses or programs—is apt to be obtrusive. Data collection in the social sciences in general runs the risk of being reactive. It is therefore important that any group seriously planning evaluation take this into account. For example, observations of classroom transactions may in themselves change the behavior of instructors (and students). This difference is not always bad, but it should be considered in interpreting the data. Webb et al. (1966) present an excellent treatment of the problems of reactive research. They suggest measures less obtrusive than those we usually use, and techniques for decreasing the reactiveness of some observations we make.

In conclusion, there are and will continue to be both political and educational pressures for evaluation in our schools and colleges. The political pressures usually demand an approach to evaluation that consists of a portrayal, as opposed to an analysis, of entire programs. The educational pressures are generally better satisfied by analyses aimed at revision and improvement of courses and programs. In either case evaluation must go beyond the mere assessment of learning.

REFERENCES

American Educational Research Association. *Monograph Series on Curriculum Evaluation*. Chicago: Rand McNally. No. 1, 1967; no. 2, 1968; no. 3, 1969; no. 4, 5, 6, 1970.

Bloom, B. S.; Hastings, J. T.; and Madaus, G. F. *Handbook on Formative and Summative Evaluation of Student Learning*. New York: McGraw Hill, 1971.

Webb, E. J., et al. *Unobtrusive Measures: Nonreactive Research in the Social Sciences*. Chicago: Rand McNally, 1966.

12

ASSESSING TEACHERS IN PUBLIC EDUCATION

Barak Rosenshine & Barry McGaw

Responsibility and accountability have always been part of educa-tion. What is new is the attempt to specify responsibilities and to determine rigorously the extent to which the responsibilities are met.

Currently, the term accountability is applied in two contexts. In one the term refers to educational outcomes, or changes in students after a period of time. In the other it refers to educational transac-tions and includes assessing how teachers and students interact in the learning situation, and how materials are used in instruction (Stake 1967). Both outcome accountability and transaction accountability will be discussed in this chapter, but the emphasis will be on issues in transaction accountability.

OUTCOME ACCOUNTABILITY

Outcome accountability is clearly the most widely emphasized form. In his introduction to an issue of the *Phi Delta Kappan* de-voted to accountability, Lieberman (1970) pointed out that all pro-posals published in that issue were efforts to relate educational "input" to educational "output" in some meaningful way. For exam-ple, Barro (1970) said accountability means that people operating school systems "should be held responsible for educational out-comes—for what children learn."

We should like to consider briefly three issues: the variety of outcomes considered important by members of various groups, the paucity of trustworthy means of measuring these outcomes, and the

Reprinted from *Phi Delta Kappan* 44, no. 10 (June 1972): 640-643. Copyright 1972 by Phi Delta Kappan.

statistical difficulties of determining how much progress is appropriate for a student or class.

First, let us look at differences of opinion on the relative importance of various outcomes. For example, although reading comprehension is commonly accepted as a major objective in education, different teachers emphasize different aspects of reading: some focus on reading for information; others teach critical thinking, literary style, or oral reading. But the standardized achievement tests in reading comprehension focus on the ability to learn new words in context, to synthesize new material, and to make inferences from unfamiliar texts. These differences between the reading outcomes emphasized by some teachers and the outcomes measured by the standardized reading tests may account for the claims of some teachers that the tests are not "valid."

A second problem is that outcome accountability can be implemented only where trustworthy and accepted measures have been developed. Unfortunately, we are a long way from developing trustworthy measures of student confidence that he can manipulate the subject matter on his own, student belief that "doing" the subject matter has value, student persistence in the subject matter after instruction has stopped (Foshay 1971). Nor do we have reliable measures of a student's self-esteem, his disposition to inquire into new problems, or his ability to make reasoned choices (Mood 1971). The concern for outcome accountability may result in concentrated work on educational outcomes that are easily measured. The danger is that other valuable but less easily measured educational outcomes may be ignored or forgotten by educators and the public.

Third, in areas where trustworthy tests are available and there is reasonable consensus on ends, the problem of determining the amount of student learning for which a teacher is responsible is a statistical quagmire. The common goal, a year's progress in a year's time, means different things to a teacher whose class begins the year near or above grade level and a teacher whose class begins two or three years below grade level. The statistical procedures usually recommended for adjusting class growth scores to take into account initial differences have been shown to have serious shortcomings (Campbell and Erlebacher 1970; McGaw 1972).

TRANSACTION ACCOUNTABILITY

These difficulties in the use of outcome accountability, as well as those elaborated by Glass in *Phi Delta Kappan* of April 1970, have led to attempts by educators and the public to hold teachers accountable for the *transactions* that occur within the classroom. Transaction accountability poses intriguing and difficult problems. We shall discuss the sources of variables for transaction accountability and then discuss some of the ingenious but misleading suggestions which have been offered for implementing transaction accountability.

Sources of Transaction Criteria

We suggest that the numerous lists of transactions for which teachers are frequently held responsible derive from four general sources: morality, taste, classroom-based research, and implicit assumptions about the importance of specified transactions for student learning. The first two sources allow for judging transactions in their own right; the second two contain assumptions about the relationship of the transactions to student outcomes. The boundary lines among these four sources are fuzzy. The sources are offered not as an authoritative classification but as an attempt to provide concepts that may be useful in considering the issues.

It seems reasonable to judge some transactions on *moral* grounds alone. Teacher behaviors which demean, humiliate, or deny the rights of individual students may be judged wrong despite any evidence that these behaviors promote desired outcomes—the end does not justify the means. Behaviors considered immoral in classrooms vary over time; verbal abuse and corporal punishment are now considered immoral, but they were once considered acceptable. However, the occurrence of immoral transactions in this sense is probably rare (Goodlad and Klein 1970).

Currently, many groups advocate contradictory educational transactions on grounds of *taste*. Arguments about the amount of regimentation in a school or classroom, or the extent and type of individualization, are frequently based on different aesthetic preferences. The extent to which the taste of individuals and groups can be applied to transaction accountability is a fascinating issue, which we would like to see someone develop. We currently believe that just as school dress codes cannot be justified by taste alone, teachers cannot be held accountable for specific classroom transactions solely on grounds of taste.

It is extremely difficult to use correlational and experimental *research* conducted in classrooms as a basis for transactional accountability. There have been relatively few studies on many of the variables of interest, and there are few teaching skills whose superiority has been clearly established (Rosenshine 1971; see also Rosenshine and Furst 1971).

At present, most of the advocacy for transaction accountability appears to rest on unverified but implicit *assumptions* that specified educational practices will lead to outcomes of worth. For example, demands that teachers maintain informal classrooms, be "indirect" in their transactions with students, specify objectives in behavioral terms, or ask fewer factual questions are not mandated by morality or supported by existing experimental or correlational studies. The demands appear to be based on assumptions that these transactions will promote desired outcomes. However, these assumptions require empirical support; a committee cannot establish the link between transactions and outcomes by vote or fiat. Appeals to authority and "educational theory," and references to a few research studies may enhance the prestige of these assumptions as hypotheses to be tested, but they do not substitute for empirical tests and cross-validation of results.

Transactions as Mini-Outcomes

Some educators and researchers argue that transactions and outcomes are part of a continuum. In such a view, student ability to summarize ideas during a lesson, for example, is seen as a "mini-outcome" that is assumed to predict the ability to summarize ideas at some future time. Thus teachers could be held accountable for initiating specified transactions because these mini-outcomes are thought to predict future abilities and dispositions in the students.

Unfortunately, the concept of a temporal continuum of outcomes is difficult to demonstrate. Researchers have recorded the occurrence of some classroom events that seemed to be reasonable mini-outcomes, and have correlated the patterns and frequencies of these transactions with end-of-course measures such as reading skills and dispositions to pursue reading outside of school. Generally, the researchers have not found high or consistent connections between observed classroom transactions and outcomes measured at the end of the courses; thus the concept of transactions as mini-outcomes has not been supported by research. If correlations cannot be shown between transactions and outcomes measured immediately following instruction, it is even more difficult to hold teachers or institutions responsible for student performances two or twenty years later. There are too many intervening influential events.

The current suggestions that teachers should promote and reward extension of student interests, individuality, and freedom of choice also contain the implicit prediction that engaging in these transactions at one time will result in certain outcomes at a future time. The implied outcomes frequently are ones for which we do not have acceptable measures, such as student independence, self-confidence, persistence, and internal locus of reinforcement. The suggestions rest on a faith that certain transactions that are difficult to code with precision are highly correlated with certain outcomes that cannot be assessed by currently available instruments.

The available research suggests that this faith is misplaced. If we are still unable to determine which reading transactions are related to measurable reading outcomes, it certainly is premature to claim that observed transactions involving student independence are related to outcomes labeled "independence." Currently, we are not sure which transactions *or* outcomes constitute "independence."

It has also been argued that even though the effect of desirable classroom transactions cannot be demonstrated by end-of-course measures, the effect will emerge in the future. This appealing idea has been supported more by rhetoric than by research. People who promote it seldom help to research it. The statement, "The tests can't measure the most important outcomes, and these outcomes will emerge at a future time," becomes an incantation to remove evil spirits and allow advocates to continue their advocacy unhampered by people who insist on empirical evidence. Research on many preschool programs has shown that positive effects demonstrated at the end of one year disappeared after the children had been in a traditional school setting for two or three years. Does someone wish to argue that the positive effects will reappear at some future time?

Rating and Counting Transactions

Several observation schedules have been proposed for use in transaction accountability, and many of them are attractive. However, although the observation schedules are useful research tools, there are several difficulties in their use for transaction accountability. The major difficulty is the untested assumption that ratings or scores on observation schedules will be highly correlated with particular outcome variables that are either too remote or too difficult to measure.

Three of the most common transactional measures are student ratings of the teacher, observer ratings of the teacher, and frequency counts of specific events in the classroom. Although thousands of items have been incorporated into hundreds of student and observer rating schedules, we do not yet know which items are correlated with various measures of student learning. Some supporters of student ratings argue that, because the student is the consumer of education, he is the best judge of the quality of his education. The student probably is the best judge of whether he was bored or stimulated, but is the student the best judge of his ability to comprehend science materials or to apply scientific principles in a new situation? This is an empirical question; an answer can be sought through empirical validation of student ratings against various outcome measures. Relatively little research of this type has been conducted using student ratings, and the results are hardly conclusive (Rosenshine 1971).

Classroom observational category systems are attractive instruments because they focus on specific, denotable teacher and student behaviors. They have gained wide acceptance because many authors claim that their instruments incorporate educational theory and research. However, the instruments have been developed for research and training, *not* for evaluating transactions. To date, it has been difficult to find relationships between items (or clusters of items) on category systems and measures of student achievement. It is premature and unwarranted to contend that there are significant relationships between items in category systems and outcomes whose measurement we cannot agree upon.

Implementation Accountability

Implementation accountability is a form of transaction accountability in which the teacher assumes responsibility for implementing specific practices, but who assumes responsibility for the outcomes is still vague and undetermined.

One version of this idea was proposed by Dyer (1970), who discussed a series of operations leading to desired student gain. Those operations included the responsibility of the school staff to know "about conditions and educational services that may be facilitating or impeding the pupils' development," and to use this knowledge to "maximize development of pupils toward certain clearly defined and agreed-upon pupil performance objectives."

Dyer's idea is important because it focuses upon the long chain of events involved in student performance, alerts us to the need to consider antecedent and out-of-school variables, and makes student fulfillment of performance objectives the ultimate responsibility of the school staff. But what happens if observers decide that the professional staff knows the necessary conditions and educational services and is using this knowledge to maximize student gain, and despite these efforts students are still reading below grade level? The occurrence of such a discrepancy is probable simply because we lack the knowledge to identify the transaction competencies that are associated with, or cause, student gain.

If this discrepancy occurs, which groups are responsible for alleviating the problem? The school staff could say that they implemented the transactions, but someone else is at fault because the transactions did not facilitate the students' performance. Such a position is tenable, but we wish that members of school staffs were more consistent in taking it. Would a teacher give an A to a student who obtained a C on the final exam but reported that he studied for the exam the way the teacher told him to?

Currently, implementation accountability may be applicable in a rare but increasingly frequent situation: where teachers are using curriculum programs or packages developed by outside, accountable groups. When a sponsoring agency assumes responsibility for developing, refining, and revising a curriculum package (for example, First Year Communication Skills Program, DISTAR, Individually Prescribed Instruction), the agency also takes responsibility for effectiveness of the materials and achievement of the outcomes. The teachers are responsible only for implementing the package according to the intentions of the sponsoring agency. "Implementation accountability" seems analogous to medical practice whereby physicians are accountable for their diagnosis and treatment but not for their cure rate.

At present, implementation accountability is most suited to curriculum programs, or packages, for which a sponsoring agency has accepted responsibility. In this case outcome responsibility is transferred to a group that has better facilities for research, development, and dissemination than individual teachers can be expected to have. Sponsoring groups that are unsuccessful will have their funding terminated, and other groups will be able to apply for both the funding and the attendant responsibility for outcomes.

Teachers need not be excluded from innovating within the curriculum packages. Teachers who believe they can improve implementation and enhance attainment of outcomes can be given freedom to innovate, so long as they accept responsibility for both their successes and failures.

WHO IS ACCOUNTABLE FOR WHAT?

What about the responsibilities of students, parents, and administrators? If a teacher assigns homework which is at the student's instructional level, and the student does not do the work, who is responsible? If a student decides that basketball practice, a job, or a political event is more important than homework, to what extent can the responsibility be the teacher's or the parent's? We doubt that the teacher alone is entirely at fault for not motivating the student.

If new materials are ordered but remain unopened in the teacher's closet, to what extent is the building principal responsible for not motivating the teacher? This problem will become more vexing, because publishing firms are now offering teacher training services along with new materials. If these services are not purchased, and the materials are not used, who is responsible? If the school district does not have funds to purchase these services, who is responsible? If the materials are purchased, training sessions are conducted, the materials are implemented, the parents and building principals are cooperative, and anticipated student change does not occur, then who is responsible?

It might be realistic to assume that students, teachers, administrators, parents, publishers, educators, and the general public are accountable for some aspect of the educational program. But if each group is responsible, how can we determine which part of a child's mathematics achievement, for example, is attributable to which of the parties?

Any attempt to use accountability should make us painfully aware of the inadequacy of our educational knowledge. The tragedy is that we seem to move from innovation to innovation, failing to conduct, synthesize, and disseminate research about each change. For all the energy spent attempting to improve education, we receive in return little information that can be used to improve the effectiveness of teachers or the learning of students. Now we are seeking to assign responsibilities and to hold people accountable when we lack adequate instruments to measure important aspects of student growth and are unable to specify precisely the processes that lead to growth.

If state legislators, accreditors, school staffs, and other groups insist on instituting accountability procedures, let all parties be aware of the paucity of our knowledge. If all parties agree, for example, that teachers should be held accountable for asking a certain percentage of "divergent questions," let them also learn what the research has shown about the effect on student growth of the use of more divergent questions. On this variable, as on many others, the research results are equivocal and disappointing. We hope that those who still choose to set such transaction standards (others use the term "teacher performance criteria") do not delude themselves into claiming educational truth where there is little information.

COOPERATIVE ACCOUNTABILITY

In the emergence of accountability procedures we sense (although we cannot confirm) an underlying competitiveness. Students, teachers, and administrators evaluate one another, making judgments on one another's competence, claiming that the others are not doing an adequate job. Everyone seems to want to grade everyone else and to hold him accountable.

But are we not all working toward the same end? Is education not a *cooperative* venture? If we agree beforehand on common goals, accountability is not something to be judged once or twice in a school year. Rather, it is an activity in which each party is asking the others how they can move together towards a common goal. In this context a negative evaluation given by one party is not a judgment of incompetence but feedback on areas that need improvement.

REFERENCES

Barro, S. M. "An Approach to Developing Accountability Measures for Public Schools." *Phi Delta Kappan* 52 (December 1970): 196-205.

Campbell, D. T., and Erlebacher, A. "How Regression Artifacts in Quasi-Experimental Evaluations Can Mistakenly Make Compensatory Education Look Harmful." In *Compensatory Education—A National Debate,* Vol. 3, *Disadvantaged Child,* edited by J. Hellmuth. New York: Brunner Mazel, 1970.

Dyer, H. "Toward Objective Criteria for Professional Accountability in the Schools of New York City." *Phi Delta Kappan* 52 (December 1970): 206-211.

Foshay, A. W. "Curriculum Design for the Humane School." *Theory into Practice* (June 1971): 204-207.

Goodlad, J. I., and Klein, M. F. *Behind the Classroom Door.* Worthington, Ohio: C. A. Jones, 1970.

Lieberman, M. "An Overview of Accountability." *Phi Delta Kappan* 52 (December 1970): 194-195.

McGaw, B. "Measurement of Change with Fallible Data." Mimeographed. Urbana-Champaign, Ill.: University of Illinois, Center for Instructional Research and Curriculum Evaluation, 1972.

Mood, A. M. "How Teachers Make a Difference." In *How Teachers Make a Difference,* pp. 1-20. Washington, D.C.: U.S. Government Printing Office, 1971.

Rosenshine, B. *Teaching Behaviors and Student Achievement.* I.E.A. Studies, no. 1. New York: Humanities Press, 1971.

Rosenshine, B., and Furst, N. "Research on Teacher Performance Criteria." In *Research in Teacher Education: A Symposium*, edited by B. O. Smith. Englewood Cliffs, N.J.: Prentice-Hall, 1971.

Stake, R. E. "The Countenance of Evaluation." *Teachers College Record* 68 (April 1967): 523-540.

13

HOW TEACHERS FEEL
TOWARD EVALUATION

Robert L. Wolf

What people want from their schools is changing—there is today a growing public interest in the process of education. Schools need to respond to the demands and questions of concerned people outside the educational system. To do so those people inside the school (teachers, administrators, and so on) must work to keep one another and themselves abreast of these demands.

Do teachers feel they are accountable to parents? Do administrators? If so, do they desire this? Or do they feel unjustly forced to be? These questions are even more relevant to their relationships with their fellow teachers, administrators, or others who work within their school.

This growing public interest suggests that schools disclose more information about their educational programs than ever before in their history. But, disclosing more information implies the concomitant process of gathering more information, which, in turn, could imply more evaluation. Schools will need to engage in more widespread evaluative activities if they are to meet the challenge and respond to the demand that accountability requires.

Accountability and evaluation are not the same. Accountability is dependent upon evaluation, but is a broader concept. The responsibility of accountability extends beyond appraisal, it includes informing constituencies about the performance of the enterprise. Similarly, it connotes responding to feedback. Schools, however, have always had difficulty in producing data about school outputs or process performance. This is their chief problem with accountability.

The issue of the impact that accountability will have on the public school is both broad and tenuous. It is further complicated by the criticism that many professional and lay factions are currently engaged in. Several critics (Silberman 1970, Holt 1971, Kohl 1969)

156

call schools "joyless institutions": institutions that are not responsive to the needs of their clients—the children they purport to educate. They suggest new evaluation strategies that will lead to meaningful change.

So it seems that solutions to both the quest for accountability and the quest for responsiveness to change and improvement hinge on the notion of evaluation. As administrators realize, however, most teachers are extremely reluctant to engage in evaluation efforts. It is precisely these efforts by teachers that can have significant impact on any schoolwide evaluation design. One real issue then is how administrators can effectively encourage teachers working in their schools to engage in evaluation that would provide more information to parents and community groups. Administrative strategies for involving teachers in evaluation are not simple. They require a better understanding of the way teachers feel about evaluation, and how those feelings and attitudes are shaped. The teachers' role in evaluation needs to be examined, particularly in the light of changing concepts in evaluation theory and practice.

RECENT TRENDS IN EVALUATION

Traditionally, the teacher's role in evaluation was that of grading and classifying students (Bloom, Hastings, Madaus 1971), a role that has done little to alter the framework of the institution. For many years curriculum evaluation consisted solely in the use and interpretation of standardized tests (Hastings 1966), results from which would provide only enough information for yes or no decisions. We have been attempting only to measure learning. But, as a measurement involves the act or process of ascertaining the extent or quantity of something, evaluation refers to the act or process of determining the worth or value. Cronbach (1963) described evaluation as the collection and use of information to make decisions about educational programs, decisions about what instructional materials and methods are satisfactory, and where specific change is needed. The relationships of the various instructional activities, or bits of data, are what Stake (1967) spoke of as the relationships that permit the improvement of educational programs, that identify outcomes contingent upon particular antecedent conditions and instructional or noninstructional transactions—a broad concept that examines the total effectiveness of the educational enterprise. The evaluation looks at the qualities that determine that effectiveness (Dressel 1960).

Evaluation broadens the scope and technique of measurement. It includes techniques such as observation, sociograms, anecdotal records, interview schedules, and the like, to supply a more complete picture of the program, its status, and its progress. Evaluation is more than simply measuring to see whether certain objectives have been achieved. It is more than simply looking at the students and their performance. Every agent of the school needs some continuous assessment. Every action, change, or interaction is part of the evidence. Teachers need to expand their knowledge of evaluation strategies.

Bloom, Hastings, and Madaus (1971) outline the procedures, complex, time-consuming, and requiring certain skills, that are necessary to report and assess the schools' progress. They define evaluation as:

1. A method of acquiring and processing the evidence needed to improve the student's learning and the teaching;
2. Including a great variety of evidence beyond the usual paper and pencil final examination;
3. An aid in clarifying the significant goals and objectives of education, and as a process for determining the extent to which students are developing in these desired ways;
4. A system of quality control in which it may be determined at each step in the process of teaching and learning whether the process is effective or not, and if not, what changes must be made before it is too late;
5. A tool in educational practice for ascertaining whether alternative procedures are equally effective or not in achieving a set of educational aims.

SUMMATIVE VS. FORMATIVE EVALUATION

In addition to being complex and time-consuming, the procedures outlined above are less summative than the traditional notion of school evaluation. Summative evaluation implies measuring the outcomes attained. In evaluating teachers' performance, summative implies a finalized statement of worth. For example, when a teacher is evaluated by a principal or supervisor, a judgment is made on the quality of his teaching. There is usually little feedback to the teacher, and the criteria are seldom explicated.

What is needed then is more formative evaluation, which consists of the collection of appropriate information by the teacher during the program to help him revise that program systematically and continuously. The continuity, which feeds information back into the system, helps monitor the direction of the activities. For this to be successful, new criteria and guidelines need to be developed that permit broad applications, adaptions, and modifications in the various aspects of education.

In formative evaluation not only are the student's needs constantly appraised but all members of the educational team evaluate their own effectiveness and its relation to the collective enterprise.

Formative Evaluation and the Teacher

If schools are to provide more information on the growth and direction of their programs, individual teachers might need to document more adequately occurrences within their classrooms. They need not only more effective ways of monitoring the progress and development of each child but also ways of evaluating whether their own program goals are being achieved. They need to know how effective they are in teaching and how they can change. The opportunities they provide for their students and the gains their students make need to be measured. For this kind of evaluation, teachers need to go beyond the test and rely on judgments made about their programs by students, parents, and professional colleagues. Self-assessment tools and procedures may also be used.

Examining the School for Clues

Little attention has been paid to the task of integrating the demands of the school organization and the demands of the teaching staff in a manner that is both organizationally productive and individually rewarding. To date, the teacher has had a limited role in evaluating the educational process, other than in evaluating student growth. If teachers are to engage in more systematic evaluation, which includes self-assessment, their own perceptions of evaluation need to change. Whether their being forced to evaluate will necessarily change their perceptions is not yet known.

Teachers' perceptions seem shaped by the institutional climate in which they teach, by the social relationships in the school, their norms, values, and orientations. This atmosphere is also determined by the various perspectives and expectations that school staff members have of one another. Role is the structural component defining the behavior of the individual teacher. How he feels toward evaluation is in part determined by the stature assigned to his role as teacher within the school. His rights, duties, and expectations suggest what he should do under what circumstances. The behavior associated with the role ranges from the required to the prohibited. The school and the community have certain expectations of the teacher's role, and a particular behavior becomes required.

Teachers tend to be very sensitive to one-upmanship by other teachers, which results in a system of rewards for seniority, socially enforced modesty about the quality of teaching or innovations, and distrust of new teachers and others who are not old associates. This is no different from peer pressure in most groups. Teachers themselves develop a set of expectations that define their role. Coffey and Golden (1957) indicate that resistance to change can be palliated by strategies that take into account an understanding of what that role is.

TEACHERS MISTRUST EVALUATION

Teachers are not fond of evaluation. They suspect any measure designed to assess the quality of their teaching, and any appraisal usually arouses anxiety. Their opposition is far from simple obstructionism. Teachers recognize the administration's need to know, but they have a stake in evaluation too. The results are the major bases for promotions, pay raises, and dismissals. Their careers are in the appraisers' hands. If teachers are to submit to an assessment of their performance, they would probably like reassurance that the criteria and method of evaluation that are to be used would produce credible results.

Teachers probably believe that the standards for evaluating what is effective teaching are too vague and ambiguous to be worth anything. They feel that current appraisal techniques fall short of collecting information that accurately characterizes their performance. They perceive the ultimate rating as depending more on the idiosyncrasies of the rater than on their own behavior in the classroom. As a result, teachers see nothing to be gained from evaluation. One suggested that present teacher evaluation practice does more to interfere with professional quality teaching than to nurture it.

Teachers as Evaluators

In most instances, the teacher sees himself as an evaluator of pupil growth more so than as an evaluator of his own effectiveness. Evaluating teaching effectiveness has traditionally been the role of the administrator. Teachers have silently resisted this kind of evaluation because of their desire to govern much more of their own behavior. (Recently, however, teacher negotiations have ended this silence.)

It seems that the role of the teacher in classroom evaluation needs to be broadened, to include perhaps an assessment of the program, as well as an evaluation of his own performance as a teacher. The teacher may rely on the judgments of others (students, parents, other teachers, and so on) but at least he will be controlling the evaluation process—we hope he will be better able to benefit from the results.

It is difficult, however, to change the role of a single member of an organization without in some way threatening the other members. The methods that evaluators need to employ to broaden the notion of evaluation among teachers must somehow circumvent the organizational dilemma of role conflict and the feeling of threat. School administrators need to be involved in this process: without the cooperation and support of building principals, supervisors, and so on, the attempts of evaluators to reduce teachers' anxiety about evaluation may be mere exercises in futility.

SURVEYING TEACHERS' FEELINGS

The attitude of teachers toward the evaluation of their teaching will influence their ability to profit from evaluation; those who hold favorable attitudes are more likely to benefit from evaluation than those who do not (Wagner and O'Hanlon 1968). Presumably, evaluation would give teachers a better awareness of their strengths and weaknesses; they might use this awareness to improve their teaching. In surveying their attitudes toward evaluation (Wolf 1971), I attempted to distinguish between teachers who held broad and narrow viewpoints. I identified variables that constitute a broad notion of evaluation and variables that might affect the ways teachers feel about evaluation. I wished to examine how the institutional climate of a school may affect the way teachers with narrow concepts of evaluation felt about it. Figure 13:1 represents the responses, which are categorized as either broad or narrow definitions of evaluation

FIGURE 13:1. CONCEPTS OF EVALUATION

Broad concepts are held by:	Narrow concepts are held by:
1. Teachers who consider evaluation to be important for decisions about the effectiveness of both teaching and learning.	1. Teachers who consider evaluation to be important for decisions about the effectiveness of learning only, or of teaching only.
2. Teachers who see the need for better communication with parents, administrators, and other teachers about their own classroom programs.	2. Teachers who do not see the need for better communication with other groups about their own classroom programs.

Broad concepts are held by:	Narrow concepts are held by:
3. Teachers who consider the judgments and opinions of their students to be valuable in an evaluation of the classroom programs.	3. Teachers who do not consider the judgments and opinions of their students to be valuable in an evaluation of the classroom programs.
4. Teachers who consider the whole notion of evaluation important.	4. Teachers who do not consider the whole notion of evaluation important.
5. Teachers who see themselves as the most important audience for the results of their own evaluation studies.	5. Teachers who do not see themselves as the most important audience for the results of their own evaluation studies.
6. Teachers who value open discussion with other teachers and administrators about the problems they are having in their own classrooms.	6. Teachers who do not openly discuss problems they are having in their own classrooms with other teachers or administrators.
7. Teachers who see the importance of assessing the results of their teaching.	7. Teachers who do not see the importance of assessing the results of their teaching.
8. Teachers who wish to report on the progress of the whole class as well as that of the individuals in it.	8. Teachers who do not see the need to report on the progress of the whole class.
9. Teachers who wish to take time to learn more about how they can effectively evaluate their own programs.	9. Teachers who cannot spare the time to learn, more about how they can effectively evaluate their own programs.

concerns. Figure 13:2 reports the institutional variables and categorizes them according to whether they support or debilitate evaluation. The items reported in figures 13:1 and 13:2 are by no means exhaustive. I have tried to represent, as simply as possible, a way of looking at the school and seeing how certain institutional parameters affect the way teachers feel about evaluation.

Notions of Evaluation

The question of whether teachers' opinions about the importance of evaluation for decisions regarding teaching effectiveness, student

FIGURE 13:2. INSTITUTIONAL VARIABLES
AFFECTING TEACHERS' EVALUATION

Supporting variables	Stifling variables
1. Teachers are encouraged by their principals or supervisors to engage in evaluation.	1. Teachers are not encouraged by their principals or supervisors to engage in evaluation.
2. When evaluating their own classroom programs, teachers perceive little external pressure from parents or administrators.	2. When evaluating their own classroom programs, teachers perceive considerable external pressure from parents and administrators.
3. Teachers are confident that they will only be blamed for negative results of school evaluations when they rightfully deserve the blame.	3. Teachers perceive that they will automatically be blamed for negative results of school evaluations regardless of who is to blame.
4. School atmosphere allows free and open discussion among faculty members about problems.	4. School atmosphere threatens and prevents free and open discussion among faculty members about problems.
5. There are sufficient rewards for evaluation.	5. There are no rewards for evaluation.

learning, or both (see figure 13:1, no. 1) seemed to be an important indicator of their concept of evaluation. Teachers who held that evaluation was important for decisions regarding both teaching and learning effectiveness tended to hold broad concepts about other issues presented. Teachers who indicated that evaluation is important only for decisions regarding learning effectiveness tended to hold narrower concepts on all other questions.

Questions that solicited information on teachers' views of evaluation tended to be related. Teachers who consider students' judgments and opinions to be valuable in an evaluation of their own classroom programs tend to consider evaluation to be important for decisions about the effectiveness of their own teaching and their students' learning. Teachers who do not value students' judgments tend also to respond in a narrow manner to the question of decisions and evaluation.

Similarly, teachers who considered themselves the most important audience for the results of their own classroom evaluation also indicated that evaluation was important for decisions about their own teaching effectiveness. Teachers who thought evaluation important for decisions about the effectiveness of student learning only tended to consider administrators the most important audience, a belief that does not seem extraordinary and is congruent with a narrower concept of evaluation. Of the 293 teachers questioned about the relative importance of evaluation for teachers and administrators, 31 percent considered teachers to be the most important, and 42 percent the least important, audience; 39 percent considered administrators the most important, and 15 percent the least important, audience for classroom evaluations.

Teachers still do not see how evaluation of their classroom programs can best serve their own interests, and not be something done to fulfill administrators' expectations. Teachers still tend not to see the value of evaluating classroom programs for their own sake.

Teachers who value open discussion with other teachers or administrators about problems in the classroom tend to view evaluation as important for decisions about teaching effectiveness as well as student learning. A willingness to discuss one's own problems suggests that such teachers are concerned with the effectiveness of their own teaching, and indicates a broader perspective of evaluation than that held by teachers who do not wish to discuss their own teaching.

Teachers who also see the importance of assessing the results of their teaching, believe that reports on the whole class are imperative, and wish to take the time to learn more about effectively evaluating their own programs. These teachers tend to also view evaluation as important for decisions about their own effectiveness in teaching. It is my feeling, however, that, whatever a teacher's opinions about evaluation might be, they are probably affected by the atmosphere or climate of the school in which he teaches. It seems logical to expect that teachers in a school that supports evaluation would be more willing to make evaluations than teachers in other schools.

Institutional Variables

Certainly one of the most likely correlates for determining teachers' feelings about evaluation is the amount of encouragement they receive from their immediate supervisor to participate in evaluations. For example, some kind of logging or record keeping is imperative for systematic evaluation. The teachers were asked whether or not they were encouraged by their principal to keep some record of what is occurring in the classroom, and were given the example of anecdotal records. The distinction was made between record keeping and evaluation, so that the teachers would not think only in terms of test administration. This question was to suggest that evaluating classroom programs is more involved than just testing students and to imply that teachers would have to engage in other, perhaps less common, evaluation activities. Of the 293 teachers questioned, 8 percent felt that they were strongly encouraged to evaluate their classroom programs, 33 percent that they were moderately encouraged, 58 percent that they were not encouraged at all, and 1 percent that they were actively discouraged.

A teacher's feelings about evaluation are likely to be affected by what he would perceive as external pressure from parents and administrators for evaluation. On the question of external pressure, 2 percent of the teachers said that they felt great pressure to evaluate their own programs; 20 percent said that they felt moderate pressure; 29 percent, little pressure; and 49 percent, no pressure at all. We speculated that teachers perceive the difference between pressure and encouragement: encouragement seems to give people more security and is less threatening than pressure.

Closely related to the issue of external pressure was the issue of blame, a measure of how threatened teachers are by the issue of evaluation. Teachers who feel that they will automatically be blamed for any negative results of school evaluations regardless of fault tend to feel more threatened by evaluation than teachers who are confident that they will be blamed only if they rightfully deserve it. Teachers who felt more encouraged about evaluation also felt that they would only be blamed for poor results if they rightfully deserved the blame. Teachers who felt more pressure to evaluate their classroom programs tended also to feel that they would automatically be blamed for any poor results. Their responses indicated that 64 percent felt that they would most definitely be blamed, whether they deserved it or not; 30 percent felt that they would be blamed only if they deserved it; and 6 percent felt that they were unlikely to be blamed at all.

In determining other factors contributing to the school climate for evaluation, we made two assumptions: the first that, in schools where the atmosphere is conducive to open discussion of classroom problems, teachers might have more opportunities to consider their own teaching effectiveness and feel less threatened in doing so; the second that teachers who are rewarded for engaging in or cooperating with formal evaluations will ostensibly be more willing to continue than would teachers who are not rewarded. We discovered that 34 percent of the teachers felt that they would be rewarded for their efforts; 66 percent felt that they would not. As can be seen from the percentages, most of the teachers felt that the atmosphere in their particular schools was not supportive of evaluation activities which they might engage in.

School Climate

If we wish teachers to do more evaluation of their own classroom programs, and their own effectiveness in those programs, we need to understand more clearly the relationships between their feelings about evaluation and the atmosphere or conditions that may shape those feelings. It appears that, although there is a moderate to strong relationship between the climate in the school for evaluation and the way teachers feel about evaluation, there are two exceptions.

We expected that the teachers' seeing the need for better communication with parents and administrators about individual classroom programs would depend on the attitude in the school toward evaluation. We reasoned that, in environments that supported evaluation and in which there was little pressure from the outside and some encouragement from the inside, teachers would be more willing to report on their own classroom programs, and that, in schools that did not support evaluation, teachers would be much more reluctant to report. No relationship was apparent.

In a similar fashion, it was expected that, in a supporting school, teachers would be more apt to see the importance of assessing the results of their teaching. But, 99 percent of the teachers we questioned see the importance, regardless of the institutional climate of the school. This should not indicate, however, that, therefore they necessarily engage in that assessment activity.

INTRODUCING NEW STRATEGIES

If the atmosphere of the school affects teachers' feelings as this survey would convey, simply working with teachers on evaluation problems is insufficient. Evaluation specialists who wish to see teachers develop both broader views and a greater sense of the need for evaluation expertise (at least as it relates to self-evaluation) should also be willing to work with other members of the school group to diminish the threat. Evaluators should spend time with parents, school board members, district administrators, building principals, and supervisors, as well as with individual teachers, pointing out important, unrecognized aspects of evaluation, such as: its usefulness in improving existing programs, and the necessity that it be continuous, used as much as possible to identify program strengths and weaknesses, and that it not be used to assign blame.

The information that results from evaluation strategies can be fed back into the system to nurture its continuous growth. A supportive environment needs to be created. Both administrators and parents could provide rewards for teachers who engage in evaluation. The rewards may encourage teachers to look for problems within their own classroom programs—a process they may find sufficiently rewarding in itself. Building principals and supervisors should try to give teachers more time for implementing new evaluation procedures, since time seems to be a common problem for teachers. Similarly, administrators can begin to evaluate their own effectiveness and secure the support of teachers in this effort, thereby providing a self-evaluation model for teachers to emulate.

Parents can provide teachers with systematic feedback based on their perceptions of the classroom program. Since emotionally charged insult or criticism tend to diminish validity, this feedback should be constructive and positive in tone.

Teachers should view themselves as an important audience for any results of classroom evaluation, such as the judgments of students about the programs, and feedback from parents and community groups. This evaluative information may be processed alone, but the principal ought to encourage more open interchange among the faculty. The approach I am advocating may be seen in the schools that are experimenting with various forms of human relations training.

In the final analysis, however, it is the school administrator who has the best opportunity to create a certain atmosphere in his school. If this atmosphere is to support evaluation activities for teachers, it needs to be one which is open and unthreatening. Problems need to be discussed and worked through, not harbored or suppressed. Building principals need to give teachers more autonomy so that the teachers can feel more responsible to themselves, as well as others. Teachers need to be rewarded for their efforts in evaluating their own programs and administrators can have an important role in setting up such a reward system. The reward for the administrator will be worth his effort: he will have better information about what is happening in his school, and a staff that is monitoring its own efforts. A school in which evaluation of the whole enterprise is an important process is a school that is likely to meet and respond to the growing public demand for accountability.

REFERENCES

Bloom, B.; Hastings, J. T.; and Madaus, G. *Handbook on Formative and Summative Evaluation of Student Learning.* New York: McGraw-Hill, 1971.

Coffey, H., and Golden, W., Jr. "Psychology of Change within an Institution." In National Society for the Study of Education Yearbook, part I, 1957.

Cronbach, L. J. "Course Improvement Through Evaluation." *Teachers College Record* 64 (May 1963): 672-683.

Dressel, P. L. "Teaching, Learning, and Evaluation." *Improving College and University Teaching* 13 (1960): 11-15.

Hastings, J.,T. "Curriculum Evaluation: The Whys of the Outcomes." *Journal of Educational Measurement* 3 (1966): 27-32.

Holt, John. *What To Do Monday.* New York: Random House, 1971.

Kohl, Herbert. *The Open Classroom.* New York: Vintage Books, 1969.

Silberman, C. E. *Crisis in the Classroom.* New York: Random House, 1970.

Stake, R. E. "The Countenance of Educational Evaluation." *Teachers College Record* 68 (1967): 523-540.

Wagner, R., and O'Hanlon, J. "Teacher Attitude Toward Evaluation." *Journal of Teacher Education* 14 (Winter 1968): 471-475.

Wolf, R. L. "The Role of the Teacher in Classroom Evaluation." M.A. dissertation, University of Illinois, 1971.

14

TEACHERS' SELF-ASSESSMENT

Richard Bodine

When the final score card is tabulated about the effectiveness of education, it will have to be based primarily on what the teacher has accomplished in the classroom. All other efforts at improvement in education must be translated eventually into *changes in the classroom,* whether in materials, or the behavior of teachers or students. The overwhelming picture so far presented by research is that most efforts at improving teacher performance by dealing with the information he possesses or the attitudes he expresses are of little or no consequence. A strange paradox exists in education. Most teaching behavior is learned by imitation, by mimicking what one's own teachers have done. In this sense, education is one of the most highly inbred of professions. Yet, once on the job, little professional interchange takes place. Two teachers can be in adjoining classrooms for years without either seeing the other teach. Neither is able, even if he wanted to, to express or act upon any responsibility for helping the other to study directly his professional behavior and to change it. The total result is to use the openness of education to expose the potential teacher to the status quo, but then to isolate him when he has reached the stage where he could meaningfully change the status quo.

A RATIONALE

The means of overcoming these shortcomings is to provide, within the school setting, the structure and the resources (time, models, support) for him to be responsible, as part of his professional behavior, for the direct improvement of his behavior through exposure of it to his own scrutiny and study. Several steps are necessary. The teacher must learn to use the same instruments of measurement of the classroom as the researcher uses, apply the measures to his own teaching performance, state one or more goals for himself in terms of the measuring instrument, try out the new teaching performance, and then repeat the first four steps.

Sources of the goals can come from models, as seen in films, at demonstrations, or in classrooms of his colleagues, readings, and examination of his own beliefs about the purposes of education. The measuring instrument used must be applied to what the teacher *does* in the classroom, and would include: an analysis of the questions used in examinations, a classification of questions used in discussions, a classification of concepts developed in textbook materials used by the teacher, descriptions by students, observations (not interpretations) by colleagues of such items as who talks how many times, audiotapes of class sessions, and so on. The teacher is motivated to assess himself by the discrepancies, which have been made visible by objective measurements, between his *ideal* and his *real*. When a person sees the discrepancy between what he ideally wants to accomplish and he really does accomplish, his task is concretely defined.

FIGURE 14:1. POSSIBLE DISCREPANCIES
BETWEEN IDEAL AND REAL TEACHING BEHAVIOR

Ideal	Real
—what a teacher hopes to do in a classroom	—what a teacher actually does in a classroom
1. Talks 40 percent of the time	1. Talks 60 percent of the time
2. Only 30 percent of the questions in exams are tests of memory	2. Eighty percent of the questions in exams are tests of memory
3. Effectively discusses the population explosion	3. Avoids discussions of the population explosion
4. Helps children with problems to express their opinions	4. Undisciplined children anger him
5. Recognizes and rewards creative behavior	5. Student ratings show that he tends to reject creative children
6. Teaches by discussion	6. Teaches by lecture

Self-assessment is probably the most powerful means yet developed for a teacher to be the master of his own professional growth. Self-assessment is bold but easy to understand, revealing and thus threatening, majestic in goal and thus giving dignity to the teaching profession.

Self-assessment, like opening a door, allows a person to look into and see what he is actually doing in the classroom. It is a mirror of his present teaching behavior. It gives the teacher objective information about his role in the classroom and enables the teacher to learn as much as he can about his own methods of working with and influencing children and other people. Through self-assessment a teacher can decide what skills and methods are important for him to apply in order to meet effectively the needs of the children in his classroom. He can scrutinize and study his professional behavior and decide whether he is successfully guiding the learning activities of his children; whether he is interacting with his children both as individuals and as a group; and whether he is exerting a positive influence on the children and on the learning environment of the classroom.

A DESCRIPTION

It has been indicated in the work on diffusion of innovations that an innovation in education takes about fifty years to disseminate. It seems critical that the process of dissemination be speeded up.

In-service training by self-assessment deals with classroom interaction among the teacher, the students, and the materials. Only if classroom behavior and classroom interactions are changed is the work with new or existing materials of any added value. When the overt behavior of the teacher changes, there is change in the classroom.

It can be implied, therefore, that in order to bring about meaningful change in teacher behavior, it is necessary to go beyond an in-service training program that stresses only information or attitudinal changes and to examine existing behavior and the practice of new behavior. It becomes imperative that the teacher be actively engaged in an in-service program dealing with actual teaching.

Effective change of teaching behavior is most likely to occur if:

1. Accurate measurement of existing behavior is given back (feedback) to the teacher.
2. Evaluation of the behavior by the teacher can be made in an emotionally supportive atmosphere (perhaps in complete seclusion).

3. Anxiety, which may lead to change, is produced by the teacher's comparing what he does with what he hopes to do, and not by threats from external authority.

4. Available research on empirical relationships is given in terms of the instruments used to measure the teaching behavior (also part of the feedback process).

5. Models of different behavior are made available.

6. Regular practice of new behavior is made possible (a margin of error must be permitted).

7. Steps 1 through 5 are repeated continually.

In short, self-assessment involves selecting a method (or an instrument such as the Class Activities Questionnaire, the Guilford Model, the Interaction Analysis, and so on) for collecting data about the teaching act, stating behavioral goals according to the instrument chosen, collecting data by using the instrument, comparing the *real* to the *ideal,* and designing strategies to bridge the gap between the *real* and *ideal.* This is, of course, a continuous process. There can be no closure.

FIGURE 14:2. THE SELF-ASSESSMENT MODEL

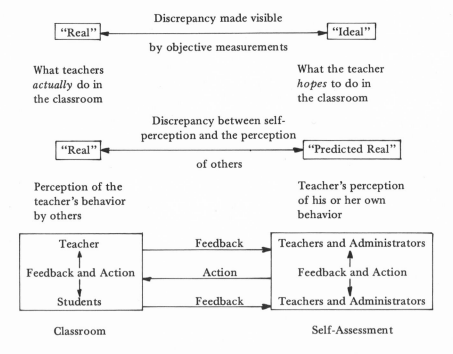

As the name suggests, self-assessment is a highly personal program. However, for the best results, it has been shown that a group of teachers all involved in self-assessment can gain much by sharing feedback and possible behavior. The rule that each teacher shares only that feedback he wishes to share with the group must be observed. Once the supportive, psychologically safe atmosphere is established in the group and the opportunity for professional exchange is present, each person has an improved opportunity to meet the goals of self-assessment, which are to:

1. Concentrate on changing overt behavior.
2. Recognize the interaction of feelings in encounters:
   feelings of threat and anxiety, stress of new tasks and change, physical factors and individual needs.
3. Set attainable goals:
   realistic levels for oneself and reasonable expectations and demands of others.
4. Provide settings for risk taking.
5. Encourage feedback on the exchange of perceptions and of data on behavior.
6. Value the person (*not* evaluate the person) by trusting the ability and potential of others and allowing for individual differences.

FOOTNOTE

The concept of in-service training by self-assessment was developed primarily by Dr. William M. Rogge, Director of the Demonstration Project for Gifted Youth at the University of Illinois.

15

BRIEFING DECISION MAKERS

Barry MacDonald

All evaluation is concerned with providing information for decision makers, but not all evaluators agree about who the important decision makers are, or what information they need. Evaluation, at least in some curriculum areas, should pay more attention to diagnosing and satisfying the needs of decision-making groups other than the program developers. This is not to question the validity of formative evaluation. Certainly we need to devise sound curriculum offerings, but we also need, if they are to be effectively used, to understand better the forces that shape their fate in the schools.

THE HUMANITIES CURRICULUM PROJECT

How is a democracy to handle controversial issues in its schools? That, in a nutshell, is the problem tackled by the Nuffield/Schools Council Humanities Curriculum Project which, after three years of research into this question, is now publishing packs of teaching materials and advising schools on ways of developing teaching skill and insight into the problems of curriculum work in this area.

The project was set up in 1967 as part of the preparation for raising the school leaving age in 1972. The central team was asked to provide stimulus, support, and materials for schools teaching the humanities to pupils between the ages of fourteen and sixteen of average and below average ability. The work of the project has been based on five major premises:

1. That, with adolescents, controversial issues should be handled in the classroom.

2. That the teacher accepts the need to submit his teaching in controversial areas to the criterion of neutrality at this stage of education, that is, that he regards it as part of his responsibility not to promote his own view.
3. That the mode of inquiry in controversial areas should have discussion, rather than instruction, as its core.
4. That the discussion should protect divergence of view among participants rather than attempt to achieve consensus.
5. That the teacher, as chairman of the discussion, should have responsibility for quality and standards in learning.

The defining characteristic of the range of subjects labeled *humanities* was a concern with important human issues, and the team decided to focus their research upon the special problems of work in controversial value areas. In this way they felt they could help schools respond to a demand (see Schools Council 1965) that the curriculum offered to adolescents should be "relevant" and that schools should tackle controversial issues with these pupils in an honest and adult way. As they saw it, the central problem faced by schools that tried to meet this demand was how to allow pupils to explore issues responsibly without being restricted by the teacher's bias or subjected to undue pressures by other pupils. They approached this problem by attempting to stimulate and study, in classroom settings, a pattern of inquiry teaching with a particular style of discussion at its core. Collections of original source material were gathered around inquiry areas and used as evidence for discussion. (*Evidence*, as the word is used by the project, has a judicial or historical connotation: that the material is relevant to the matter under discussion.) Teachers, in the role of discussion group chairmen, took responsibility for providing evidence for the pupils to study and interpret. They undertook not to give their own views on the issues, and to protect divergence of view among pupils. This neutrality of the teachers, although by no means a new idea in this context (see, for instance, Adams 1927), attracted a great deal of public attention during the project, and has been perceived by some to be its defining feature, a judgment that may overstress one element in the teacher role that the project has been exploring. The project team produced initial collections of material on such topics as war, education, the family, relations between the sexes, people and work, and poverty. (Collections on race, law and order, and living in cities followed.) Between 1968 and 1970, these collections were used by approximately 150 teachers in 36 schools throughout England and Wales.

The central team put forward hypotheses about teaching strategies, and asked these teachers to test them by adhering to suggested rules. The teachers were also asked to comment on the usefulness of the material when these rules were followed, to suggest alternative rules or hypotheses, and to develop other inquiry activities that needed to be built up around the discussion.

Early in 1970 revised packs began to be published commercially and training schemes for teachers were set up throughout the country to meet the response from individual schools and local education authorities. During the 1971/72 academic year about six hundred schools have bought the materials, which are available on the open market. Although most of these schools expressed the intention of adopting the research strategy explored by the central team, fewer than half of them have, to date, attended training courses. (The Evaluation Unit, which is attempting to document the overall pattern of adoption and use of the materials, is notified by the publishers of all sales, and asks all purchasers for information about how they intend to use the materials.)

The evaluation of this project began in 1968, when I was appointed. My job was not closely specified, but it was broadly intended that I should study the work of the project, provide feedback to the central team about the progress of the experiment in the schools, and design a suitable evaluation program for implementation during the period from 1970 to 1972. In the past year I have been joined by three colleagues.

The problems of evaluation struck me as formidable when I began. When a curriculum experiment is mounted in a largely unresearched field, which was the case with the Humanities Project, there is little experience to draw upon in order to predict its impact or anticipate the problems it will encounter. There is, of course, the accumulated wisdom of previous innovation (see, for instance, Miles 1964). Measured against this, a gloomy prognosis emerged. The project, at first glance, seemed to have many of the earmarks of past innovation failures. It required induction courses for teachers, it was difficult to use, it was costly in terms of school resources, it conflicted with established values. In short, the project showed distinct promise as a case study in the pathology of innovation, from symptoms to post-mortem. This prognosis assumed that the project should be judged by the amount of pupil learning it produced in a given period. This seems to me now an inappropriately narrow criterion for judging the merits of a curriculum development of this kind. A closer look at some key features of the project may help to underline this, and will also allow me to explain the influence of the project's design upon the development of the evaluation.

Design

The first point concerns the design of the project. The most widely advocated model of curriculum development begins by specifying learning objectives in terms of pupil behavior at the end of a course. The content of the program and the method by which it is taught are then varied until the desired behavior is elicited. These program objectives provide, for the evaluator, criteria of success. His main task is to assess the extent to which they have been achieved.

This model is clearly most useful where these statements of objectives are easy to make and command wide agreement, where side effects are likely to be insignificant or easily detected and controlled, and where strict adherence to the objectives is unlikely to undermine educational values that they do not contain. The Humanities Project team, considering that the nature of their experiment precluded such conditions, had reservations about the usefulness of the objectives approach, and decided to take a different line. (For a full account of these reservations, see Stenhouse 1971.) To put it simply, they set out to answer three questions: What content is worthwhile? What general aim would be appropriate in teaching this content? What kind of learning experience is most conducive to furthering that aim? Answering the last of these questions would involve extensive experimentation in classrooms. Using hypotheses about effects, rather than objectives, the team hoped to develop the general lines of an effective teaching strategy consonant with the particular value position they had adopted toward the teaching of controversial issues.

The assumption in the design is that teachers can, from their understanding of a general aim, develop effective teaching strategies. The emphasis in such a model is upon the attempt to embody the aim in classroom process. It places a heavy burden on the teacher, who is responsible for seeing to it that what he does in the classroom is consistent with the aim and pedagogically effective.

In this nonobjectives approach there is no ready-made niche for the evaluator. He must await events, see what happens, trace the different ways in which the work unfolds, and try to link patterns of effect to patterns of teaching. *Outcome* and *process* both demand his attention. A particular problem is to determine *which* effects to study. In an evaluation program, it is no use providing answers to questions that no one is asking.

Aim

The second point concerns the aim of the project, "To develop an understanding of social situations and human acts and of the controversial value issues which they raise." In adopting "understanding" as their aim, the central team expressed a faith in "educational" rather than "social adjustment" approaches to controversial issues. But the practical implications of this aim, in terms of pupils and teacher roles and relationships, meant setting up, in many schools, a pattern of behavior that conflicted with established assumptions and habits. Given the likelihood that such conflict would influence the work of the project, and the certainty that the degree of conflict would differ from school to school, I decided that the evaluator must give attention to the *context* in which the program is to operate.

Curriculum Innovation

The third point concerns the project team's general approach to the problems of curriculum innovation. Whereas most externally conceived attempts at curriculum reform have been characterized by efforts to minimize their dependence on the judgment of teachers (making the curriculum "teacher proof"), the central assumption of the project's design is that there can be no effective, far-reaching curriculum development without teacher development. To promote this development the team asked teachers to accept the project as a means of exploring for themselves the problems of teaching controversy rather than as an authoritative solution devised by experts. It was important for the success of the project that teachers should understand this position, should see themselves as creators of curriculum change and not as mere spectators.

For the evaluator this indicated that some study of the project team's communications and personal contacts with the schools would be called for in order to gain information about the success or otherwise of this effort. In short, some attention to input from the project would be necessary.

What I had to cope with, then, was an attempt at creative curriculum development with variable components, obvious disturbance potential, and a novel approach. My aim, at that stage, was simply to describe the work of the project in a form that would make it accessible to public and professional judgment. In view of the potential significance of so many aspects of the project, I felt that I should commit myself initially to a complete description of its experience and to making myself aware of a full range of relevant phenomena.

Evaluation design, strategies, and tactics would, I hoped, evolve in response to the impact of the project on the system and the structure of the evaluation problems which that impact would throw up.

THE PROJECT IN THE EXPERIMENTAL SCHOOLS

The thirty-six schools that mounted the experiment in the fall of 1968 were not selected by normal sampling methods. They were nominated by their administering authorities and reflected, by their variety, interesting differences in judgments and priorities among the local education authorities. Only in a few cases were the criteria of nomination made explicit. In most cases they had to be elicited or inferred. Pursuing the reasons that lay behind the choices made by the Local Education Authorities (LEAs) was an important evaluation exercise. It helped me to understand the characteristics of the school sample, to learn something about the LEA policies of and strategies for curriculum development, to assess how well different LEAs knew their schools and by what means they judged them. Clearly there were a variety of criteria involved in nomination. In some instances schools were nominated if they were likely to reflect well upon the authority concerned; in others we had schools that were considered to need an injection of new ideas. It appears that, occasionally, an old school was offered participation in an innovation to compensate for having to put up with very poor material conditions and facilities. In other areas the showpiece school was chosen. The grounds for nomination were sometimes more doubtful. In one district there appeared to be an understanding that the head of the school would not use the project as an excuse to demand an unfair share of resources, such as new equipment. Some schools were, of course, self-selected in the sense that the initiative had come from the head or the staff who, having heard about the experiment, pressed their claim upon the authority. On the whole, LEAs seemed to nominate schools that they considered to be "good" in some not very precisely specified way. Close acquaintance with the experimental schools suggested that some LEA decision makers do not know their schools very well and tend to make judgments about them on limited criteria, particularly community image. Such comments on LEA choices should not be allowed to disguise the fact that a primary consideration in most nominations was the perceived suitability of the school for the experiment.

The participating teachers met the central team during the summer of 1968 at regional conferences where the nature and design of the experiment were explained to them and their task outlined. By all accounts most of them went away from these conferences with some enthusiasm for the task.

The experimental schools were distributed throughout England and Wales, and located variously in rural, suburban, urban, and conurban environments. Questionnaires completed for me by each school showed differences in type, size, organizational structure, and in the formal characterization of their client populations. As a consequence of the central team's policy of sharing decision making, this contextual diversity was compounded by differences in the decisions the schools made about how to introduce, organize, and implement the experiment. For instance, the time allocated to the work came to two hours in one school but seven and a half in another, while the number of staff taking part varied from one teacher to ten. Some schools chose to involve their able fifteen-year-old pupils, while others worked with their most limited fourteen-year-old leavers. The situation was further complicated by variables that became clearer as time went on, variables in the motivation, understanding, and expectations of the people participating in the experiment. Yet another variable was the extent and nature of the support each school received from its local authority.

Immediate Effects

The immediate impact of the project was, on the whole, alarming. There was enormous confusion and misunderstanding, leading to a general failure on the part of the schools to respond appropriately to the specifications of the central team. There were many unexpected problems, and widespread misperception of the demands that the project was making. Some elements of this confusion were:

1. The importance of principals in innovation was underestimated by the central team, who did not see, initially, the scale of the demands they were making on rather inflexible administrative institutions. It was not easy for schools to create the necessary conditions for the experiment, nor was it easy for teachers to undertake such difficult and novel work without the principal's understanding and support.
2. The teachers did not anticipate the extent to which many pupils had developed, in their previous schooling, a "trained" incapacity for this work, nor the depth of alienation from any kind of curriculum offering that many pupils felt, nor the degree to which they themselves and their pupils had been successfully socialized

into a tradition of teacher dominance and custodial attitudes. They were confounded when pupils, invited to discuss, maintained a sullen or embarrassed silence. Many were surprised by how dependent pupils appeared to be upon the teacher's taking and maintaining the initiative, or by the skepticism with which the proferred invitation to "talk freely" was received. It would appear that almost all schools and teachers are more authoritarian than they realize. The implications of the project for the school's authority structure became increasingly clear. Many of the teachers found themselves locked in role conflicts, or in attempts to bridge an unforeseen credibility gap between themselves and their pupils. Thus the following comment from a teacher:

> I'm very tolerant in the discussion group to what the group wants to say . . . but then at other times when they approach me in an easy offhand way I find my adult pride springing up in me and I find I have to sort of take a position over them you know—authority . . . sort of show my superiority in a sense in relation to them and this causes a bit of anguish on my part, inside me.

3. It emerged that the central team had failed at the outset to communicate successfully the nature of the enterprise. From the teacher's point of view the ethos of the project was evangelical rather than exploratory, and the suggested teaching strategies looked like tests of teacher proficiency rather than research hypotheses. Many felt as if they were on trial. This both reduced their capacity to profit from the experience and adversely affected their feedback to the center.

Had the picture from the schools been so uniform as these points suggest, the evaluation might have developed differently. But it was not. Although the program proved generally to be demanding, difficult, and disturbing, there were striking exceptions and many contradictions. While many schools reported severe problems, for example, with the reading level of the materials or the attitudes of the pupils, others expressed surprise at accounts of difficulties that they had not themselves encountered. Limited explanations of perceived failure or success, such as pupil ability, teacher behavior, or institutional ethos, could not readily be generalized. Nor was it easy to reduce, through experience, the number of theoretically postulated variables. Teachers working in the northeast of England suggested that the difference in the response to small-group discussion of boys

and girls could only be explained in terms of a powerful sex differential in expectations and aspirations in that region's working-class
culture, while teachers in a Welsh school claimed, only half in jest,
that the reason they couldn't get discussion going was that there's no
such thing as a controversial issue in the Welsh valleys. The matter
seemed increasingly complex, even leaving aside such regional arguments.

Information

During the first year, while the central team grappled with the
problems of the schools in an effort to sustain the experiment, I
concentrated on trying to establish precisely what was happening in
the schools, and on gathering information that might help to explain
differing patterns of action and response. I studied the activities of
the team and the interaction among them, the local authorities, and
the schools, gathered data for each school about the external forces
of support and opposition that were mobilized by the introduction
of the experiment, produced a checklist of hard and soft data items
that added up to an institutional profile of each school, tried to
assess, by questionnaires administered at conferences, the participating teachers' understanding of project theory, and their attitudes
towards it, and organized a feedback system of audiotapes of classroom discussion with written supplementary data. I also made videotape recordings of classroom work through the generous cooperation
of a number of educational television units throughout the country.
An edited master tape of these recordings is now available, from the
Evaluation Unit, as a visual report on the project. The needs of the
central team and of the evaluator overlapped sufficiently to form a
continuing basis of cooperation, even if the demands of the team's
support role made it increasingly difficult to match priorities.

I embarked on a series of visits to the schools, intending initially
to study all of them at first hand. After visiting about half of them
this plan was abandoned in favor of making case studies of a small
number, principally because I could not understand the causes of the
behavior that I had observed in discussion groups. Why were the
differences among schools in this respect so much more marked than
the differences within schools? Why was one group of pupils enthusiastic about the work, and a group, with similar formal characteristics
in another school, so hostile? Other questions accumulated as I began
to seek contextual clues. Why did some staff groups support the
project, while others were indifferent, and still others openly hostile?
Why did some schools react in dissimilar ways to apparently similar

problems? A host of questions like these arose as the diversity of institutional, teacher, and pupil response unfolded.

Toward the end of the first year, and throughout the second year of the experiment, clinical field studies of about six schools were carried out. These schools were selected on multiple criteria, but did represent the range of response to the experiment of the schools as a whole. Case study strategies included observation of classrooms, interviews with staff, pupils, and parents, and gathering detailed information about the various forces and circumstances, both inside and outside the school, that might be exerting an influence on the project. It is not possible here to give an account of these studies, but I can list some of the propositions arising out of them that the evaluation is exploring.

1. Human behavior in educational settings is susceptible to a wide range of variable influences. This is a commonplace, yet in curriculum evaluation it is sometimes assumed that what is intended to happen is what actually happens, and that what happens varies little from setting to setting.

2. The impact of an innovation is not a set of discrete effects, but an organically related pattern of acts and consequences. To understand fully a single act one must locate it functionally within that pattern. It follows from this proposition that innovations have many more unexpected consequences than is normally assumed in development and evaluation designs.

3. No two schools are so alike in their circumstances that prescriptions of curricular action can adequately supplant the judgment of the people in them. Historical or evolutionary differences alone make the innovation "gap" a variable that has significance for decision making.

4. The goals and purposes of the program developers are not necessarily shared by its users. We have seen the project used variously as a political resource in an existing power struggle between staff factions, as a way of increasing the effectiveness of a custodial pattern of pupil control, and as a means of garnishing the image of institutions that covet the wrappings, but not the merchandise, of innovation. The latter gives rise to the phenomenon of innovation without change.

RATIONALE AND FRAMEWORK OF THE EVALUATION

To avoid possible misunderstanding, I should point out that evaluation of the project is not an activity engaged in solely by specialized personnel. All members of the development team have devoted much of their time to evaluating their work in order to increase their understanding and improve the quality and appropriateness of their support to schools. Many of the schools have, with the assistance of the team, devised examinations, syllabuses, and forms of pupil assessment. However, I am responsible only for the work of an independent evaluation unit attached to the project, and it is that work that I am here concerned to describe.

Evaluations may be judged by whether they get the right information to the right people at the right time. But who are the right people, what is the right information, and when is it needed?

Decision Makers

Faced with a central team who were opposed to the use of "objectives," I had to look elsewhere for a concept of evaluation to guide me. In any case, as I became aware of the complexity and diversity of what was going on in the experimental schools, I became increasingly skeptical of the notion of confining evaluation to the measurement of intention achievement. I then explored the possibility of defining my responsibilities in relation to the likely readers of my report. The ideas of evaluation for consumers attracted me. In time "consumers" became redefined as decision makers and four main groups of decision makers emerged—sponsors, local education authorities, schools, and examination boards. The task of evaluation was then defined as that of answering the questions that decision makers ask. This task definition was subsequently perceived as unsatisfactory principally because it assumed that these groups knew in advance what questions were appropriate—an unjustified assumption when educational process is so little understood that the effects of intervening in it cannot be fully anticipated.

At the present time we see our task as that of feeding the judgment of decision makers by promoting understanding of the considerations that bear upon curricular action. This task definition has two main advantages. In the first place it greatly increases the number of people for whom the evaluation is potentially useful. In the second it goes some way toward meeting the oft-voiced complaint that evaluation data come too late to affect decisions about the program. Where the evaluation findings are specifically tied to the program and do not generalize beyond it, this criticism is telling. Our findings ought to be relevant to recurring problems of educational choice, and contribute to a cumulative tradition of curriculum study.

With these considerations in mind, we can define the objectives of the evaluation unit as follows:

1. To ascertain the effects of the project, document the circumstances in which they occur, and present this information in a form that will help educational decision makers to evaluate the likely consequences of adopting the program.
2. To describe the present situation and operations of the schools we study so that decision makers can understand more fully what it is they are trying to change.
3. To describe the work of the project team in terms that will help the sponsors and planners of such ventures to weigh the value of this form of investment, and to determine more precisely the framework of support, guidance, and control that are appropriate.
4. To make a contribution to evaluation theory by articulating our problems clearly, recording our experience and, perhaps most importantly, by publicizing our errors.
5. To contribute to the general understanding of the problems of curriculum innovation.

Not everyone would agree that all of these are defensible objectives for an evaluation unit set up to study one project. I would argue firstly that objectives are, in part, a function of opportunities, and secondly that, at a time when curriculum development is becoming increasingly the concern of a number of new and relatively inexperienced agencies, there is a need for those involved in the field to contribute what they can toward an understanding of the problems of change.

There still remains the problem of the "right" information. As an American friend put it, "It's not a see-through blouse if nobody's looking." Decision-making groups differ in their data requirements. Teachers may be mainly interested in pupil development, principals in teacher development, LEAs in school development, planners in project strategies, boards in the adequacy of examinations for the assessment of pupil learning. Moreover, individuals differ in the degree of confidence they place in different kinds of data, and in the levels of confidence at which they are prepared to act. Faced with such diverse interests and requirements, we are making a broad study of the project, combining both subjective and objective approaches (to use a convenient, if misleading, dichotomy), in our acquisition of relevant information.

Evaluation Design

The design we are working with contains clinical, psychometric, and sociometric elements. Basically we are seeking information from two overlapping school samples, one large and one small. The idea is to study in some detail over a period of time the experience of a small number of schools, while gathering sufficient information about what is happening in a large number of schools to permit interpretation from one sample to the other. The design looks like this:

In the Large Sample of Schools (approximately 100)
1. Gathering input, contextual, and implementation data by questionnaire.
2. Gathering judgment data from teachers and pupils.
3. Objective measurement of teacher and pupil change. (We have, at the beginning of this year, carried out pretests of pupils on twenty-one objective tests, which represent the combined judgments of teachers, pupils, the central team, and ourselves, of likely dimensions of pupil change. This is a massive operation, but will be justified if it can help us establish the effects of the project on the pupils, and enable us, next year, to use a small but accurate test battery.)
4. Tracing variations in teaching practice through the use of specially devised, multiple-choice, feedback instruments that require minimal effort by the teacher and are monitored by pupils.
5. Documenting the effect on the school by asking the teachers to write semistructured diaries.

In a Small Sample of Schools (approximately 12)
1. Case studies of patterns of decision making, communication, training, and support in local areas.
2. Case studies of individual schools within these areas.
3. Study of the dynamics of discussion by audiotape, videotape, and observation.

To sum up, we now have the job of describing the experience of hundreds of schools embarking on work with Humanities Project materials and of describing that experience in ways that will be helpful to those who have judgments to make in this field. We believe that much evaluation work in the past has been oversimplified in its approach, or so subservient to the canons of traditional research that its attention has been too narrowly focused. Perhaps at this stage of our understanding bolder evaluation designs can give us a more adequate view of what it is we are trying to change, and what is involved in changing it. That is why we have adopted such a comprehensive plan of evaluation. By interweaving the studies outlined above, we hope to advance understanding of the interplay of forces in this curriculum innovation.

REFERENCES

Adams, John. *Errors in School.* London: University of London Press, 1927.

Miles, M. B., ed. *Innovation and Education.* New York: Columbia University Press, 1964.

Schools Council. "Raising the School Leaving Age." Working Paper no. 2. London: Her Majesty's Stationery Office, 1965.

_____. *The Humanities Project, an Introduction.* London: Heinemann, 1970.

Stenhouse, Lawrence. "Some Limitations of the Use of Objectives in Curriculum Research and Planning." *Paedogogica Europa* 6 (April 1971): 73-83.

IV

IF EVERYONE AGREES . . .

Evaluation with a Consensus on Goals

Many evaluation experts seem to assume that everybody agrees on educational goals and that all that is needed for a successful evaluation is that those goals be specified clearly enough so that they can be measured readily. This is the theme of the "behavioral objectives" school, begun by Ralph Tyler many years ago, which has dominated the evaluation world until the last several years.

The first chapter of this section deals with the use of behavioral objectives as such. Stake analyzes in depth the dangers of both specifying and measuring behavioral objectives, especially in performance contracts.

The remaining three chapters deal with so-called systems approaches to evaluation. Systems approaches also assume that there are no disagreements about goals and that the problem of evaluation is to maximize the goals that already exist. Such approaches are termed "systems analysis," "cost-benefit analysis," "program, planning, and budgeting systems," and "operations research." They assume that all objectives can be specified, but add other techniques such as cost analysis. They are elaborated versions of the objectives model. The first chapter describes such techniques and various modifications and criticisms of how the techniques work. The second casts systems techniques into the context of educational systems. The third article challenges the efficacy and desirability of the whole approach.

Stake's contribution is not comforting to the testing expert or the performance contractors. He contends that our tests were actually designed to measure the correlates of learning, that is, to predict later performance rather than to measure current performance. The "errors" of testing cannot be eliminated; they have been tolerated because they have not involved important decisions. But, with errors running as high as a full grade equivalent, our standardized tests are less than adequate as the sole measure of educational output.

Performance contracting is precisely the situation in which decisions are made without relying on professional observers. In performance contracting there are the errors of attending to the wrong objectives, of selecting the wrong tests, of misinterpreting the test scores, and of depersonalizing school life. Contrary to common belief, prespecifying objectives has many disadvantages. It requires much time and effort. Almost always the objectives easiest to measure and least controversial are emphasized. Prespecification also decreases emphasis on subject matter. Perhaps most damaging, there is little empirical evidence that prespecification leads to better results. In fact, one study indicates that teachers attend less to immediate pupil concerns when using behavioral objectives.

A second major set of difficulties awaits the performance contractor in the lack of test reliability and validity. For performance contracting, "validated" tests do not exist. Tests are usually validated against future grades, which is quite different from current learning. It is unrealistic to expect the benefits of instruction to be entirely apparent in the performances of learners when they are tested. In addition, the reliability of the tests is such that a standardized test cannot measure the specific outcomes of an individual student with sufficient precision. Stake also discusses how test results vary with the school calendar, the problem of grade equivalents, and many other problems. He argues strongly against the simplistic overuse and reliance on objectives and tests that are often encountered among accountability advocates.

The remainder of Part IV is devoted to the systems approach to evaluation, particularly to those cost-cutting measures such as program planning and budgeting. Hartley concisely and clearly outlines the nature of these management tools. He notes that they are an attempt to control the future rather than react to it. The outstanding features of such systems approaches are the emphasis on the outputs of the educational process and the relating of inputs to outputs in terms of effectiveness. There is great emphasis on evaluation activities, especially on quantitative measures. In such a system it is critical to have accurate measures of effectiveness. Hartley identifies this way of thinking as deriving from "economic rationality," an encroachment on the devices of "political rationality" such as negotiation and compromise.

In spite of being in favor of such approaches, Hartley warns that they are not panaceas. Performance criteria are badly deficient or lacking and there is a shortage of trained personnel. Such approaches may also increase costs because of the additional personnel required. More substantive dangers may also lurk. There are real dangers that such processes might distort educational goals, lead to increased centralization through central data banks, and accentuate conflict through exposing latent social antagonisms. Hartley also notes that most districts that claim to have adopted such systems have not actually done so. He cites three exemplary projects.

Burnham applies the systems model to the evaluation of educational programs. Pointing out that past organizational analysis had assumed that organizations are rational and determinate systems, he contends that the open system model is more appropriate. The open system is interdependent with the environment and hence has strong elements of uncertainty and indeterminateness. He sees evaluation as a comparison of the effects of a program against some criterion of desirability. Evaluation becomes a "test of efficiency" only when the standard of desirability is specific and a cause and effect model is clear. When causes and effects are not clear, evaluation becomes an "instrumental test." And when neither the cause and effect relationships are clear nor the standards specific, evaluation becomes a "social test"—seeing which social reference group's standards will prevail. Education fits the last case most of the time.

School bureaucracies are also faced with a need to appear rational, so they fall back on "fitness measures" as evaluative standards, for example, compliance with the rules, whether quotas for manpower are met, and the expressed confidence of the public. The question becomes, "Does the organization meet the expectations of those groups with which it is interdependent?" Under these circumstances, schools will prefer "symbolic extrinsic evaluation." They will try to demonstrate historical improvement, for example, accreditation evaluation, or try to satisfy the most important group, usually that with economic interests.

House attacks the systems approach and the current accountability movement. Cautioning that accountability is not always good and that we are already accountable in many ways, he maintains that such an approach will work neither technically or politically. Proponents of accountability perceive education as a vast corporation with accountability rising upward. The basis of this system is economic efficiency and its purpose is to control the behavior of teacher and student.

Business techniques are used to obtain such control. Since, in a pluralist society goal agreement cannot be reached easily, the result is to agree on a few set goals and shape students to those prespecified ends. Education becomes engineering and finally industrial production. Evaluation becomes simply a comparison of the final product to the prespecifications. The loss is cultural pluralism. An example of such schooling is presented.

House attacks the California PPB system for education, calling it a batch of hazy generalizations having nothing to do with education. The outcome of such systems is that the individual is more accountable to the institution but the institution is not accountable to the individual. He then sketches the characteristics of a scheme for institutional accountability.

16

MEASURING WHAT
LEARNERS LEARN

Robert E. Stake

"Can there be teaching if there is no learning?" Hear again one of the lines from the educator's catechism. The question is not to be taken literally. Good teaching, elegant teaching, without student benefit, of course is possible—though doubly wasteful. The question is rhetorical. Professionals and laymen alike sanctify the teaching-learning contract that results in better student performance.

Measuring the learning is no small problem. Teachers, as a matter of course, usually are able to observe that individual students are or are not learning. Sometimes they cannot. And increasingly, outsiders are reluctant to take the teacher's word for it. Gathering "hard-data" evidence of student learning is a new and ominous challenge. Of course, we have tests. But the results of our testing have seldom been adequate grounds for the continuing faith we have in education.

PRESENT DEMANDS

Expectations of testing are on the rise because schools have been told to be accountable—to demonstrate publicly what they are accomplishing (Lieberman 1970; Bhaerman 1970). Increasing educational costs and mounting frustration with social and political problems have brought higher demands for answers to an important question: what are we getting for our education dollar?

Educators have been challenged to become more explicit and more functional in lesson plans and school budgets; to identify the gains and losses children make in reading, singing, and the many human talents; and to realize that the events of the classroom are not unrelated to the events of the street, the marketplace, and the city hall

193

(Cohen 1970). Educators have been told to learn about systems analysis, operations research, cost-benefit analysis, program planning and budgeting, and other models for orderly and dispassionate treatment of institutional affairs (Lessinger 1970).

Some critics of contemporary education are bothered that educational practice is so intuitive, impulsive, inefficient, and resistant to change. Others continue to be bothered more by passionate but naive efforts to substitute technical procedures for personal attention. Thorndike (1921), Tyler (1950), and Krathwohl (1969) have been persuasive advocates of a more rational, explicit, performance-oriented school. But Atkin (1968b), Oettinger (1969), and Dyer (1970) have cautioned that formal analyses and production models can be narrow, irrelevant, and even oppressive. It is safe to say that all specialists in testing and instruction believe that it is possible to measure many specific educational outcomes and to use such measurements in improving educational decisions. But a few of these same specialists are among the most vehement critics of present testing (Glaser 1963; Grobman 1970).

PERFORMANCE CONTRACTS

The performance contract is an agreement between a group offering instruction and a school needing services (Lennon 1971). Reimbursement is to be made in some proportion to measured student achievement. Especially for children with special needs, such as those who are handicapped, gifted, or unable to read, a new way of getting special instruction is appealing. A "hard-data" basis for evaluating the quality of instruction is appealing. In performance contracting student gains are the criterion of successful teaching.

In the first federally sponsored example of performance contracting for the public schools, Dorsett Educational Systems of Norman, Oklahoma, contracted to teach reading, mathematics, and study skills to over 200 poorly performing junior and senior high school students in Texarkana, Texas. Commercially available, standardized tests were used to measure performance gains.

Are such tests suitable for measuring specific learning? To the person not intimately acquainted with educational testing it appears that performance testing is what educational tests are for. The testing specialist knows that this is not so. These tests have been developed and administered to measure correlates of learning, not learning itself, as are most tests. Correlation with important general learning is often high, but correlation of test scores with performance on many specific educational tasks is seldom high. Tests can be built for specific competence, but there is relatively little demand for them and many do a poor job of predicting later performance either specifically or generally. General achievement tests predict better. The test developer's basis for improving tests has been to work toward better predictions of later performance rather than better measurement of present performance. Assessment of what a student is now capable of doing is not the purpose of most standardized tests. Especially when indirect-measurement tests are used for performance contracting, but even with direct-assessment tests, errors and hazards abound.

THE ERRORS OF TESTING

Answering a *National School Board Journal* (November 1970) questionnaire on performance contracting, a New Jersey board member said, "Objectives must be stated in simple, understandable terms. No jargon will do and no subjective goals can be tolerated. Neither can the nonsense about there being some mystique that prohibits objective measurement of the educational endeavor." Would that our problems would wither before stern resolve. But neither wishing nor blustering rids educational testing of its errors. They exist.

Just as the population census and the bathroom scales have their errors, educational tests have theirs. The technology and theory of testing are highly sophisticated; the sources of error are well known (Lindquist 1951; Cronbach 1969). Looking into the psychometrist's meaning of "A Theory of Testing," one finds a consideration of ways to analyze and label the inaccuracies in test scores (Lord 1952). There is mystique, but there is also simple fact: no one can eliminate test errors. Unfortunately, some errors in testing are large enough to cause wrong decisions about individual children or about school-district policy.

The whole idea of educational testing is thought to be an error by some educators and social critics (Hoffman 1962; Holt 1969; Silberman 1970; Sizer 1970). Bad social consequences of testing, such as the perpetuation of racial discrimination (Goslin 1970) and pressures to cheat (McGhan 1970) continue to be discussed. But, as would be expected, most test specialists believe that the promise in testing outweighs these perils. They refuse responsibility for gross misuse of their instruments and findings, and concentrate on reducing the errors in specific tests and test programs (Lennon, n.d.).

Some technical errors in test scores are small and tolerable, but some are intolerably large. Today's tests can, for example, measure vocabulary and word-recognition skills sufficiently accurately. Today's tests cannot adequately measure listening comprehension or the ability to analyze the opposing sides of an argument. Today's test technology is not refined enough to meet all the demands put on it. The tests are best when the performance is highly specific—when, for example, the student has to add two numbers, recognize a misspelled word, or identify the parts of a hydraulic lift. When a teacher wants to measure higher mental processes (Bloom et al. 1956), such as those used in generating a writing principle or synthesizing a political argument, our tests give us scores that are less dependable. See figure 16:1 for several examples.

FIGURE 16:1. HIGH AND LOW VALIDITY ITEMS
IN CONVENTIONAL STANDARDIZED ACHIEVEMENT TESTS

High validity—"basic mental process" items:
1. Which one of the following phrases about wave motion defines period?

  a. the maximum distance a particle is displaced from its point of rest
  b. the length of time required for a particle to make a complete vibration
  c. the number of complete vibrations per second
  d. the time rate of change of distance in a given direction

2. Directions: In each group below, select the numbered word or phrase that most nearly corresponds in meaning to the word at the head of that group, and put its number in the parenthesis at right.

  ( ) antelope

  a. fruit   b. animal   c. prelude   d. feeler   e. gallop

3. The first movement of a sonata is distinguished from the others by:

  a. rapidity and gaiety
  b. length and complexity
  c. emotional abandon
  d. sweetness and charm
  e. structural formality

4. Which of these would help you decide whether or not you used the word *filter* correctly in a sentence?

  a. encyclopedia
  b. dictionary
  c. thesaurus
  d. English grammar textbook

Lower validity—"higher mental process" items:

5. A and B were arguing about the desirability of adopting a nationwide system of compulsory health insurance in the United States. B said that, while he had no fundamental objection to health insurance, he felt strongly that people should not be compelled to participate in it. "Now look here," he said, "do the people want health insurance or don't they? I don't think they do, but in either case, compulsory insurance is bad. If the people really want health insurance, there is no need for compulsion. If they don't want it, it is impossible to force them to participate. So the answer is clear."

Which of the following statements most nearly expresses the logical conclusion of B's argument?

    a. Health insurance is bad
    b. Compulsory health insurance is bad
    c. Compulsion is impossible
    d. Compulsion is unnecessary
    e. Compulsion is either unnecessary or impossible

6. *Directions:* In each situation below, you are given introductory information about a person's action or conclusion. This is followed by several independent statements of evidence. Decide whether the added information in each statement makes it more or less probable that the action or conclusion is correct. For each statement, mark the answer space under a if the added information makes it *more* probable that the conclusion is correct; under b if the added information makes it *less* probable that the conclusion is correct; under c if the added information makes it *neither more nor less* probable that the conclusion is correct.

Situation: I predict that our team will win the basketball tournament next week. With the exception of one player, our team is the same as last year when we won easily. Furthermore, we have a 13-3 won-lost record this season.

Statements:

    a. Another team in the tournament has been undefeated against substantially the same teams.
    b. Our closest competitor will be relying mainly on sophomores to carry it to victory.
    c. The first game will be played Monday morning instead of Monday afternoon as previously announced.

SOURCES:
Questions 1 through 5: Benjamin S. Bloom et al. *A Taxonomy of Educational Objectives: Handbook 1, The Cognitive Domain.* New York: David McKay, 1956, pp. 25, 79, 151.
Question 6: George A. Prescott, coordinating editor. *Analysis of Learning Potential.* Advanced I Battery, Form A. New York: Harcourt Brace Jovanovich, 1970. Reproduced here by permission.

Unreached Potentials

Many educators feel that the most human of human gifts, for example, the emotions, the higher thought processes, interpersonal sensitivity, moral sense, are beyond the reach of psychometric testing. Most testing specialists disagree. While recognizing an ever-present error component, they believe that anything can be measured. The credo was sounded by Thorndike:

> Whatever exists at all exists in some amount. To know it thoroughly involves knowing its quantity as well as its quality. Education is concerned with changes in human beings; a change is a difference between two conditions; each of these conditions is known to us only by the products produced by it—things made, words spoken, acts performed, and the like. To measure any of these products means to define its amount in some way so that competent persons will know how large it is, better than they would without measurement. To measure a product well means so to define its amount that competent persons will know how large it is, with some precision, and that this knowledge may be conveniently recorded and used. This is the general *Credo* of those who, in the last decade, have been busy trying to extend and improve measurements of educational products.

> We have faith that whatever people now measure crudely by mere descriptive words, helped out by the comparative and superlative forms, can be measured more precisely and conveniently if ingenuity and labor are set at the task. We have faith also that the objective products produced, rather than the inner condition of the person whence they spring, are the proper point of attack for the measurer, at least in our day and generation.

> This is obviously the same general creed as that of the physicist or chemist or physiologist engaged in quantitative thinking—the same, indeed, as that of modern science in general. And, in general, the nature of educational measurements is the same as that of all scientific measurements (1918).

Testing men believe it still. They are not so naive as to think that any human gift will manifest itself in a forty-five-minute paper-and-pencil test. They believe that, if given ample opportunity to activate and observe the examinee, any trait, or talent, or learning that manifests itself in behavior can be measured with reasonable accuracy. The total "cost" of measuring may be a hundred times that of administering the usual tests, but they believe it can be done. The final observations may rely on professional judgment, but it would be a reliable and validated judgment. The question for most test specialists is not "Can complex educational outcomes be measured?" but "Can complex educational outcomes be measured with the time, and personnel, and facilities available?"

If we really want to know whether or not a child is reading at age-level, we have a reading specialist listen to him read. She observes his reading habits. She might test him with word recognition, syntactic decoding, and paragraph-comprehension exercises. She would retest where evidence was inconclusive. She would talk to his teachers and his parents. She would arrive at a clinical description which might be reducible to such a statement as "Yes, Johnny is reading at (or above) age-level."

The scores we get from group reading tests can be considered estimates of such a clinical judgment. These test scores correlate positively with the more valid clinical judgments. Though more objective, such estimates are not direct measurements of what teachers or laymen mean by the ability to read. Achievement gains for a sizable number of students will be poorly estimated by them. It is possible that the errors in group testing are so extensive that—when fully known—businessmen and educators will refuse to accept them as bases for contract reimbursement.

Professional Awareness

Classroom teachers and school principals have tolerated standardized test errors as much as they have because they have not been obliged to make important decisions on the basis of test scores alone. Actually, it is seldom in day-to-day practice that they use test scores (Hastings, Runkel, and Damrin 1961), but, when they do, they use them, in combination with other knowledge, to estimate a child's progress in school and to guide him into an appropriate learning experience. They do not use tests as a basis for assessing the quality of their own teaching.

In performance contracting the situation is supposed to be drastically changed. Tests are indicated as the sole basis for contract reimbursement. The parties must decide how much to pay the contractor for instructing each child. An error in testing means money misspent. Graduation and reimbursement decisions are to be made without reliance on the knowledge and judgment of a professional observer, without asking persons who are closest to the learning (that is, the teachers, the contractors, the students) whether or not they see evidence of learning. They are to be made entirely by objective and independent testing. The resulting human errors and technical misrepresentations will be numerous.

CHOICE OF OBJECTIVES

It is important to recognize that at no time—in any real educational practice—are instructional objectives completely and finally specified. No statement of objectives is final. Changes in aim, as well as changes in priority, occur throughout training even in the more highly structured instructional programs. Some people feel that this is what is wrong with much classroom instruction: it cannot pick a target and stay fixed on it. But other people are convinced that classroom instruction is too fixated, too inflexible, that teachers are too unwilling to adapt to the changing goals of students and society.

No statement of objectives says exactly what it ought to. Every statement has its ambiguity; each word can be misunderstood; we cannot expect any list to say exactly what its authors want it to. Verbal statements of objectives cannot perfectly represent human purpose. All this does not mean that educators should not state their objectives, but it does mean that educators should continue to look for better ways of representing their objectives. They should expect them to change from beginning to end of the semester and beyond. They should regard any statement as an approximation. Objectives remain in flux, never completely free of misrepresentation by our tests and observations, in even the most stable curricula.

Specification Benefits

Identifying the goals of education in formal, rational terms is recognized as a powerful way to change professional practice (Tyler 1950; Mager 1962). To recognize that objectives will change is not to argue that they should not be stated in advance of training. An awareness of purpose by both teacher and student is usually desired. Only occasionally will an educational experience be highly successful if there is no advance expectation of what should occur. Usually the activity will be improved if the opportunity to learn is deliberately provided. Often instruction will be improved if lesson plans focus on desired behavior rather than entertain spontaneous interests and distractions.

Outside evaluation of the success of instruction is made much simpler and possibly more effective by the prespecification of objectives. Popham (1969) has identified these and other benefits that accrue to those who state their instructional objectives in advance and stick to them.

Specification Costs

But each of these possible benefits carries with it a cost. Stating objectives properly is a lot of work. Some other possible costs are less obvious. To specify what is to be accomplished always fails to represent the sum total of what is desired. Language fails to portray exactly what we want. The error may be small and unimportant, or it may not. But to some extent there will be a misrepresentation of purpose.

The singularity of any list of objectives—even if it has 100 separate objectives—disregards the disparity in what teachers, students, and citizens need and want. In a pluralist society, different people have different priorities. Gooler (1971), for example, found that teachers put more emphasis on humanist curricular objectives than parents do. Schrag (1970) said:

> Any single, universal public institution—and especially one as sensitive as the public school—is the product of a social quotient verdict. It evaluates the lowest common denominator of desires, pressures, and demands into the highest public virtue. It cannot afford to offend any sizable community group be it the American Legion, the B'nai B'rith, or the NAACP.

Publicized statements of objectives are likely to represent nobody's objectives.

Any public display of educational goals evokes political and social reaction (Lortie 1967). Educators—as other people—are seldom candid in the face of hostile criticism. They are likely then to state (and possibly emphasize in the classroom) objectives that are less controversial. Pressure to state objectives is transformable into pressure to change objectives.

The schools presently pursue many more objectives than any educator can specify; more than he chooses to admit (Gooler 1971).

The result of a specification of objectives, for good or ill, is to increase substantially the emphasis on some objectives and to decrease substantially the emphasis on others. Some objectives are more easily specified and more easily measured than others. It is almost certain that easily measured objectives will get increased emphasis when a statement of objectives is drawn up.

The language of behavioral specification is such that behavioral processes (recalling, solving, writing, observing, and so on) are given greater emphasis, and subject matter (the Civil War, use of quotation marks, conservation of energy, the nature of knowledge, and so on) will get less. Gagné has claimed (1967) that subject matter is preserved to any desired extent by behavioral objectives, but the AAAS Elementary Science Curriculum, whose creators relied heavily on his counsel, is a curriculum that attends relatively little to the traditional categories and relationships of science. Increased emphasis on performance is likely to bring decreased emphasis on content.

Furthermore, when curricular objectives are spelled out in advance, it is more difficult for a teacher to seize an opportunity to teach something the students are obviously ready for and wanting to learn (Atkin 1968a). And it is more difficult for a teacher to assign needed remedial work when the schedule, and perhaps the syllabus, call for completion of specific units.

The listing of trade offs could go on. There are many things that happen when you try to state educational objectives in "simple, understandable terms." McNeil (1967), Jenkins and Deno (1969), Baker (1970), and Zahorik (1970) carried out empirical studies to examine the good and bad effects of specification and planning. Improved student performance *on the specified objectives* in some circumstances appears to be attributable to the specification itself. But Zahorik found that planning resulted in less attention to the immediate concerns of the pupils. More research on the overall effects of specification is needed. For each effort to identify more specifically what will be learned, to identify it earlier, and to identify it formally as a statement of instructional objectives, it seems that there are both potential benefits and hazards for the instructional process.

CRITERION TESTING PROCEDURES

Among test developers the most vexing problem has always been "the criterion problem," the problem of correlating test scores to a true criterion. For validating a new test, the developer needs to ascertain that, at least for a small, carefully measured reference group of students, there is a high correlation between what the test measures and what is already known about that group that the test is supposed to indicate. A high correlation signifies that, for that criterion chosen, the test is valid. The high scorers on a study-skills test, for example, would be the students who independently and by direct observation are judged to have the best study capabilities. True criterion observations—whatever the criterion might be—are not readily available on most students. Because of the difficulty and expense, any one standardized test will be validated against only one, or a very few, criterion variables. The most common criterion variables are a course grade given by a teacher or a grade-point average.

For performance testing, the standardized test—the right, already-validated, standardized test—is not likely to exist. The purposes of the contract instruction are relatively clear, for example, to increase reading speed and comprehension, and the available tests have been validated against a more general criterion, for example, grades in reading. The educator has a choice between using a not-quite appropriate available test and building an expensive and questionably valid test. The problem is a vexing one: how to select or construct the appropriate items, observations, or test to serve as the criterion of learning for the purpose of the contract. There is a question about relying on performance as a criterion indicator of benefit from instruction, a question about measuring complex performances with simple tests, and a question of "teaching for the test." The first two are related to hazards in the choice of objectives as described in the previous sections.

Savings

An objection to the performance test is that it does not reveal one of the outstanding benefits of instruction: savings. In learning-research jargon, *savings* is the increased ease of relearning something just because it was studied before. Whether or not a student masters something, he usually forgets some or all of it. When he needs to know it, in school or out, he usually has an opportunity to relearn it. *Immediate recall* is just not as important as test designers assume.

It is usually much easier to learn the second time than the first. It is, of course, easier to learn on that later occasion than it would have been had the learner not studied the lesson before. Sometimes it is easier because the learner knows how to go about learning it the second time. This savings is an important benefit from instruction.

Learning how and when to use reference sources for particular topics is a major, but poorly recognized, instructional objective. Such learning shows up as savings. Savings and long-range retention are among several things, in addition to immediate retention performance, that should be considered in deciding whether or not instruction deserves reimbursement. Others include: improving typical as well as maximal behavior; developing awareness of contexts where special skills are needed; increasing structure and "organizers" for learning; providing opportunity to learn; increasing desire to learn; using good adult models; treating students with dignity and humanity, and so on. Perhaps the school officials should be paid a bonus if they identify an appropriately broad set of objectives or fined if they do not.

Complex Performances

It is unrealistic to expect that a project director can find or create paper-and-pencil test items, administrable to large numbers of students in an hour by persons untrained in psychometric observation and standardized diagnostics, objectively scorable, valid for the performance contract, and readily interpretable. The more complex the training, the more unrealistic the expectation. One compromise is to substitute criterion test items measuring simple behavior for those measuring the complex behavior targeted by the training. For example, the director may substitute vocabulary-recognition test items for reading-comprehension items or a knowledge of components in place of the actual dismantling of an engine. In this situation tendencies to teach for the test must be checked. The substitution may be sound, but the criterion test should be validated against performances directly indicated by the objectives. It almost never has been.

It would be unrealistic to expect that the benefits of instruction will be entirely apparent in the performances of learners taking the test. The tests to be used will probably evoke relatively simple behavior. Ebel said:

> most achievement tests . . . consist primarily of items testing specific elements of knowledge, facts, ideas, explanations, meanings, processes, procedures, relations, consequences, and so on (1971, p. 130).

He went on to point out that more than simple recall is involved in answering even the simplest vocabulary item.

Much more complex behavior is needed for answering a reading-comprehension item. An example of an excellent reading-comprehension item, from the Iowa Tests of Basic Skills, is shown in figure 16:2. The items here are clearly calling for more than the literal meanings of the words. The student must paraphrase, interpret—what we expect readers to be able to do.

FIGURE 16:2. A READING COMPREHENSION TEST

Paragraph 1

When your teacher says "O.K.," you know that all is well. Do you know how we happen to use two letters of our alphabet for words? Do you know the words for which the two letters stand?

Paragraph 2

The custom of using O.K. to mean that all is correct is now 100 years old. It began during the election year of 1840. William Henry Harrison, a candidate for president, came to Urbana, Ohio, to make a speech. A large number of people went out to meet him. When they returned to town, one of the wagons carried a large banner on which was written, "The people is oll korrect." The spelling, of course, was wrong; the sign meant "all correct."

Paragraph 3

The enemies of General Harrison made fun of the poor spelling of his friends. Harrison's friends, however, used the saying to advertise their candidate. They said he was the candidate of the common man. Since many people of that day could not spell well, saying that Mr. Harrison's friends could not spell made him still more popular with the common people. Soon, instead of saying "oll korrect," people were saying just "O.K.'

Paragraph 4

After the election Daniel Leffler, an innkeeper of Springfield, Ohio, put a sign over the door of his house which read, "The O.K. Inn." This inn was on the great national road. Many people stopped to eat and many others saw the strange sign as they drove by. Harrison had been elected president, and people remembered the "Oll Korrect" and the "O.K." of the election. The sign on the inn kept the memory alive. Besides, the food at the inn was "oll korrect" as advertised. People began to say "O.K." when things were right.

Questions
0. What two letters are mentioned in the first line?
    1) A.B.   2) O.K.   3) X.Y.   4) P.S.

1. Why did Mr. Harrison come to Urbana?
    1) To see the "oll korrect" sign
    2) To get people to vote for him

    3) To visit some old friends

    4) To stay at the O.K. Inn

2. What is the purpose of paragraph 1?
    1) To tell where the expression "O.K." originated
    2) To get the reader interested in the article
    3) To tell that letters can be used for words
    4) To ask the reader if he knew what O.K. meant

3. Who first used the letters "O.K." for the words "Oll Korrect"?
    1) Wm. H. Harrison
    2) Daniel Leffler
    3) The innkeeper
    4) The article does not give his name

4. What is the topic of paragraph 2?
    1) The origin of the term "O.K."
    2) The election of Harrison
    3) The poor spelling of Ohio men
    4) The meaning of the term "O.K."

5. What is the author's purpose in paragraph 4?
    1) To show that the innkeeper's sign developed from the misspelled campaign banner
    2) To show that the innkeeper's sign helped make O.K. a popular expression
    3) To tell about the location and food of "The O.K. Inn"
    4) To tell who first used the term "O.K."

6. Why did the misspelled words on the banner make Harrison more popular?
    1) They made people believe Harrison was "oll korrect," as the banner said
    2) They suggested that Harrison was a common man
    3) The innkeeper of a popular inn put them on his sign
    4) Most people disliked good spellers

7. Why was Daniel Leffler mentioned?
    1) Because he helped Harrison win the election of 1840
    2) Because he carried a banner saying, "The people is oll korrect"
    3) Because he owned an inn that had very good food and service
    4) Because he helped to make O.K. a common expression

8. What is the author's purpose in writing this article?
    1) To make the reader curious by asking questions
    2) To show why it is sometimes good to misspell words
    3) To show how the English language has developed in the last 100 years
    4) To tell how one of our common expressions started

9. What kind of speller was Mr. Harrison?
    1) Good
    2) Average

3) Poor
4) The article does not give any clue

10. The expression "O.K." probably would have been forgotten if one of the following were true. Which one is it?
1) If Daniel Leffler had been a better speller
2) If the people had known who Daniel Leffler was
3) If Mr. Harrison had been an unpopular candidate
4) If Mr. Harrison's enemies had been good spellers

SOURCE: *Iowa Every-Pupil Tests of Basic Skills,* Test A, Form N, Advanced Battery. Boston: Houghton Mifflin, 1942. Reprinted by permission.

These items and ones for problem solving and the higher mental processes do measure high-priority school goals, but growth in these areas is relatively slow, and most contractors will not risk reimbursement on the small chance that evidence of growth will be revealed by these criterion tests.

Using judgments of clinically experienced teachers to increase attention to the complexities of performance is considered too subjective (which it is not) and too expensive (which it is). For all these reasons we can expect some of the complex objectives of instruction to be underemphasized in the typical performance contract testing plan.

The success of Texarkana's first performance-contract year is still being debated. Late-winter (1969/70) test results looked good, but spring test results were disappointing. (The official evaluation report was written by Andrew and Roberts [1970]. Summaries and commentaries have been written by Dyer [1970], Schwartz [1970], and Welsh [1970].) Relatively simple performance items had been used. But the debate did not get into that. It started when the project's outside evaluator ruled that there had been direct coaching on most, if not all, of the criterion test items. The criterion test items were known by the contractor during the school year. Critics claimed an unethical "teaching for the test." The contractor claimed that both teaching and testing had been directed toward the same specific goals, as should be the case in a good performance contract. The issue is not only one of ethics, it deals with the very definition of education.

Teaching for the Test

Test specialists have recognized an important difference between preparation for a test and direct coaching for a test (Anastasi 1954). To prepare an examinee, the teacher teaches the designated knowledge-skill domain and has the examinee practice good test-taking behavior (for example, don't spend too much time on overly difficult items; guess when you have an inkling though not full knowledge; organize your answer before writing an essay item), so that relevant knowledge-skill is not obscured. Direct coaching is to teach the examinees how to make correct responses to the specific items on the criterion test.

This is an important difference when criterion test items represent only a small sample of the universe of items representing what has been taught or when the criterion test items are indirect indicators, that is, when they are correlates, rather than direct measurements. (See Nunnally 1959). The breach also represents the distance between an established teaching profession and challenging instructional technologists. It ceases to be an important difference when the criterion test is set up to measure directly and thoroughly that which has been taught. In this case, teaching for the test is exactly what *is* wanted.

The solution of the problem of teaching for the test probably lies in identifying for each objective a very large number (or all) of the items that indicate mastery or progress. Items from standardized tests, if used (publisher's permission needed), would be included as separate items, not as tests-as-a-whole. The item pool would need to be exhaustive in that, if a student could get a perfect score, there would be no important aspect of the objective that the student would not do well on. A separate random sample of items would be drawn for pretests and posttests for each child. Although attractive to a public concerned about the individual child, instructional success would be based on the mean gain of all students of a kind rather than on the gain of individual students. Finding a sufficiently large pool of relevant, psychometrically sound test items is a major chore; but if it can be done, this procedure will prevent "teaching for the test" without introducing a criterion unacceptable to the contractor.

Joselyn (1971) pointed out that the performance contractor and the school should agree in advance about the criterion procedure, though not necessarily about the specific items. To be fair to the contractor, the testing needs to be reasonably close to the teaching. To be fair to the school patrons, the testing needs to be representative of the domain of skills or abilities they are concerned about. A contract to develop reading skills would not be satisfied adequately by gains on a vocabulary test, according to the expectations of most people. All parties need to know how similar the testing is going to be to the actual teaching.

A Dissimilarity Scale

Unfortunately, neither the test specialist nor anyone else has developed scales or grounds for describing the similarity between teaching and testing. (Richard C. Anderson and his colleagues at the Training Research Laboratory, University of Illinois, have been working on the problem [Anderson, Goldberg, and Hidde 1971; Wittrock and Hill 1968].) This is a most grievous failing. There is no good way to indicate how closely the tests match the instruction. Complete identity and uniqueness are recognizable by everyone, but at present important shades of difference are not even susceptible to good guessing.

Some idea of the importance of dissimilarity can be learned from the research literature on transfer of training.

Working with nonsense syllables, Yum (1931) found that recall memory scores dropped substantially as the test-item stimulus symbol became different from the one learned. He taught persons to say *jury* when he presented the stimulus *toq-bex,* and thirteen other such stimulus-response combinations. One-third of the learners were retested a day later with the same stimuli; another third were retested with stimuli with one vowel changed; another third with both vowels changed. The results averaged for each subgroup were:
1. Same stimuli on retest: 50 percent correct recall
2. Single-letter change: 33 percent correct recall
3. Double-letter change: 11 percent correct recall
As was expected, the greater the dissimilarity, the more difficult the question. In this work and elsewhere (Watts 1970), another point has been made clear: small variations can make large changes in the difficulty of items.

The problem is complicated by the fact that there are many ways for criterion questions to be made dissimilar, for instance, by:
1. Syntactic transformation
2. Semantic transformation
3. Change in context or medium
4. Application, considering the particular instance
5. Inference, generalizing from learned instances
6. Implication, adding quickly taught information to generally known information
For examples of some of these transformations, see table 16:1.

Hively, Patterson, and Page (1968) and Bormuth (1970) have discussed procedures for using some of these transformations to generate test items.

TABLE 16:1. TRANSFORMATION OF INFORMATION
TAUGHT INTO TEST QUESTIONS

Information Taught:	Point Barrow is the northernmost town in Alaska.
Minimum Transformation Question:	What is the northernmost town in Alaska?
Semantic-Syntactic Transformation Question:	What distinction does Point Barrow have among Alaskan villages?
Context-Medium Transformation Question:	The dots on the adjacent map represent Alaskan cities and towns. One represents Point Barrow. Which one?
Implication Question:	What would be unusual about summer sunsets in Point Barrow, Alaska?

The difficulty of these items depends on previous and intervening learning as well as the thoroughness of teaching. A considerable difference in difficulty and perceived relevance might be found between the least and most dissimilar questions. (The reading items of any contemporary standardized achievement test—as illustrated in figure 16:2—are likely to be more dissimilar to reading teaching (performance contract or regular classroom) than any of the "dissimilarities" shown in table 16:1.) It is apparent that performance contracting in the absence of good information about the similarity between test items and instructional objectives is scarcely an exercise in rationalism.

ANALYSIS OF GAIN SCORES

The testing specialist sees not one but at least four hazards attendant to the analysis and interpretation of learning scores: grade-equivalent scores, the "learning calendar," the unreliability of gain scores, and regression effects. All show how measures of achievement gain may be spurious. Ignoring any one of them is an invitation to gross misjudgment of the worth of the instruction.

Grade-Equivalent Scores

Standardized achievement tests have the appealing feature of yielding grade-equivalent scores. Teachers and parents like to use grade-equivalent scores. Raw scores, usually the number of items right, are transformed to scores indicating (for some national reference group population of students) the grade placement of all students who got this raw score. These transformed scores are called grade equivalents. The raw scores are not meaningful to people unacquainted with the particular test; the grade equivalents are widely accepted by teachers and parents. It is probably true that more of them *should* question the appropriateness of the distribution of scores made by the little-defined reference group as a yardstick for local assessment, but the grade equivalent score is information that the public can readily put to use. (A shortage of understandable indicators is one reason the schools have not been accountable to the public. However, House [1971] claimed that it is unlikely that educators will use better report procedures even if available because there is much more risk than reward in doing so.) Grade equivalents are common in the terminology of performance contracts.

Unfortunately, grade equivalents are only available from most publishers for tests, not for test items. Thus the whole test needs to be used, in the way prescribed in its manual, if the grade equivalents are to mean what they are supposed to mean. Among the problems of using whole tests is that the average annual "growth" for most standardized tests is a matter of only a few raw-score points. Consider in table 16:2 the difference between a grade equivalent of 5.0 and 6.0 with four of the most popular test batteries. Most teachers do not like to have their year's work summarized by so little a change in performance. Schools writing performance contracts perhaps should be reluctant to sign contracts for which the distinction between success and failure is so small. But to do so requires the abandonment of grade equivalents, at least until the grade equivalence of a large pool of appropriate items can be identified. Then we would ask, "At what grade level do half the students get this item right?" The score for a student would be the grade equivalents of the most difficult items he passes, with perhaps a correction for guessing.

Instructional specialists (Glaser 1963; Hively, Patterson, and Page 1968) have questioned the appropriateness of grade equivalents or any other "norm referencing" for interpreting items. They object to defining performance primarily by indicating who else performs as well. Clearly the items on all standardized tests have been selected on the basis of their ability to discriminate between the more and less

TABLE 16:2. GAIN IN ITEMS RIGHT NEEDED
TO ADVANCE ONE GRADE EQUIVALENT ON
FOUR TYPICAL ACHIEVEMENT TESTS

	Items Right for Grade Equivalent		Items Needed To Improve One Year in
	5.0	6.0	Grade Equivalent
Comprehensive Test of Basic Skills, Level 3: Reading Comprehension	20	23	+3
Metropolitan Achievement Test, Intermediate Form B: Spelling	24	31	+7
Iowa Tests of Basic Skills, Test A1: Arithmetic Concepts	10	14	+4
Stanford Achievement Test, Form W, Intermediate II: Word Meaning	18	26	+8

sophisticated students rather than to distinguish whether or not a person has mastered his task. Joselyn (1971) said that the items left may do the poorest job of describing performance. Jackson (1970) summarized the research and writing of those who endorse only those standardized test items that *directly* indicate successful attainment of the instructional objectives. But the items Jackson's authors would like educators to use usually do not exist—or if they do, their whereabouts are unknown. Creating and field-testing new test items is a difficult, time-consuming, costly task. For a local performance contracter, the cost of developing his own criterion items could easily exceed the entire cost of instruction. In the years ahead, such criterion items must become available for purchase. Grade equivalents, as Lennon (1971) concluded, in spite of their apparent utility, are too gross to measure individual short-term learning.

The School Calendar

For most special instructional programs in the schools, criterion tests will be administered at the beginning of and immediately after instruction, often in the first and last weeks of school. There is a large amount of distraction in the schools those weeks, but choosing other times for pre- and posttesting has its hazards too. Getting progress every several weeks during the year is psychometrically preferred (Wick and Beggs 1971), but most instructional people are opposed to "all that testing."

Children learn year round, but the evidence of learning that gets inked on pupil and personnel records comes in irregular increments from season to season. Winter is the time of most rapid academic advancement, summer the least. Summer, in fact, is a period of setback for many youngsters. Beggs and Hieronymus (1968) found that punctuation skills spurt more than a year's worth between October and April but drop almost half a year between May and September. Discussing their reading test, Gates and MacGinitie (1965) said,

> In most cases, scores will be higher at the end of one grade than at the beginning of the next. That is, there is typically some loss of reading skill during the summer, especially in the lower grades.

The picture will be different, of course, depending on what the learners do in and out of school. A spring slowdown and summer setback sometimes occur in conventional school programs. If the instructional program began in March or in June, the results would not necessarily be the same.

The first month or two of the fall, when students first return to school, is the time for getting things organized and restoring general skills lost during the summer. According to some records, spring instruction competes with only partial success with other spring attractions. Thus, the learning year is lopsided, a basis sometimes for miscalculations.

TABLE 16:3. LEARNING CALENDAR FOR A
TYPICAL FIFTH-GRADE CLASS

			Month					
S	O	N	D	J	F	M	A	M
Mean Achievement Score 5.0		5.3		5.6		5.9		6.2	6.3

The two-monthly averages in table 16:3 are fictitious, but they represent test performance in a typical classroom. The growth for the year appears to be 1.3. No acknowledgement is made there that early-September standardized test results were poorer than those for the previous spring. For this example the *previous* May mean (not shown) was 5.2. The real gain, then, for the year is 1.1 grade equivalents rather than the apparent 1.3. It would be inappropriate to pay the contractor for a mean gain of 1.3.

Another possible overpayment on the contract can result by holding final testing early and extrapolating the previous per-week growth to the weeks or months that follow. In Texarkana, as in most schools, spring progress was not as good as winter's. If an accurate evaluation of contract instructional services is to be made, repeated testing, perhaps a month-by-month record of learning performances, needs to be considered. Wrightman and Gorth (1969) described Project CAM as a model for a continual (perhaps every two weeks) performance monitoring record.

Perhaps the biggest problem in timing the tests arises from the common belief that schooling is not supposed to aim at terminal performance at the project's end, but at continuing performance in the weeks and months and years that follow. Many diverse instructional specialists (Gagné, Mayor, Garstens, and Paradise 1962; Traub 1966; Atkin 1963) agree that the instructor should use different tactics to maximize long-term rather than short-term gain. Teachers are inclined to emphasize long-term aims; the performance contractor has proposed to deal with short-term aims. They will disagree about the allocation of teaching time. The contractor points out that he is there because the school recognized that some students need immediate remedial work. He, the contractor, is not going to dilute his remedy just because there are many other important objectives for the school. He is not going to spend time analyzing the coordination between his instruction and what the student will get in simultaneous and subsequent instruction. His is a defensible position. Whether or not he should be placed in a position that will substantially reduce emphasis on long-range educational goals is an issue needing attention early in any discussion about performance contracting.

Unreliable Gain Scores

Most performance contracts pay off on an individual student basis. The contractor may be paid for each student who gains more than an otherwise expected amount. This practice is commendable in that it emphasizes the importance of each individual learner and makes the contract easier to understand, but it bases payment on a precarious landmark: the gain score.

Let us see how unreliable the performance test gain score is. For a typical standardized achievement test with two parallel forms, A and B, we might find the following characteristics reported in the test's technical manual:

Reliability of Test A = +.84
Reliability of Test B = +.84
Correlation of Test A with Test B = +.81
Almost all standardized tests have reliability coefficients at this level. By using the standard formula (Thorndike and Hagen 1969), we find a disappointing level of reliability for the measurement of improvement.
Reliability of Gain Scores (A - B or B - A) = +.16
The manual would indicate the raw score and grade-equivalent standard deviations. For one widely used test they are 9.5 items and 2.7 years, respectively. Using these values we can calculate the errors to be expected. *On the average,* a student's raw score would be in error by 2.5 times, his grade equivalent would be in error by 0.72 years and his grade-equivalent *gain score* would be in error by 1.01 years. The error is indeed large.

Consider what this means for the not unusual contract whereby the student is graduated from the program and the contractor paid for his instruction on any occasion that the performance score rises above a set value. Suppose that the student leaves whenever his improvement is one year grade equivalent or better. Suppose also, just to make this situation simpler, that there is *no* intervening training and that the student is not influenced by previous testing. Here are three ways of looking at the same situation:

1. Suppose that a contract student were to take a different parallel form of the criterion test on three successive days immediately following the pretest. The chances are better than 50:50 that on *one* of these tests the student would have gained a year or more in performance and would appear to be ready to graduate from the program.

2. Suppose that three students were to be tested with a parallel form immediately after the pretest. The chances are better than 50:50 that one of the three students—entirely due to the errors of measurement—would have gained a year or more and appear ready to graduate from the program.

3. Suppose that 100 students were admitted to contract instruction and pretested. Later, with no further training, they were tested again and the students gaining a year were graduated. After another period of time, another test and another graduation. After the fourth terminal testing, even though no instruction had occurred, the chances are better than 50:50 that two-thirds of the students would have been graduated.

In other words, the unreliability of gain scores can give the appearance of learning that actually does not occur.

The unreliability also will give an equal number of false impressions of deteriorating performance. These errors (false gains and false losses) will balance out for a large group of students. If penalties for losses are paid by the contractor at the same rate that bonuses are paid for gains, the contractor will not be overpaid. But according to the way contracts are being written, typified in the examples above, the error in gain scores does not balance out; it works in favor of the contractor. Measurement errors could be capitalized upon by unscrupulous promoters. Appropriate checks against these errors are built into the better contracts.

Errors in individual gain scores can be reduced by using longer tests. A better way to indicate true gain is to calculate the discrepancy between actual and expected final performances. (Tucker, Damarin, and Messick [1965] have discussed change scores that are independent of and dependent on the initial standing of the learner. A learning curve fitted to test scores could be used to counter the unreliability of individual scores.) Expectations can be based on the group as a whole or on an outside control group. Another way is to write the contract on the basis of mean scores for the group of students, which would have the increased advantage of discouraging the contractor from giving preferential treatment within the project to students who are in a position to make high pay-off gains. Corrections for the unreliability of gain scores are possible, but they are not likely to be considered if the educators and contractors are naive about statistics.

Regression Effects

Regression effects are probably the source of the greatest misinterpretation of the effects of remedial instruction. They are easily overlooked but need not be; also they may be corrected. For any pretest score the expected regression effect can be calculated. Regression effects make the poorest scorers look better the next time tested. Whether measurements are error-laden or error-free, meaningful or meaningless, when there is differential change between one measurement occasion and another (that is, when there is less-than-perfect correlation), the lowest original scorers will make the greatest gains and the highest original scorers will make the least. On the average, posttest scores will, relative to their corresponding pretest scores, lie in the direction of the mean. This is the regression effect. Lord (1963) discussed this universal phenomenon and various ways to set up a proper correction for it.

The demand for performance contracts has occurred where conventional instructional programs fail to develop—for a sizable number of students—minimum competence in basic skills. Given a distribution of skill test scores, the lowest-scoring students, those most needing assistance, are identified. It is reasonable to suppose that, under unchanged instructional programs, they would drop even further behind the high-scoring students. If a retest is given after any period of conventional instruction, of special instruction, or of no instruction, these students will no longer be the poorest performers. Some of them will be replaced by others who then appear to be most in need of special instruction. Instruction is not the obvious influence here—regression is. Regression effect is not due to test unreliability—but it causes some of the same misinterpretations. *The contract should stipulate that instruction will be reimbursed when gains exceed those attributable to regression effects.* The preferred evaluation design would call for a control group or groups of similar students to provide a good estimate of the progress the contract students would have made in the absence of the special instruction. Wardrop (1971) has discussed the problem of control groups that do not provide an appropriate control.

THE SOCIAL PROCESS

The hazards of specific performance testing and performance contracting are more than curricular and psychometric. Social and humanist challenges should be raised too. The teacher has a special opportunity and obligation to observe the influence of testing on social behavior.

I have referred frequently to the *uniqueness* of making major personal and scholastic decisions on the sole basis of student performances. This is a unique circumstance in schooling partly because it puts the student in a position of strong administrative influence. He can make the instruction look better or poorer than it really is (Anastasi 1954). More responsibility for school control possibly should accrue to students, but performance contracts seem a devious way to give it.

Even if he is quite young, the student is going to be aware that his good work will bring rewards to the contractor. Sooner or later he is going to know that, if he tests poorly at the beginning, he is able to do more for himself and the contractor. Bad performances are in his repertoire—he may be more anxious to make the contractor look bad than to make himself look good. He may be under undue pressure to do well on the posttests. These are interactions between pupils and teachers that should be watched carefully.

To motivate the student to learn and to make him want more contract instruction, many contractors use material rewards or opportunities to play. (Dorsett used such merchandise as transistor radios.) Other behavior modification strategies (Meacham and Wiesen 1969) are common. The proponents of such strategies argue that, once behavior has been oriented to appropriate tasks, the students can gradually be shifted from extrinsic rewards to intrinsic. That they *can* be shifted is probably true, that it will happen without careful deliberate work by the instructional staff is unlikely. It is not difficult to imagine a performance-contract situation in which the students become even less responsive to the rewards of conventional instruction than they were before.

Still another hazard of performance contracting and many other uses of objectives and test items is that by using them as we do, without acknowledging how much they indirectly and incompletely represent educational goals, we misrepresent education. People inside school and out pay attention to grades, and tests, and monetary reimbursement. We may not value factual knowledge and simple skills proportionately to the attention they get, but we have ineffective ways of indicating what our priorities really are (Stake 1970).

It is difficult for many people to accept the fact that in conventional classrooms a vast number of educational goals are simultaneously pursued (Gooler 1971). Efforts to get teachers to specify those objectives result in a simplified and incomplete list. The performance contractor has an even shorter list. Even if performance contracting succeeds in doing the relatively small job it aims to do, adequate arguments have not been made that this job should be given the priority and resources that the contractors require.

In early 1971 performance contracting appears to be popular in Washington with the current administration because it encourages the private-business sector to participate in a traditionally public responsibility. It is popular among some school administrators because they can obtain federal funds which are difficult to get, because it is a novel and possibly cheaper way to get new talent working on old problems, and because the administrator can easily blame the outside agency and the government if the contract instruction is unsuccessful. It is unpopular with the American Federation of Teachers because it reduces the control the union has over school operations and it reduces the teacher's role as a chooser of what learning students need most. It is popular among most instructional technologists because it is based on a number of well-researched principles of teaching and because it enhances their role in school operations. The accountability movement as a whole is likely to be a success or failure on such sociopolitical items. Cohen (1970) reminded evaluators to look for the issues the decision makers are concerned about. All too seldom do these include the measures of performance I have mentioned. The measurement of the performance of "performance contracting" is even more hazardous than the measurement of students' performances.

SUMMARY

Without yielding to the temptation to harass new efforts to provide instruction, educators should continue to be apprehensive about evaluating teaching on the basis of performance testing alone. They should know how difficult it is to represent educational goals with statements of objectives. They should know how costly it is to provide suitable criterion testing. They should know that the commonsense interpretation of these results is frequently wrong but that many members of the public and the profession think that special designs and controls are extravagant and mystical.

Performance contracting emerged because people inside the schools and out were dissatisfied with the instruction some children are getting. Implicit in the contracts is the expectation that available tests can measure the newly promised learning. The standardized test alone cannot measure the specific outcomes of an individual student with sufficient precision. This limitation and other hazards of performance measurement are applicable, of course, to the measurement of specific achievement in regular school programs.

NOTE

This chapter was prepared with financial support from the National Educational Finance Project and the Office of the Superintendent of Public Instruction, State of Illinois.

REFERENCES

Anastasi, Anne. *Psychological Testing.* New York: Macmillan, 1954.

Anderson, R. C.; Goldberg, S. M.; and Hidde, J. L. "Meaningful Processing of Sentences." *Journal of Educational Psychology* 62 (1971): 395-399.

Andrew, D. C., and Roberts, L. H. "Final Evaluation Report on the Texarkana Dropout Prevention Program, Magnolia, Arkansas: Region VIII." Mimeographed. Magnolia, Ark.: Education Service Center, 1970.

Atkin, J. M. "Behavioral Objectives in Curriculum Design: A Cautionary Note." *The Science Teacher* (May 1968): 27-30. (a)

_____. "Research Styles in Education." Paper read at the annual meeting of the National Association for Research in Science Training, February 1968, Chicago. (b)

Baker, E. L. "Experimental Assessment of the Effects of the Probe System." Paper read at the annual meeting of the American Educational Research Association, March 1970, Minneapolis.

Beggs, D. L., and Hieronymus, Al. "Uniformity of Growth in the Basic Skills throughout the School Year and during the Summer." *Journal of Educational Measurement* 5 (1968): 91-97.

Bhaerman, Robert. "A Paradigm for Accountability." *American Teacher* 55, no. 3 (1970): 18-19.

Bloom, B. S.; Englehart, M. D.; Furst, E. J.; Hill, W. H.; and Krathrohl, D. R. *A Taxonomy of Educational Objectives: Handbook I, The Cognitive Domain.* New York: David McKay, 1956.

Bormuth, John. *On the Theory of Achievement Test Items.* Chicago: University of Chicago Press, 1970.

Cohen, D. K. "Politics and Research: Evaluation of Large-Scale Education Programs." *Review of Educational Research* 40, no. 2 (1970): 213-238.

Cronbach, L. J. "Validation of Educational Measures." *Proceedings of the 1969 Invitational Conference on Testing Problems,* pp. 36-52. Princeton, N.J.: Educational Testing Service, 1969.

Dyer, H. S. "Performance Contracting: Too Simple a Solution for Difficult Problems." *The United Teacher* (29 November 1970): 19-22.

Ebel, Robert L. "When Information Becomes Knowledge." *Science* 171 (1971): 130-131.

Gagné, Robert M. "Curriculum Research and the Promotion of Learning." In *Perspectives of Curriculum Evaluation.* American Educational Research Association Monograph Series on Curriculum Evaluation, no. 1, edited by R. E. Stake, pp. 19-38. Chicago: Rand McNally, 1967.

Gagné, R. M.; Mayor, J. R.; Garstens, H. L.; and Paradise, N. E. "Factors in Acquiring Knowledge of a Mathematical Task." *Psychological Monographs* 76, no. 7 (whole no. 526), 1962.

Gates, A. I., and MacGinitie, W. H. *Technical Manual for the Gates-MacGinitie Reading Tests.* New York: Columbia University, Teachers College Press, 1965.

Glaser, Robert. "Instructional Technology and the Measurement of Learning Outcomes: Some Questions." *American Psychologist* 18 (1963): 519-521.

Gooler, D. D. "Strategies for Obtaining Clarification of Priorities in Education." Ph.D. dissertation, University of Illinois at Urbana-Champaign, 1971.

Goslin, D. A. "Ethical and Legal Aspects of the Collection and Use of Educational Information." Paper read at the Invitational Conference on Testing Problems, October 1970, New York.

Grobman, Hulda. *Developmental Curriculum Projects: Decision Points and Processes*. Itasca, Ill.: Peacock, 1970.

Hastings, J. T.; Runkel, P. J.; and Damrin, D. E. "Effects on Use of Tests by Teachers Trained in a Summer Institute." Cooperative Research Project no. 702. Mimeographed. University of Illinois, College of Education, Bureau of Research, 1961.

Hively, Wells, II; Patterson, H. L.; and Page, S. H. "A 'Universe-Defined' System of Arithmetic Achievement Tests." *Journal of Educational Measurement* 5, no. 4 (1968): 275-290.

Hoffman, Banesh. *The Tyranny of Testing*. New York: Collier Books, 1962.

Holt, John. *The Underachieving School*. New York: Pitman, 1969.

House, E. R. "The Conscience of Educational Evaluation." Paper read at the Ninth Annual Conference of the California Association for the Gifted, February 1971, Monterey, California.

Jackson, Rex. *Developing Criterion-Referenced Tests*. Princeton, N.J.: Educational Testing Service, ERIC Clearing House on Tests, Measurement, and Evaluation, 1970.

Jenkins, J. R., and Deno, S. L. "Effects of Instructional Objectives on Learning." Paper read at the annual meeting of the American Educational Research Association, February 1969, Los Angeles.

Joselyn, E. G. "Performance Contracting: What It's All About." Paper read at Truth and Soul In Teaching Conference of the American Federation of Teachers, January 1971, Chicago.

Krathwohl, D. R. Presidential address to the annual meeting of the American Educational Research Association, February 1969, Los Angeles.

Lennon, R. T. *Testimony of Dr. Roger T. Lennon as Expert Witness on Psychological Testing*. New York: Harcourt, Brace and World, n. d.

_____. "Accountability and Performance Contracting." Paper read at the annual meeting of the American Educational Research Association, February 1971, New York.

Lessinger, Leon. "Engineering Accountability for Results in Public Education." *Phi Delta Kappan* 52, no. 4 (1970): 217-225.

Lieberman, Myron. "An Overview of Accountability." *Phi Delta Kappan* 52, no. 4 (1970): 194-195.

Lindquist, E. F., ed. *Educational Measurement*. Washington, D.C.: American Council on Education, 1951.

Lord, F. M. "Elementary Models for Measuring Change." In *Problems in Measuring Change*, edited by Chester W. Harris, pp. 21-38. Madison: University of Wisconsin Press, 1963.

_____. "A Theory of Test Scores." The Psychometric Society, Psychometric Monograph no. 7. Philadelphia: George E. Ferguson, 1952.

Lortie, D. C. "National Decision-Making: Is it Possible Today?" *The EPIE Forum* 1 (1967): 6-9.

Mager, R. F. *Preparing Objectives for Programmed Instruction*. San Francisco: Fearon, 1962.

McGhan, B. R. "Accountability as a Negative Reinforcer." *American Teacher* 55, no. 3 (1970): 13.

McNeil, J. D. "Concomitants of Using Behavioral Objectives in the Assessment of Teacher Effectiveness." *Journal of Experimental Education* 36 (1967): 69-74.

Meacham, M. L., and Wiesen, A. E. *Changing Classroom Behavior: A Manual for Precision Teaching.* Scranton: International Textbook, 1969.

National School Board Journal Staff. "Two out of Three Boardmen Buy Performance Contracting." *National School Board Journal* (November 1970): 35-36.

Nunnally, J. C., Jr. *Tests and Measurements: Assessment and Prediction.* New York: McGraw-Hill, 1959.

Oettinger, A. G. *Run, Computer, Run.* Cambridge, Mass.: Harvard University Press, 1969.

Popham, W. J. "Objectives and Instruction." In *Perspectives of Curriculum Evaluation.* American Educational Research Association Monograph Series on Curriculum Evaluation, no. 3, edited by R. E. Stake, pp. 32-52. Chicago: Rand McNally, 1969.

Prescott, G. A., ed. *Analysis of Learning Potential.* Advanced I Battery, Form A. New York: Harcourt Brace Jovanovich, 1970.

Schrag, P. "End of the Impossible Dream." *Saturday Review* 53, no. 38 (1970): 68.

Schwartz, Ronald. "Performance Contracting: Industry's Reaction." *The Nation's Schools* 86 (1970): 53-55.

Silberman, C. E. *Crisis in the Classroom: The Remaking of American Education.* New York: Random House, 1970.

Sizer, T. R. "Social Change and the Uses of Educational Testing: An Historical View." Paper read at the Invitational Conference on Testing Problems, October 1970, New York.

Stake, R. E. "Objectives, Priorities, and Other Judgment Data." *Review of Educational Research* 40 (1970): 181-212.

Thorndike, E. L. *The Measurement of Educational Products.* National Society for the Study of Education, Seventeenth Yearbook, part II. Bloomington, Ill.: Public School Publishing, 1918. Reprinted in *Psychology and the Science of Education,* edited by G. M. Joncich, p. 151. New York: Columbia University, Teachers College Press, 1962.

Thorndike, R. L. *The Original Nature of Man.* Vol. 1, *Educational Psychology.* New York: Columbia University, Teachers College Press, 1921.

Thorndike, R. L., and Hagen, Elizabeth. *Measurement and Evaluation in Psychology and Education,* 3d ed. New York: Wiley, 1969.

Traub, R. E. "Importance of Problem Heterogeneity to Programmed Instruction." *Journal of Educational Psychology* 57 (1966): 54-60.

Tucker, L. R.; Damrin, F.; and Messick, S. *A Base-Free Measure of Change.* Research Bulletin RB-65-16. Princeton, N. J.: Educational Testing Service, 1965.

Tyler, R. W. *Basic Principles of Curriculum and Instruction.* Chicago: University of Chicago Press, 1950.

Wardrop, J. L. "Some Particularly Vexing Problems in Experimentation on Reading." *Reading Research Quarterly* 6, no. 3 (Spring 1971): 329-337.

Watts, G. H. "Learning from Prose Material: Effects of Verbatim and 'Application' Questions on Retention." Ph.D. dissertation, University of Illinois at Urbana-Champaign, 1970.

Welsh, James. "D. C. Perspectives on Performance Contracting." *Educational Researcher* 31 (October 1970): 1-3.

Wick, John, and Beggs, D. L. *Evaluation for Decision-Making in the Schools.* New York: Houghton Mifflin, 1971.

Wittrock, M. C., and Hill, C. E. "Children's Preferences in the Transfer of Learning." Final Report, Project no. 3264, U. S. Department of Health, Education, and Welfare. Mimeographed. Los Angeles: University of California, 1968.

Wrightman, L., and Gorth, W. P. "CAM: The New Look in Classroom Testing." *Trend* (Spring 1969): 56-57.

Yum, K. W. "An Experimental Test of the Law of Assimilation." *Journal of Experimental Psychology* 14 (1931): 68-82.

Zahorik, J. A. "The Effect of Planning on Teaching." *The Elementary School Journal* (December 1970): 143-151.

ADDITIONAL REFERENCES

Blaschke, Charles. "Performance Contracting in Education." Washington, D.C.: Educational Turnkey Systems, 1970.

Dyer, H. S.; Linn, R. L.; and Patton, M. J. "A Comparison of Four Methods of Obtaining Discrepancy Measures Based on Observed and Predicted School System Means on Achievement Tests." *American Educational Research Journal* 6 (1969): 591-605.

Elam, Stanley. "The Age of Accountability Dawns in Texarkana." *Phi Delta Kappan* 15, no. 10 (1970): 509-514.

Linn, R. L.; Rock, D. A.; and Cleary, T. A. "The Development and Evaluation of Several Programmed Testing Methods." *Educational and Psychological Measurement* 29 (1969): 129-146.

Phi Delta Kappa Commission on Evaluation. *Educational Evaluation and Decision Making.* Itasca, Ill.: Peacock, 1971.

Popham, W. J., and Husek, T. R. "Implications of Criterion-Referenced Measurement." *Journal of Educational Measurement* 6 (1969): 1-9.

Scriven, Michael. "The Methodology of Evaluation." In *Perspectives of Curriculum Evaluation.* American Educational Research Association Monograph Series on Curriculum Evaluation, no. 1, edited by R. E. Stake, pp. 39-83. Chicago: Rand McNally, 1967.

Stake, R. E. "The Countenance of Educational Evaluation." *Teachers College Record* 68 (1967): 523-540.

Tyler, R. W. *Educational Evaluation: New Roles, New Means.* National Society for the Study of Education, Sixty-eighth Yearbook. Chicago: University of Chicago Press, 1969.

Webb, H. V. "Performance Contracting: Is It the New Tool for the New Boardmanship?" *American School Board Journal* 185, no. 5 (1970): 28-36.

17

PPBS AND AN ANALYSIS
OF COST EFFECTIVENESS

Harry J. Hartley

The design of conventional school budgets is such that local officials may be inclined to emphasize saving at the expense of accomplishing. At the risk of encouraging cynics to affirm that budgetary incrementalism and nonprogrammatic planning procedures currently employed in schools are easier to deplore than change, the premise for this chapter is that educational budgets should portray programs to be accomplished in addition to objects to be purchased. The purpose of subsequent paragraphs is fourfold: to delineate the major conceptual and operational elements of a PPB System; to describe exemplary program budgeting installations of urban schools in three states; to discuss performance indicators that may be used in cost-effectiveness analysis; and to examine some of the limitations of PPBS.

CONCEPTUAL AND OPERATIONAL ELEMENTS

PPBS is part of the new generation of interrelated management procedures that are designed to enhance organizational rationality. The extension of the time horizon in educational planning with the program budget is a way of attempting somewhat to control the future instead of merely reacting to it and being controlled by it. The conceptually distinct elements of planning, programming, and budgeting constitute the process by which objectives and resources, and the interrelations among them, are taken into account to achieve a coherent and comprehensive program of action for an organization

Reprinted from Educational Administration Quarterly 5, no. 1 (Winter 1969): 65-80. Copyright 1969 University Council for Educational Administration.

as a whole. An essential operational characteristic of PPBS is the projection of total resource and dollar needs for a suitable number of years and in relation to key decision variables of the organization.

Characteristics and Advantages

The twenty theses that follow (Hartley 1968*a*) are aimed at describing, in concise outline form, the concept of program budgeting as it should operate in local educational planning.

1. Output Emphasis. The budget is structured on the basis of outputs, missions, functions, activities, services, or programs, rather than on conventional input items. A program is related to operational objectives, and consists of activities to be performed, subprograms, and program elements such as human resources, materials, space, and facilities.

2. Input-output Coordination. PPBS seeks to relate inputs to the programs of an organization in a way that enhances a rational means-ends calculus.

3. Evaluation. Comparison of desired outcomes, as expressed by programmatic objectives, may be made with actual accomplishments. Performance indicators are utilized, such as indices that measure changes in pupil cognitive development, psycho-motor skills, and the more elusive affective domain.

4. Long-range Fiscal Planning. The annual budget is integrated with multi-year projections on a continuing basis. Typically, a program budget document portrays estimates of needs and costs over a time horizon of at least five years. Annual planning calendars and cycles are constructed.

5. Quantitative Analysis. In order to analyze comparative benefits, quantitative measures are applied if they are available. These include such techniques as: input-out analysis (Burkhead, Fox, and Holland 1967), benefit-cost analysis, cost-effectiveness evaluation, operations analysis, management information systems, linear programming, simulation, queuing, gaming and others. Qualitative measures are also included and they should play a major role in educational planning.

6. Multiplicity of Options. PPBS provides a framework for the consideration of all relevant alternatives for a particular course of action.

These are then placed in order on the basis of desirability, feasibility, least cost, available resources, and other criteria.

7. Programming. Lines of action are drawn to coordinate the planned objectives, programs and activities, and costs along an extended time dimension.

8. Program Review and Revision. In addition to program formulation and analysis, procedures for periodic review and modifications of programs are specified. This process is dynamic, viable, and promotes the adoption of innovations. Intraprogram studies are encouraged.

9. Subprograms and Program Elements. Each of the major programs contains delineated subprograms that minimize overlapping. Supporting program elements for each are specified.

10. Future Needs. More explicit assumptions can be made about future demand and production functions of the organization. Risk is reduced and assumptions are specified. Total cost implications of present decisions pertaining to long-term undertakings are expressed.

11. Economic Rationality. There are at least two schools of budgetary theory, one subscribing to economic rationality and the other to political rationality. PPBS is essentially an economic concept designed to serve in the political arena. It represents an encroachment of economics upon politics and is an embodiment of classical political economy.

12. Flexibility. PPBS should not impose structural constraints. Programs can be defined in any way suitable to a particular organization. This approach is suitable both for internal programming and control and for development of future policies and programs.

13. Openendedness. Expenditure items are not treated as givens. The amount available for the total system is determined and the highest utility alternatives are selected for the specified budget programs. The major objective is not expenditure control in the fiduciary sense.

14. Policy Determination. Budgeting becomes an integral part of the administrative process with PPBS. The financial administrator shares in policy formulation, and provision should be made for a continuing interaction of the policy maker, systems analyst, budget officer, and the organization members affected by such policy.

15. Decision Centers. Within some organizations using PPBS, decision centers and cost centers are developed so that administrators can have at their fingertips historical and projected information from all phases of activity. These are retrievable from a computer data bank. Simulations of the budget can be developed.

16. Cost Neutrality. PPBS is neutral on the issue of cost reduction. A cult of efficiency, measured by less spending, per se, is not the criterion of success for PPBS.

17. Structural Variability. Organizational structural variability is maintained, because the operations may be either centralized or decentralized. If the latter, participatory planning is encouraged so that policymaking is shared by all members of the organization. If the former, lowest departmental level budget estimates form the building blocks for the next level where they are aggregated, reviewed, and transmitted upward to the highest level.

18. Accountability and Performance Measurement. PPBS can be used for control and internal management purposes to review personnel data, output data, and resource data. It seeks to measure performance and affix accountability. Cost accounting procedures are generally a part of the PPBS format, although it may be necessary to redesign an existing accounting system so that it will provide information to meet line-item, legal accounting requirements and also provide data on program costs.

19. Concise Budget Document. The PPBS presentation document should be concise, but complete, and should be understandable even to a lay reader. Local school budgets frequently use terminology and nonprogrammatic categories that are too technical and unclear for the citizenry. With PPBS, the programs should be clearly stated so that the public can grasp their content easily.

20. Preservation of the Past. The program budget encompasses the best features of previous budgeting formats: the executive budget, line-item object budgets, and performance budgeting. It need *not* replace conventional budgeting procedures. For the time being, line-item *and* program budgets probably should be maintained concurrently as a means of describing an organization's expenditures on both an input and output basis.

Program budgeting is not a panacea. It does not abolish the vulgarity of concern over dollars, nor does it ensure that this ideal-type blueprint will be maintained successfully in actual practice. The "original sin" in the world of school finance is not budgeting, but comprises numerous intervening variables that existed long before the program budget: human errors, poor judgment, dishonesty, resistance to accountability, administrative shortsightedness, adherence to orthodoxy, manifest political factors, and the like.

EXEMPLARY PPBS INSTALLATIONS

The range of projects that are designed to develop PPBS encompasses the United States government, industry, state and municipal governments, higher education, and local school systems. For these diverse organizations, the common aim is to chart the direction of future events less in response to impulse than to reasoned strategy. Although program budgeting is still in a formative stage in education, a number of urban school districts claim to be phasing-in at least several aspects of a program budget format. Close observation of their procedures reveals that some have simply continued their conventional planning and budgeting approaches, but under the disguised name of program budgeting.

Perhaps the most common misuse of PPBS by school districts is to assume that the concept applies only to a school's fiscal operations. Most districts that claim to be moving toward a PPBS design apparently do not involve curriculum-instructional specialists until a later phase, if they are involved at all. If this new approach is to be successful, it is imperative that instructional specialists be involved from the very inception in the design of the program structure and classification of the program components. Progress has been impeded by the newness of the concept, the lack of familiarity of most school officials with recently developed management science techniques, perennial resistance to innovation that plagues education, and insufficient venture capital to engage in research and development projects of any kind.

Representative Districts

Among the urban districts that purport to be using program budgeting are Baltimore, Chicago, Dade County (Miami, Florida),

Los Angeles, Memphis, New York City, Philadelphia, Sacramento, Seattle, and an intermediate district in Westchester County, New York. Detailed information for each project is generally available upon request. In my judgment, three of the most interesting and noteworthy projects are those of Dade County, New York City, and Sacramento.

Dade County Public Schools. In early 1968, the district announced that it received approval for a Title IV (ESEA) research proposal for the three-year $600,000 comprehensive project in program budgeting. Although this project may have a national impact upon schools that are seeking directional assistance, it is likely to take several years before definitive guidelines and technical manuals are prepared by Dade County and made available to interested outside parties. A unique feature of this project is that it is sponsored jointly by the district and the nationwide Association of School Business Officials (ASBO), the latter organization serving as the dissemination agent for this venture. (ASBO supported a number of other school districts across the nation in a three-year project, between 1969 and 1972. The results were published by the ASBO [1971].)

The district developed a comprehensive program, called a "Strategy for Teaching," that pertained to the overall improvement of its instructional program. It also designed a three-part management system (instructional services, administrative services, operational services) to provide support to teachers. A data bank was installed along the lines of a management information system. A summary of the research proposal for Dade County is contained in table 17:1. It depicts the objectives, procedures, and products of research that the "Strategy for Teaching" project is intended to yield. The Dade County project appears to be quite promising.

New York City Public Schools. In early 1967, the City of New York Board of Education announced first phase plans for the development of a comprehensive PPBS, promising that this would be the first such installation in a large city school district. The entire State of New York adopted PPBS in 1964, and the municipal government of New York initiated PPBS in 1967, so that the decision of the school district was an extension of earlier efforts. Because of its fiscal dependence status, the school district's policies tend to follow those of the city government.

Pursuing a strategy sharply different from that of other government units that are installing PPBS (fifteen governmental units are developing PPBS procedures as part of the State and Local Finances

TABLE 17:1.

SUMMARY OF A PROGRAM BUDGET RESEARCH PROJECT FOR A LOCAL SCHOOL DISTRICT[a]

	Function 1 Research of Over-all System Design	Function 2 Cost Analysis Research	Function 3 Program Identifica-tion Research	Function 4 Accounting Proce-dures Research	Function 5 Budget Procedures Research	Function 6 Data Processing Applications Research	Function 7 Planning & Evalu-ation Procedures Research
OBJECTIVES	The preliminary de-sign of organiza-tional system con-ducive to the suc-cessful operation of the budget tech-niques.	To establish cost schedules of direct and indirect costs of instructional programs.	To identify present instructional pro-grams as they re-late to (1) Strategy of Education (2) cost accounting (3) program budget.	To design account-ing procedures to accommodate cost accounting and the program budget for federal, state and local funds, and management requirements.	To design budget-ing procedures which accommo-date the program budget and exer-cise the best fi-nancial planning techniques.	To design an EDP sub-system which best satisfies the requirements of the Strategy of Educa-tion.	To design a plan-ning and evalua-tion function under the superintendent.
PROCEDURES	1—Identify goals 2—Determine sup-port require-ments 3—Synthesize or-ganization 4—Design data flow and anal-ysis system 5—Design evalua-tion procedures	1—Analyze instruc-tional support function costs in terms of direct and indirect costs 2—Establish formu-las for periodic revision of costs 3—Compose and publish initial cost schedules	1—Establish pro-gram definitions accommodate goals, support organization cost, cost ac-counting, and program budget-ing in terms of present instruc-tional programs 2—Identify present programs for budgeting 3—Analyze future program objec-tives 4—Continued re-finement of goal and program design	1—Determine all functions requir-ing accounting services and re-ports, internal and external 2—Determine ac-counting, per-sonnel, payroll, purchasing and other interre-lated functional procedures 3—Establish ac-counting proce-dures to satisfy all requirements	1—Determine the report require-ments for fed-eral, state and local agencies 2—Determine finan-cial planning procedures for revenues and appropriations 3—Determine best procedures for budgeting pro-grams 4—Design coordi-nation proce-dures with plan-ning and sup-port functions 5—Establish bud-get presentation and review pro-cedures	1—Analyze guid-ance from senior consultants, ref-erence Step 1 2—Observe and an-alyze old and new organiza-tion to deter-mine interim and planned CDP require-ments 3—Design and de-velop EDP pro-cedures which accommodate data flow plan of the senior consultant	1—Design proce-dures for goal revision and policy formation and dissemina-tion 2—Design planning function based on goal, policy, priority and re-source alloca-tion 3—Design an over-all supporting system evalua-tion function in-cluding statis-tical analysis
PRODUCTS OF RESEARCH	Preliminary report for establishing guidance for Steps 2 through 7.	A manual of cost schedules applicable to programs with revision proce-dures.	A list of programs which is adaptable to cost accounting, budgeting and EDP.	A manual of ac-counting proce-dures which ac-commodate the Strategy of Educa-tion.	A manual of bud-get policies and procedures.	A manual of op-timum procedure description for data processing to meet all system require-ments, reference—Step 1.	A manual of goal and policy formu-lation planning and evaluation proce-dures.

[a] Dade County Public Schools, A Program Budget Research Proposal (Miami, Florida: Dade County Board of Public Instruction, November, 1966), p. 3. Permission to reproduce this was granted by E. L. Whigham, Superintendent, and Jack W. Whitsett, Project Manager for Support Systems, January 15, 1968.

Project, which is supported by a grant from the Ford Foundation to the George Washington University, and consists of five states, five counties, and five cities), New York City's "overall approach has deliberately been opportunistic, rather than systematic and comprehensive. We have concentrated our efforts on analysis, rather than on program structure and accounts, and we have focused on sectors of high apparent yield (Hayes 1967)." A partial justification for this approach is that the massive effort to classify city expenditures by program category and to articulate and quantify all program objectives might suffocate the basic intent of rational planning.

The city suggested that a number of factors contributed to its limited capacity to engage in conceptual budgeting: the absence of a highly developed budget-making apparatus, inadequate information systems, a lack of personnel and inexperience in program planning, the centralization of budget control, the line-item basis for budget construction and administration, the predominance of established practice in key municipal programs (for example, police, fire, education), and the lack of funds for innovation and experimentation.

A number of first steps were taken in 1967 and 1968 toward the PPBS format that are suggestive of preliminary procedures needed for rational educational planning:
1. Recruitment efforts to employ program analysts.
2. The establishment of a Policy Planning Committee.
3. An analysis of the capital and operating budgets by objective.
4. A review of projects by community area within the city.
5. Efforts to establish proximate goals for new projects.
6. The establishment of a Division of Program Planning.
7. PPBS probes in key areas.
8. The use of cost-effectiveness procedures.
9. Project information and scheduling systems.
10. Proposals for a think tank to analyze city problems.

In addition, the city hired Rand Corporation to do a six-month study of selected agencies. Rand, which conducted most of the initial research on PPBS for the federal government, committed more than 5 percent of its 1968 budget to the problems of the city.

The City School District, with an expense budget exceeding $1.5 billion and serving more than 1.1 million pupils with 60,000 teachers, hopes that the new budgeting system will provide better accountability and guide the Board of Education in policy decisions. One objective was to obtain a breakdown of every function of the school system into component cost factors, so that policy makers could determine whether the amount allotted to each function, or general program, was yielding its stated objective in the most efficient manner. A second objective was to facilitate long-range planning. After a complete examination of alternative ways of achieving a given objective, the district hopes to be able to spell out in detail the objectives it seeks to accomplish over a five-year period and relate these to available resources. A third objective is to decentralize budget administration, even though PPBS appears to possess a centralizing bias. The district's budget tends to be highly centralized for reasons of administrative efficiency.

Initially, the district chose rather crude output measures; for example, high schools used eight output measures, and one representative school provided the following data:
1. Pupil attendance—94.4 percent
2. Extra-curricular pupil participation—25 percent
3. Number of diplomas granted
    a. academic—280
    b. general—360
    c. other—100
    d. not graduating—85
4. Number of scholarships and awards earned—65
5. Pupils taking five or more major subjects—30 percent
6. Pupils with grade averages of 85 percent or more—10 percent
7. Number of pupils discharged
    a. with employment certificates—45
    b. seventeen years of age and over—35
8. Test results
    a. Metropolitan Achievement Tests (reading)
       mean grade equivalent: grade 9—9.6
       mean grade equivalent: grade 10—10.4
    b. other test measures
       pupils passing Regents Exam—75 percent
       pupils passing Uniform School Exam—70 percent
It is too soon to judge the worth of program budgeting in New York.

Sacramento (California) City Unified School District. The public schools of Sacramento operate within a program budget type of framework. This school district, with about 55,000 pupils and total expenditures of $37 million for 1967/68, prepares its budget in terms of three program areas: administrative services, instructional programs and services, and supporting services. The largest of the three program areas is instructional programs and services, and it is further subdivided, largely on a grade-level basis, into twelve programs: instructional administration, curriculum development, special services, special programs, elementary schools, junior high schools, senior high schools, schools for adults, continuation high schools, summer school programs, staff training and summer demonstration schools, and special projects.

> The Sacramento Schools' budget is a combination, or a hybrid, of a budget by programs and a program budget. By use of account codes in the computer, it is run in three formats: 1) by state required classifications, which is an object budget; 2) by programs which is the working budget; and 3) in publication format for presentation to the Board of Education and to the public. Some programs, notably federal ones, include appropriations for indirect costs. Most programs include only appropriations for direct costs (Henry J. Moeller: personal communication).

As of 1968, it is probably accurate to state that there is insufficient evidence to predict the extent to which program budgeting and operations analysis procedures would be installed successfully in local school systems. Each of the projects described above was somewhat exploratory and is not yet a finished product. If they are evaluated by the same people who initiated them, undoubtedly they will be "doomed to success."

COST EFFECTIVENESS

It would be premature to establish overall measures of effectiveness in local schools before suitable program structures have been devised. The very heart of the PPBS concept is the *program structure,* for it makes the outputs of a school viable and identifies the resources required to yield these outputs.

Alternative Program Structures

Where does one look for ideal-type program structures? Several program analysts have observed that "programs are not made in heaven"; rather, they are imposed on the natural world by man. There is no single *best* program format for schools. Inasmuch as the local schools across the nation differ in organizational structure, size, clientele, staff expertise, pupil needs, and fiscal resources, they will probably also differ in the goals they specify, the curricular programs they offer, the priorities they assign to competing program elements, and in their achievement as measured by performance indicators.

There are at least three basic approaches to devising a program structure. The first is to use organizational, or grade-level, categories. Programs might include: early childhood, primary grades, intermediate grades, middle school, technical high school, comprehensive high school, junior college, adult education, and so on.

A second approach, and probably the ideal type, is to devise programs on the basis of curricular (subject-matter) organization. Direct and indirect costs are apportioned to subject areas, such as: language arts, science, mathematics, social science, creative arts, special education, and so on. The third option is a hybrid format that combines grade level organization at the elementary level with subject-matter organization at the secondary level. Generally this reflects existing state certification procedures whereby instructors are certified as elementary teachers through grade six and as mathematics, language, or social studies teachers at the secondary level. The latter two approaches are the most desirable, yet most difficult types to develop, and so it is the first approach, which is most widely used among the ten local school districts mentioned. Cost-effectiveness analysts might heed the advice of one school finance official:

> If program activity and subactivity statements and performance statistics were required, this alone would be a herculean task. For a superintendent to evaluate the effectiveness of each account appears to be impossible. Surely, for those who wish to embark on the path towards program accounting only an absolute minimum of programs and activities should be costed out. And what is equally important they should be costed out on an accrual rather than a cash basis.

> What the structure of program costs should be, no one really knows. Some persons think that school districts, particularly the large systems, should seek to attain the ideal—in other words, program costs for subject matter by grade level, with costs assigned to each school in the system. *The literature abounds with such proposals particularly by college professors.* Before anyone takes his school system down this primrose path, he should weigh seriously the benefits to be derived against the costs involved. Program costs by subject matter by grade level by school involve a vast amount of work because it necessitates

the gathering and manipulation of numerous cost items (Furno 1967, p. 13).

Criteria of Effectiveness

Nearly all attempts to apply benefit-cost and cost-effectiveness analysis to education have been made on a national or regional basis, or have been devoted to specific programs such as vocational education or compensatory programs (Title I, in particular). Becker (1964), Blaug (1965), Bowman (1966), and others calculated private and social rates of return to secondary and higher education that indicate that education has a positive effect upon lifetime earnings, reduced unemployment, reduced juvenile delinquency, and inter-generation benefits. Bowman reviewed the main analyses of human capital formulation, a development that she calls "the human investment revolution in economic thought." The United States Office of Education has conducted symposia on operations analysis that focus upon operations analysis procedures, including benefit-cost analysis. Kiesling (1967) attempted to quantify educational benefits from compensatory elementary and secondary programs. For a sample of children in the Higher Horizons program, benefit-cost ratios were calculated as 0.59 for elementary programs and 0.88 for junior high school programs. Another calculation was made in one school district that showed gains from a compensatory program. Here it was found that the experimental groups gained 7 percent a year more than a control group in grades three, four, and five. This was calculated to have an average financial benefit of $168, discounted back to the fifth grade. Program cost per child was $114 for the three years, yielding a benefit-cost ratio of about 1.5.

Also at the local level, a few attempts have been made to model the educational process. Nonlinear models have been devised that relate aggregate school district operations to average achievement (as defined by specific test processes). These permit exploration for optimizing operating conditions, but they are rather crudely designed at the present time. The major weakness appears to be the lack of performance indicators.

Performance Indicators

Cost-effectiveness analysis can be conducted after a program structure has been devised and criteria to assess performance have been specified. Even in broadly defined cost-effectiveness analysis, as described by Quade (1965a, b) and Schwarz (1968), the need exists for means of measuring the performance of educational systems in a way that is easily interpretable by educators and policy makers and at the same time avoids, as far as possible, assumptions that cannot be empirically supported. Standardized tests of academic achievement have long been used as indicators of system performance, although they may have created more problems than they resolved. A common approach has been to try to predict from a pupil's IQ scores what his achievement *should* be and then to compare his actual achievement test scores with the predicted scores. Critics have noted a number of fallacies in this procedure.

Several attempts to devise better performance indicators in education include the Quality Measurement Project (QMP) of New York State and recent projects undertaken by the Educational Testing Service (ETS) of Princeton, New Jersey. QMP was an attempt by the New York State Education Department to develop a series of differentiated achievement test norms that would provide data by which a local school administrator could compare the performance of his district's students with that of students in other systems of similar economic condition and IQ (Firman 1966).

Dyer, an ETS measurement specialist, noted (1967) that "a further step along the road toward believable educational performance indicators was taken by Educational Testing Service in the development of a plan for measuring the quality of education provided by the school systems in Pennsylvania." This was a refinement and a more comprehensive version of New York's QMP; it was mandated by the Pennsylvania legislature. The state board of education was given the charge to develop in two years' time "an evaluation procedure designed to measure objectively the adequacy and efficiency of the education programs offered by the Commonwealth." If successful, this evaluation procedure eventually could provide two kinds of results: it could enable each district to appraise the effectiveness of the programs shown in a program budget in sufficient detail to indicate what should be done to strengthen them, and it could provide state education departments with program performance standards to aid in allocative decisions to all districts across a state. Dyer explained that, in order to depict how a system is performing, ETS constructed a matrix of performance indices (time dimensions that indicated years of schooling; changes in cognitive development, attitudinal development, interpersonal behavior, and so on). Regression equations were developed and matrices constructed for each district to show the general areas where it may be strong or weak, and to suggest where increased effort and money might have the highest payoff. Thus, performance indicators developed by ETS provide a series of estimates of how well a school district is doing in comparison with other districts working under presumably comparable advantages and handicaps.

A highly publicized study that used student performance measures to test hypotheses about the relationships between educational ends and means is Coleman's *Equality of Educational Opportunity* (1966). Numerous implications for making decisions about program resource allocations are contained in the study, but a number of criticisms have arisen. For example, Levin, of the Brookings Institution, argued (1968) that the Coleman analysis was: "overwhelmingly weighted in a direction that would understate the importance of school resources in explaining variations in achievement," and "biased by a research design which overstated the importance of family background and derogated the influence of school resources on student achievement." Nevertheless, such studies may lead to improved utilization of cost-effectiveness procedures in local schools.

LIMITATIONS

Perhaps the report of PPBS in local educational planning could be told by emphasizing potential usage rather than past achievement. In no school district is PPBS fully implemented. Converting function-object line budgets into a multiyear framework focused on operational objectives inevitably encounters bottlenecks. Few competent cost-effectiveness analyses have been completed, and even fewer are integrated into the program budgeting process. In addition to shortages of data and measurement criteria, there are conceptual questions for analysts to answer. If costs are incurred at one point in time, and benefits are received in another, should benefits occurring far out in time be valued less than those with immediate payoff? What discount rates should be used? Are the benefits to be specified as individual or social?

A number of factors may contribute to the current limitations of PPBS. There is a shortage of trained systems personnel. Program budgeting may increase costs for a local district because it requires additional personnel, facilities, and hardware. Goals may be distorted because there is a tendency to try to achieve those goals that most easily lend themselves to quantitative measurement. A "cult of testing" may be created if output is equated with standardized test results. A centralization syndrome could result if computerized central data banks are misused. Organizational strains and teacher resistance may arise as the schools' objectives are exposed in analytical terms. Transfer problems will occur because generic systems models must be altered to fit specific situations of local schools. And finally, there may be a wisdom lag. Recent advances in technology and science far transcend any comparable advances in human wisdom. We possess the capacity to analyze intricate school problems with computers, but often we do not know how to estimate the value of obtainable data (Hartley 1968b). Quantitative analysis may occasionally substitute elegance for relevance. The tragedy of our era is that human intellectual capacity, as addressed to problems of human relationships and education, seems, if anything, regressive.

After its installation in a local school, program budgeting may initially serve to accentuate conflicts and engender antagonisms as organizational objectives and priorities are exposed in the cold, bold figures of the dollar. It can be anticipated that, with the introduction of PPBS, bureaucratic inertia, vested interests, old prides, honest differences of opinion, and political factors will not suddenly disappear. Even though the schools may soon be characterized by a systems syndrome, these kinds of factors will influence the degree of success brought on by the PPB System. Schools are not politically unencumbered. It is apparent in systems analysis that the best way to control the quality of programmatic output is to control the quality of input. However, public schools have no such intake valve; they must serve all.

Finally, underlying the general advancement in educational planning, procedural, and allocative strategies are three major causes: demands for greater efficiency are being placed upon school officials, improvements are taking place in the methods of framing the problems and organizing available data, and more detailed analyses of the data are possible because of more precise economic tools.

REFERENCES

Association of School Business Officials. *Educational Resources Management System.* Chicago: ASBO, 1971.

Becker, Gary S. *Human Capital.* Princeton, N.J.: Princeton University Press, 1964.

Blaug, Mark. "The Rate of Return on Investment in Education in Great Britain." *Manchester School of Economics and Social Studies* 33 (September 1965): 205-226.

Bowman, Mary J. "The Human Investment Revolution in Economic Thought." *Sociology of Education* 39 (Spring 1966): 111-137.

Burkhead, Jesse; Fox, T. G.; and Holland, J. W. *Input and Output in Large-City High Schools.* Syracuse, N. Y.: Syracuse University Press, 1967.

Coleman, James S. *Equality of Educational Opportunity.* Washington, D. C.: U. S. Government Printing Office, 1966.

Dyer, Henry S. "The Pennsylvania Plan." *Science Education* 50 (April 1966): 242-251.

_____. "The Concept and Utility of Education Performance Indicators." Paper read at the Systems Science and Cybernetics Conference, 12 October 1967, Boston.

Firman, W. D. "The Quality Measurement Project." *Science Education* 50 (April 1966): 259-279.

Furno, Orlando F. "Program Budgeting and School Quality." *Association of Educational Data Systems Monitor* 5, no. 9 (April 1967).

Hartley, Harry J. *Educational Planning-Programming-Budgeting: A Systems Approach.* Englewood Cliffs, N.J.: Prentice-Hall, 1968. (a)

_____. "PPBS: The Emergence of a Systemic Concept for Public Governance." *General Systems* 13 (1968): 149-155. (b)

_____. "PPBS: A Status Report with Operational Suggestions." *Educational Technology* 12, no. 4 (April 1972): 19-22.

_____. "PPBS: Status and Implications." *Educational Leadership* 29, no. 8 (May 1972): 658-661.

Hayes, Frederick O'R. "PPBS in New York." Mimeographed. New York: City of New York Budget Department, 1967.

Kiesling, Herbert J. "Some Program Analysis of Title I of ESEA." Mimeographed. Indiana University, Department of Economics, 1967.

Levin, Henry M. "The Coleman Report: What Difference Do Schools Make?" *Saturday Review*, 20 January 1968, p. 55-66.

Quade, E. S. *Some Comments on Cost-Effectiveness*, P. 3091. Santa Monica, Ca.: Rand Corporation, 1965. (a)

_____. *Cost-Effectiveness: An Introduction and Overview.* P-3134. Santa Monica, Ca.: Rand Corporation, 1965. (b)

Schwarz, Brita. "Introduction to Programme Budgeting and Cost-Effectiveness Analysis in Educational Planning." In *Budgeting, Programme Analysis and Cost-Effectiveness in Educational Planning.* Paris: Organization for Economic Cooperation and Development, 1968.

18

SYSTEMS EVALUATION AND GOAL DISAGREEMENT

Robert A. Burnham

The practicing administrator is confronted with a plethora of problems of varying degrees of uncertainty. To assist in the search for answers a variety of problem-solving techniques are available, ranging from highly intuitive hunches to precise, formal, rigorous, mathematical solutions. The administrator needs to know what technology can do for him (or to him) as an aid to evaluation and decision making.

SYSTEMS EVALUATION

First of all, systems are made of sets of interrelated components that function together. The systems approach is a way of thinking about these overall systems and their components. Systems approaches, according to Churchman (1968), are the ways different advocates use systematic problem solving. Such systems approaches are used by specialists who apply them to specific aspects of systems analysis, design, control, operation, and evaluation. The methodologies are similar; the frame of reference differs substantially. Systems analysis usually includes the evaluation of alternative means to accomplish a particular objective. The systems analyst generates a series of alternative courses of action that will lead to a desired outcome, evaluates these in terms of their consequences, desirability, and probability, and ranks them in order of their objective attainment potential. A higher level decision maker is presumably then able to make a rational choice among the evaluated alternatives.

In a similar fashion systems evaluation frequently involves the critical examination of accomplishing a given objective and assessing the extent to which the desired outcome is achieved. This evaluation, usually as an effectiveness ratio, compares input to output, or as an efficiency measure compares actual output to some a priori criterion of efficiency. Systems approaches seem to offer straightforward evaluation of different means of accomplishing a relatively specific goal.

The context for decision making, however, in which the school administrator finds himself is one in which, except at a technical operating level, the consensus on goals is not uniform. How then can the administrator give the analyst a standard against which to measure performance? The system scientist has considerable difficulty in attempting to resolve human value conflicts about objectives so that he can proceed with analysis using precise systems models. Perhaps the analyst or evaluator can do no more than assess the potential organizational policies (or means) for achieving over-arching goals. His greatest service may be to clarify goal statements. Of necessity, the evaluation becomes far more ambiguous when both means and goals are moving targets. The application of the logic of systematic approaches to goal formulation and policy analysis is the subject matter of the rapidly growing field of policy sciences.

Students of complex organizations have recently become aware of the pervasive influence of our cultural bias that favors harmony in social interaction. Many of our earlier theories of organizational analysis and policy making stress the need for harmony to maintain organizational and social equilibrium. There is a shift away from such models toward "controlled" conflict theoretical frameworks that can accommodate pluralism, disagreement, and partial nonconsensus. Although we are just learning how to institutionalize this conflict—via negotiating councils of teachers and administrators, student involvement in policy making, school group political processes, and various adversary proceedings in education—many theoreticians see conflict as the dynamic force that will enable educational institutions to adapt successfully.

Now what is it that we are going to evaluate? Space limitations require us to generalize about output evaluation; that is, evaluation of the outcomes of the functional processes carried on by the organization. Also, we can evaluate organizational policies that represent attempts at operationalizing means-ends chains. In some organizations, and schools are a good example, we are increasingly aware of the need to map and measure interdependencies between the primary technical operation (teaching) and supportive services (for example, counseling and guidance) or facilities (the classroom and the schoolhouse itself). Unless we fully understand the interactive nature of these separate but interrelated components of the school system, we are in danger of falsely evaluating what are assumed to be independent aspects of the school program. We may evaluate one part of the instructional program and give it a spuriously high rating because the combined effects of related activities have not been taken into account. If the interactions can be accounted for, then suboptimization is appropriate. We are partially aware of the external influences of the community and peer groups on performance, but even our understanding of internal influences—organizational climate, the environment of teaching and learning, and so on—is meager.

EVALUATION IN THE OPEN SYSTEM

My theoretical framework for analyzing evaluation in the school as an open system was derived from Thompson's work (1967). He provides the conceptual means for examining and evaluating organizations and their processes, pointing out that much of the organizational analysis of the recent past has been done by students of performance and efficiency striving to eliminate uncertainty by assuming that organizations are rational, determinate systems that attempt to maximize their performance outcomes. In such closed systems goals are frequently taken as givens. Rationality is a valued notion in our western culture. Organizations, however, seldom seem to fit these rational, closed systems models. Thus, the open or natural system model appears to have greater utility in analyzing organizations and evaluating what they do.

The open system model portrays a complex organization as a set of interdependent components constituting a whole that is, in turn, interdependent with some larger environment. Components and their interrelationships are assumed to be determined by evolutionary processes and "satisficing" outcomes are substituted for maximum efficiency output.[1] Thompson combines the concepts of natural systems and complex environments by conceiving of

> complex organizations as open systems, hence indeterminate and faced with uncertainty, but at the same time as subject to criteria of rationality and hence needing determinateness and certainty (ibid., p. 10).

Goals of open system organizations are not viewed as givens, rather they are constantly evolving as the organization adapts to its environment.

Technical rationality is determined by the extent to which organizational activity—given the state of knowledge about critical variables, their cause and effect relationships, and their manipulation—produce desired outcomes. Thompson states that

> technical rationality can be evaluated by two criteria: instrumental and economic. The essence of the instrumental questions is whether the specified actions do in fact produce the desired outcome, and the instrumentally perfect technology is one which inevitably achieves such results. The economic question in essence is whether the results are obtained with the least necessary expenditure of resources (ibid., p. 14).

A Hierarchy of Evaluative Tests

In abstract terms within a systems framework, evaluation involves comparing the actual or perceived effects of causal actions with some criterion of desirability. As a prerequisite we must have some knowledge of what those effects are, what the relations of cause and effect might be, and have some conception of the standard of desirability. Understanding of these factors exists to greater and lesser degrees.

The rational economic model reduces the standard to one of maximizing profit, the interaction to a linear function, and the variables to the components of production, for example, land, labor, and capital. The evaluation constitutes a *test of efficiency*. When the standard of desirability is specific, as in the economic model, and the knowledge of cause and effect is presumed to be complete, the efficiency test is appropriate.

When there is agreement on the desirability of a standard but the knowledge of cause and effect is incomplete, the evaluation determines whether or not the desired outcome was achieved without attempting to determine the actual effects of causal action. Evaluation under these circumstances is an *instrumental test*.

When the criterion is ambiguous or simply not agreed upon, regardless of the presumed knowledge of cause and effect relationships, neither efficiency tests nor any instrumental tests are appropriate. We resort to *social tests* that aid us in defining, in terms of various reference groups, a standard. This frequently is a political process to decide which reference group's (or coalition's) standard will prevail. Differences of opinion exist and the standard tends to be ambiguous so as to appeal to the largest possible coalition. The coalitions shift over time.

Given the stress on rationality and the need for determinateness and certainty, we would expect that evaluators would prefer efficiency tests over instrumental tests and instrumental tests over social tests.

Quasi Evaluation

Under the press of rationality and the quest for certainty, schools fall back on bureaucratic measures of fitness that are based on notions of organizational rationality. The yardsticks for measuring fitness are: compliance with rules, attainment of processing quotas to supply trained persons to the next higher level, and expression of confidence by coordinate units in the activities performed. These tests may be categorized as social reference-group tests: they determine whether or not the focal component is able to meet the expectations of other interdependent units. They tell us little about technical or instrumental performance.

Thompson asserts that school districts will tend to be antagonistic to evaluation since the goals of education are ambiguous, there are numerous assessors to be satisfied, and the functional technology (based on theories of learning) is incomplete. Thompson hypothesizes that, under these conditions, school districts are more likely to prefer symbolic extrinsic evaluation. An example of this is the negative evaluation given to the educational enterprise when Sputnik was launched by the Russians and the more positive report card issued when the U.S. won the "race to the moon." School districts, according to Thompson, will prefer to measure their fitness in terms of satisficing by demonstrating historical improvement and by favorable comparison to similar organizations. Accreditation agencies are prime examples of the institutionalization of this type of evaluation. Thompson notes that

> when organizations cannot show improvement on all
> dimensions, they seek to show improvement on those
> of interest to important elements of the task environ-
> ment. Organizations especially emphasize scoring well
> on criteria which are most visible to important ele-
> ments (ibid., p. 97-98).

School districts appear especially anxious to demonstrate improvement to the critical source of their finances. Greater attention is given to superficial but newsworthy efficiency, cost reduction programs, and center stage budget cutting. What could be more rational?

SYSTEMS APPROACHES

Without question, the techniques subsumed under systems approaches are based on highly rational notions. Rationality has taken on a nearly pejorative connotation in much educational literature. If we go further and claim systems approaches to be the utilization of scientific knowledge, we are charged with being overly presumptuous. Nonetheless, the evaluation techniques described below have some scientific basis and we can enhance their scientific usefulness by defining the situations and conditions under which they are valid.

There are six universal elements (or steps) in the systems techniques applicable to educational evaluation. These common elements appear repeatedly in the systems analysis literature although the nomenclature and emphasis varies somewhat. The commonalities are:

1. State the system's *objectives*. This refers to the outcome/s of the system or subsystem being evaluated.
2. Establish a criterion *measure*. The objective should be measurable or quantifiable to some extent. The more specific the objective, the better the measure, and the more rigorous the evaluation.
3. Define the relevant *variables*. These are usually categorized as uncontrollable (constraints) and controllable (decision) variables.
4. Explicate the *interactions* between variables. How are the variables (be they men, material, money, tasks, or time) interrelated?
5. Analyze the interrelated variables in some technical *model* and enter the values each variable can assume. This may be a mathematical equation, which can be solved, or a flow chart approximating a causal model.
6. *Evaluate* the solution, or the objective function, the input/output ratios, the extent of goal attainment, or simply the logic of the flow chart through the use of some decision rule.

Efficiency Tests

Decision makers increasingly are able to rely upon the operations researcher and the operations analyst for tools to improve decisions. Input/output analysis, cost-benefit, and cost-effectiveness models are analytic schema for investigating relationships of means and ends. One of the most useful of the cost-benefit approaches is linear programming, which is a mathematical technique for finding the best or optimal solution to a given specific problem.

Linear programming has been used in education to assign pupils and teachers to courses, to select the best mix of properly sized furniture for a new school, to plan the best bus routes, in terms of the pupils' travelling distances, and to plan lowest cost school lunch menus offering a balanced diet (Van Dusseldorp et al. 1971). The basic elements in a linear programming problem are:

1. Identification of the object variable to be optimized.
2. Identification of the decision variables that are assumed to have a linear relationship to the objective.
3. Specification of the constraints or side conditions under which the process must operate.

For computational purposes all variables must be greater than or equal to zero. Computer programs are readily available to aid the evaluator or administrator in solving linear equations with multiple unknowns.

Linear programming has the potential to enable us to determine optimal solutions to objective functions. We may maximize: student achievement, the availability of instructional material, the use of facilities, subject and course offerings, the nutritional value of lunch menus. We may minimize: the cost of facilities, the interest paid on bonds, the ratios of pupils to teachers, transportation time, and the cost of equipment and supplies. Only with very specific objective functions, however, are we able to identify decision variables that affect the problem objective. If our objective function is to maximize the reading skills of eighth grade students, as measured by a criterion referenced reading test, we must determine which factors have a major influence on reading scores. The variables might include the students' skill at entry, class size, reading texts and materials, facilities, the teacher's verbal skills and training, contact between teacher and pupils, and so on. The solution would be subject to constraints imposed by scarcity of resources such as the number of reading teachers available during any one period, the number of classrooms available, contact time limitations, and so on. Numeric values (parameters) must be assigned to the decision variables to determine how much effect each decision variable will have on reading test scores, given the constraint set.

By examining the six universals we can evaluate the appropriateness of linear programming as an efficiency test. Where the objective is highly specific and commonly valued, as well as being measurable in a discrete way, we have fulfilled the first two requirements. An array of controllable and uncontrollable variables could be identified that may account for the main effects in the objective function. We are forced to assume that each decision variable interacts in a linear fashion with the objective. Assigning parameters or numeric values to each of the variables may be undertaken using objective or empirical evidence, but frequently it is based on subjective estimates of the effects. The linear equation itself represents the analytical model. The prescribed decision rule is to maximize (or minimize) the objective.

Clearly we can evaluate the utilization of facilities, class scheduling, or the nutritional value of different lunch menus more objectively and quantitatively than we can the optimization of student achievement scores. The more we must resort to subjective and arbitrary weighting or assigning of numeric values to variables the less appropriate the test.

Other efficiency tests available as systems approaches are Program Evaluation Review Techniques (PERT) and Critical Path Method (CPM). These provide the decision maker with a planning and evaluation tool. Again, they have the six elements common to other systems approaches. The primary objective is the completion of the overall project whether it is a new school ready for occupancy or the completed design of a new instructional program. A PERT project is based on a work breakdown structure that factors the work into discrete subtasks or activities for which time estimates can be determined. The sequence of activities is based on conventional logic of what functions must precede others and is represented by a flow chart, or a functional flow block diagram. Final scheduling of PERT/CPM projects involves the allocation of men, material, money, and time. The overall elapsed time of the longest path through the network—the critical path—is replanned to see if a better critical path can be devised to reduce the duration of the project. Once underway, the project is routinely evaluated to see if subphases of the project are being completed according to the preplanned schedule. If subtasks on the critial path are taking longer than estimated, the completion of the project by the final deadline is jeopardized and the project administrator must take action. PERT/CPM methodology is an appropriate device for planning, managing, and evaluating complex projects with multiple interdependent activities where the final goal or objective is given or self-evident and where experience provides a guide for the sequence of events and assigning estimates of the time the various activities will take.

The tools of operations research are valuable aids to the

educational evaluator. Increasingly they will be used as tests of efficiency in education. The determination of the best outcomes is based on assumptions of specific objectives, known cause and effect relations, and quantified variables. Where these conditions are not obtained the efficiency test is of little use and we employ the more general instrumental test to see if any aspect of the desired outcome is being satisfied.

Instrumental Tests

Systems analysis techniques are employed to evaluate outcomes against inputs—the crux of instrumental tests. Educational program and systems evaluation in general attempts to answer the questions, "Are we achieving what we said we wanted to accomplish?" and "Is there a better way to accomplish our objective?"

An educational system's objectives tend to be diffuse and global. Further, there is little consensus on which goals are most relevant and the evaluator often finds the goals can only be represented by a myriad of criterion variables. In terms of the measurability of criteria, some quantification is possible but sometimes only for minor variables, and side effects are often as important as main effects. Similarly, the extant knowledge for identifying the variables that are constraints and those that are controllable is poor, thus residual unknowns are great. There are reasonably valid technologies for analyzing several dependent variables and an array of independent variables, especially where assumptions of linearity pose no problem. Technology must be perfected, however, to handle the range and multiplicity of input and output variables with highly interactive and nonlinear relationships. Over all, we can comply with the six universal aspects of systems approaches only by approximation; there are few unequivocal responses. Nonetheless, even a soft analysis and evaluation of a management information subsystem or a pupil accounting system will provide the decision maker with an informed basis for taking action.

Although there have been excellent systems analyses of governmental and social action programs, the analysis of educational systems is in its infancy. Generalized systems analyses have evaluated alternative means of providing government services; for example, police and fire protection networks, judicial processes and services, and urban administrative structures. More theoretical approaches to public investment have relied upon economic benefits as criterion measures. (See, for example, Nichol 1967.) Since the economic benefits of education extend across many years it is exceedingly difficult to use monetary benefits to evaluate educational programs.

Rivlin (1971) provides an interesting account of the problems involved in instrumental evaluation of educational services. She reviews some of the work that systems analysts have done in seeking some "functional relationship between the types and proportions of resources used and the results produced." She finds that

> one major conclusion shows up in all these studies:
> variations in school inputs have limited power to
> explain differences in student performance. . . . Even
> when a significant positive relation is found between
> school performance and some school input, the rela-
> tionship is generally weak (ibid., pp. 72-73).

Granting that such relationships should exist, Mrs. Rivlin suggests that stronger and clearer relations between school input and performance are not found because:

1. Relationships have been measured to determine effects in a single year. Longitudinal studies need to be made.
2. Output measures—usually achievement tests—may be poor.
3. Proxy variables chosen to represent school input factors may be inadequate.
4. Statistical methodologies employed may be inadequate.
5. The unit of observation frequently is the classroom, school, or even school district, rather than the child.

She also sees inadequate sources of data as a shortcoming. Considerable information is generated on the performance of pupils, but it is not collected, reduced, and analyzed for instrumental evaluation.

Another recent effort at outlining a systems analysis of educational programs was made by Mushkin and Pollak (1970). They refer to analysis as a "process of comparing and assessing costs and benefits of competing programs to support choice." This educational program analysis "calls for the application of methodology of modern science to a reasoning about costs and benefits of competing programs and program levels within a conceptual framework that is drawn largely from economic theory (ibid., p. 329)."

Instrumental tests demand increasingly complex analysis and, for the most part, only prototype models are available. Efficiency tests are frequently misapplied in evaluating performance outcomes. Extremely simplified assumptions are made that reduce the power of the systems evaluation approaches. The potential for assessing only trivial outcomes is great.

One harbinger of new technology that may be of tremendous importance to systems evaluation is dynamic simulation modeling. Systems Dynamics is a rapidly growing technique that uses computers to explore long-term interdependencies of a set of key variables. Systems Dynamics evaluation of many of our urban planning policies that have been based on intuition have found them to be counterproductive in the long run. Early efforts at analyzing world dynamics do not portray a very optimistic scenario of the future. Many of the predicted outcomes indicate that intuitive policies of industrial growth are leading to ecological disaster (Forrester 1968; see also Forrester 1971).

Efficiency and instrumental tests operate fairly well in areas of relative certainty where goals are specific, are supported by a solid consensus, and tested theories and models are available. Such tests are grossly inadequate when our concern is with evaluation in matters where theoretical understanding is weak and acceptance on faith is the mode. For political reasons goals are sometimes made deliberately vague, that is, they are stated in abstract terms in order to gain more adherents. Technical evaluation is no longer appropriate since it requires a consensus on a specific goal. While it may be useful to categorize these systems approaches to evaluation, these tests are not discrete techniques in themselves. It may be advantageous to combine technical and policy analysis particularly in the evaluation of educational programs. Thus, given the ambiguity about the real objectives of education and the state of the art of systems approaches, Mushkin and Pollak say that

> because analysis is concerned with public programs, it requires the imaginative search of policy options and an intuitive sorting out of the politically feasible. Public programs often have multiple purposes or outputs.

> The defining of outputs is only a rudimentary stage: moreover, the relationships between program inputs and the outputs achieved have yet to be fully researched. The formulation of output concepts is partly an imaginative, conceptual undertaking. Selection of methods of analysis from among the tools available calls for an intuitive building of models that can bring to light the essential relationships through simplifying selection of strategic determinants. Analysis is thus a mood of questioning, an art of selection

and combining, and an inventive process (1970, pp. 329-330).

Social Tests

Evaluation where objectives are ill-defined or not agreed upon is much more of a political process than technical evaluation. Systems approaches are obviously useful in policy analysis and evaluation (Dror 1969). The evaluation task under these circumstances may be the comparison of one body of goals or policies to another to determine their logical (or ideological) consistency. Wildavsky (1969) supports the contention that policy analysis is similar to a broadly conceived version of systems analysis. He states:

> Policy analysis aims at providing information that contributes to making an agency politically and socially relevant. Policies are goals, objectives, and missions that guide the agency. Analysis evaluates and sifts alternative means and ends in the elusive pursuit of policy recommendations (p. 190).

In educational evaluation, the systems universals are less well defined. In fact, the primary focus of the social test is on the definition of objectives as reflected in policy formulation. The political aspects of policy making involve a considerable amount of time spent in putting together and maintaining coalitions and seeking a consensus on policies within the coalition. Evaluation by way of the social test is in part based on ideology—the criterion is that which does the most good and for the largest number of people in the dominant coalition. The advocate of scientific systems approaches is frustrated by the lack of a theoretical base for sorting and defining desirable outcomes in education. Theories of learning provide little basis for the evaluation of educational programs since any one theory is not widely accepted in the professional culture. Educators are reduced to adopting a particular theory and hoping that others, including evaluators, will have faith in what is avowed. Variables are seen as mostly uncontrollable from the rationalist frame of reference. One controllable variable is the recruitment of political power, or coalition formation, essential in gaining a temporal image of the future as the "desired outcome" criterion around which policy analysis can take place. Interactions between the presumed variables are exceedingly complex: in reality they are often undifferentiated.

Rules to give the evaluator a guide for establishing the desirability of policies are lacking. Various social groups, for example, will assign different values to curriculum components. Disagreement over curriculum goals is ubiquitous. It is only the *logic* of the systems approach that is useful to the analyst in sorting out curricular policies for "evaluation" through a political process.

Kirst and Walker (1971) deal with the value problem in their systematic analysis of curriculum policy making:

> What are schools *for*, anyway? So long as there is disagreement on the proper basis for assessing the worth of the curriculum, there are bound to be conflicting views concerning its composition. *The authoritative allocation of these value conflicts is the essence of what we mean by the political process in curriculum decision-making* (emphasis added) (p. 483).

The resolution of these value conflicts is a political process involving various groups and individuals—it is what we are referring to as a social test.

Historically this social test has been the political determination of whose values are to prevail. The majority vote determines the outcome. But does it? How was the issue to be voted upon identified, conceptualized, and tied into existing policy? Who is affected by the policy? What is the legislative or policy maker's intent? School board policies frequently defy rational analysis. Even at the level of the state legislatures the amount of contradictory and unconstitutional legislation that is enacted in any one session prompts us to say that policy analysis has been haphazard. After-the-fact reconstruction of legislative intent is an exercise in ambiguity.

The role of the policy analyst is to provide information to answer such questions. His task is to draw out the strands of complex problems involving policy and to define these strands and their interrelationships. He must know the key decision points in the policy making system, both in relation to timing and to the point of entry into the process. A thorough analysis takes considerable time, a commodity the decision makers never have enough of. The unfortunate result is that an issue is decided or voted upon before the analysis is completed, or the vote is postponed pending completion of the analytic report giving rise to the charge of delay—"paralysis by analysis" to use Victor Thompson's phrase. There are those who say that such inadvertent, countervailing actions and "muddling through" are a good thing since they permit only gradual change.

The policy analyst's objective is to identify coherent policy alternatives that are logically consistent in their capability for attaining goals. His analysis is a systematic presentation of the problem and alternative policy solutions. The policy analysis step preceeds decision making in the hope that more purposeful issues will be acted upon by an informed decision-making body.

Interdisciplinary policy science groups are working on models to aid the analyst and evaluator in systematizing the social test. Educational policy study centers have been established at several places, for example Berkeley, Harvard, Syracuse, Stanford, Penn State, Buffalo, and MIT, in addition to the policy "think tanks" such as the Rand Corporation and Systems Development Corporation. Many policy analysts are looking for rational political systems approaches to evaluate educational policy, what Dror (1970) refers to as meta-policy, or policy on policy making.

CONCLUSION

How effective is systems analysis? Has anyone ever put it to the test? The former assistant secretary of Health, Education, and Welfare, Mrs. Rivlin, evaluated the progress of large-scale systems analysts in improving the decision-making base for social action programs. The foreword to her book succinctly summarizes the progress as she viewed it:

> The grades are mixed. The author finds that there has been considerable progress in identifying social programs and estimating who would gain if social programs were successful. But little progress has been made in comparing the benefits of different social programs—the analysts cannot say whether another million dollars would be better spent to cure cancer or to teach children to read. Far more serious, little progress has been made in distinguishing more effective from less effective approaches even to well-defined social ends. The author maintains that education, health, and welfare systems are not organized so as to provide information on the effectiveness of alternative ways of delivering these services. We are not likely to discover more effective ways until we conduct systematic experiments with different ways of delivering social services and analyze the results (1971, p. vii).

In addition to the politically sensitive issue of the use of evaluation findings, there are other important political aspects. Wildavsky (1966) has enumerated the political aspects of systems approaches. He notes that cost-benefit analysis is an economic model based on a political theory:

> The idea is that in a free society the economy is to serve the individual's consistent preferences revealed and rationally pursued in the marketplace. Governments are not supposed to dictate preferences nor to make decisions (p. 294).

Systems analysis has begun to uncover some of the shortcomings in educational policy making, policy-making structures, and postures. Iannaccone (1967) found that local educational authorities, educators, and board members operated in a closed system, shielded from social influence and frequently rejecting new policy inputs from the community. As long as the local educational authority can maintain a sizeable coalition, any disagreement with the system over goals is brushed aside. Thus, policies are not effectively put to the social test. The systems analyst, of course, would see the remedy as a better policy-making system as well as the opening up of educational systems to make them more responsive.

There is, perhaps, well-founded fear that institutional information systems (including national social accounting systems) might be misused as a basis for efficiency tests. The demand for data systems, however, stems from the requisite for essential information needed in policy making. Social indicator data, for example, are the raw material for policy analysis to buttress policy making in the social action arena. Likewise, educational policy-making systems might well be improved by the provision of management information systems linked to other governmental policy subsystems that would provide relevant and timely information to policy makers. At the present there are too few analysts available to convert the raw data to intelligible information. And the uninitiated decision maker is likely to feel inundated with facts.

Innovative changes in both urban and educational metapolicy are needed to meet these problems. We need conceptually different kinds of educational forums for deciding policy matters when disagreement is the norm (Dror 1970). The policy-making system must be sensitive enough to tap the views of all parties on an issue, reliable enough to avoid distortion of information, and cohesive enough to manage conflict.

The accompanying table briefly summarizes the uses of systems approaches in the technical and policy domains. Examples of appropriate evaluation topics and techniques are given. Before the school administrator can begin to employ systems evaluation he must satisfy three general prerequisites. He must:

1. Be able to understand the technical processes utilized in the program or component to be evaluated and discern how these activities relate causally to specified outcomes.
2. Understand enough about systematic methodologies to be aware of their strengths, weaknesses, and underlying assumptions.
3. Be able to aid the analyst in conceptualizing the goals to be attained, determining whether or not a consensus exists, or, as a minimum, whether there are common values.

Additionally, the administrator must *want* to expose his organization, procedures, and policies to analysis and evaluation. Evaluation may be time-consuming and expensive.

Most districts can handle efficiency tests as in-house evaluation. The techniques are not arcane. Analysts and evaluators are being trained by a number of colleges and businesses. Computer service bureaus have programs available to do the computational work associated with linear programming much as they presently contract for class scheduling and grade reporting.

The more involved instrumental tests can be undertaken by staff analysts, university consulting groups, and management firms. There is greater danger in misplacing the stress on efficiency in the instrumental area (where specified outcomes and cause and effect relations are unknown) than in the efficiency area (where outcomes can be specified and causal relations are understood). The administrator must be especially alert to evaluation or analysis that would lead him toward greater efficiency in doing the wrong thing. Continual emphasis on reducing class size without regard to the learning situation, or substantive content, or the effectiveness of the teacher is an apt example.

Policy analysis is much more complex and our understanding is weak. Neither procedures nor forums are immediately available in most school districts to assist the decision maker in making routine social tests. Major issues and national issues, usually crises, may be evaluated and solved with policy analysis approaches, but such applications are situational and infrequent. The social test at present tends to be an external assessment of a system's policies.

The evaluator or analyst and the administrator have a common interest in defining a pertinent problem and in relating organizational

TABLE 18:1. EVALUATION TECHNIQUES USING SYSTEMS APPROACHES

Technical Analysis		Policy Analysis
Efficiency Test	Instrumental Test	Social Test
Desired outcomes: Specific Cause and effects: Known Evaluation question: Are desirable effects achieved economically?	Desired outcomes: General Cause and effects: Incomplete knowledge Evaluation question: Are desirable effects achieved?	Desired outcomes: To be determined Cause and effects: Indeterminate Analysis question: Are there coherent policies? Are these logically consistent?[1]

Analysis and evaluation in educational logistics area by *Linear Programming*
Examples:
  Teacher assignment
  Class scheduling
  Pupil assignments for desegregation
  Menu planning
  Salary schedule construction
  School bus routing
  Facilities utilization
Facilities planning and project programming, by *PERT/CPM*
Pupil population prediction and financial forecasting, by *Linear and Multiple Regression*
Equipment and some manpower utilization problems, by *Linear Programming*
	Learning methods and devices
	Master planning of facilities location
	Manpower planning and training
	Communication, control, and incentive system
	Economic implications of education
	  All by *Systems Analysis and Evaluation Techniques*
	Educational subsystem integration and articulation, by *Input/output Analysis*
		Curriculum
		Fundamental educational policy making
		Basic substantive content of programs
		Social, political, and ideological implications of education
		Resource allocation and priority setting
		  Analysis by *Political Systems and Policy Analysis Techniques*
		
		1. Final evaluation is decided by social groups through a political process.

activities to a set of unifying objectives. The evaluator seeks answers to questions pertaining to how well the activities do in fact lead toward obtaining objectives. Both evaluator and administrator think in terms of resource allocation in the same light. The systems person can clarify underlying issues and, if creative, suggest some alternatives. Final decision making is properly left up to the administrator, and policy making to the electorate or their representative.

FOOTNOTE

1. "To optimize requires processes several orders of magnitude more complex than those required to satisfice. An example is the difference between searching a haystack to find the *sharpest* needle in it and searching the haystack to find a needle sharp enough to sew with (March and Simon 1958, p. 141)."

REFERENCES

Churchman, C. West. *The Systems Approach*. New York: Dell, 1968.

Dror, Yehezkel. *Systems Analysis for Development Administration: Some Problems and Requisites*. Santa Monica, Ca.: Rand Corporation, 1969.

_____. *Urban Metapolicy and Urban Education*. Santa Monica, Ca.: Rand Corporation, 1970.

Forrester, Jay W. *Principles of Systems*. 2nd prelim. ed. Cambridge, Mass.: Wright-Allen Press, 1968.

_____. *World Dynamics*. Cambridge, Mass.: Wright-Allen Press, 1971.

Iannaccone, Laurence. *Politics in Education*. New York: The Center for Applied Research in Education, 1967.

Kirst, Michael W., and Walker, Decker F. "An Analysis of Curriculum Policy-Making." *Review of Educational Research* 41, no. 5 (December 1971): 479-509.

March, James G., and Simon, Herbert A. *Organizations*. New York: John Wiley, 1958.

Mushkin, Selma J., and Pollak, William. "Analysis in a PPB Setting." In *Economic Factors Affecting the Financing of Education*, edited by R. L. Johns; I. J. Goffman; Kern Alexander; and D. H. Stollar. Gainesville, Fla.: National Educational Finance Project, 1970.

Nichol, Helen O. "Guaranteed Income Maintenance: A Public Welfare Systems Model." In *Planning Programming Budgeting: A Systems Approach to Management*, edited by Fremont J. Leyden and Ernest G. Miller. Chicago: Markham Publishing, 1967.

Rivlin, Alice M. *Systematic Thinking for Social Action*. Washington, D.C.: The Brookings Institution, 1971.

Thompson, James D. *Organizations in Action*. New York: McGraw-Hill, 1967

Van Dusseldorp, R. A.; Richardson, D. E.; and Foley, W. J. *Educational Decision-Making Through Operations Research*. Boston: Allyn and Bacon, 1971.

Wildavsky, Aaron. "The Political Economy of Efficiency: Cost-Benefit Analysis, Systems Analysis, and Program Budgeting." *Public Administration Review* 27, no. 4 (December 1966): 292-310.

_____. "Rescuing Policy Analysis from PPBS." *Public Administration Review* 29, no. 2 (March/April 1969): 189-202.

19

THE DOMINION OF ECONOMIC ACCOUNTABILITY

Ernest R. House

While recognizing that it may be a passing fad, and that some manifestations are ephemeral, I believe that the idea of accountability is going to be around for a while. If for no other reason, it is a way of lassoing the wild stallion of educational spending. Groups competing for funds at the federal, state, and local levels ensure that educational spending will not continue to climb as rapidly as it has in the past. So whatever else accountability may be, it is a way of holding down spending. Although some good may come from it, I am disturbed at the form it is taking.

It has been said in support of accountability that it will result in favorable changes in professional performance "and these will be reflected in higher academic achievement, improvement in pupil attitudes, and generally better educational results (Barro 1970)." I would contend that accountability will not automatically do good things, that we are already accountable for many things that we do, that being accountable in fact makes our lives miserable in certain ways, and often actually prohibits favorable changes in professional performance and better educational results. For example, college professors are quite accountable for publishing articles, yet one would be hard-pressed to show how this arrangement helps, say, the public schools. Similarly public school teachers are accountable for keeping their classrooms quiet, and I have heard it said that this is an impediment to good teaching.

So, when one hears talk about accountability as if it did not now exist and that all good things are going to happen when we get it, one must regard this argument as too simplistic and look more squarely

Reprinted from *The Educational Forum* 37, no. 1 (November 1972): 13-23. Copyright 1972 by *The Educational Forum*, Kappa Delta Pi.

at what is being proposed. It is safe to assume that somebody wants something he is not now getting.

Not long into any discussion on accountability, someone always raises the question "Who is accountable to whom?" Almost invariably the response is that one is accountable to his superior. In fact, most people apparently perceive society as being a vast hierarchy in which each person is accountable to his boss, and his boss is accountable to someone else, and so on. In this ubiquitous conception the school district, the society, the world are perceived as being organized like a vast bureaucracy, a gigantic corporation. Accountability is upward. Each person is accountable to the institution.

Nowhere is this better illustrated than in an issue of the *Phi Delta Kappan* (December 1970) devoted to the theme of accountability. Explicitly or implicitly several articles in the magazine harbor this view. But the apotheosis is the lead article written by a Rand Corporation economist. He proposes that pupil performance measures be given to all the students in a school district and then, through a series of multiple regression equations, each teacher, each principal, and the superintendent be held accountable for that bit of pupil performance that the analysis attributes to him. Mrs. Smith, for example, is responsible for 3 percent of verbal reasoning while Mr. Jones only managed to get in 1 percent. Presumably Mrs. Smith and Mr. Jones will be rewarded differently for those contributions. Good girl, Mrs. Smith. Bad boy, Mr. Jones.

The technical and political problems that this approach would encounter are so insurmountable that they will never be overcome. Technically the conditions necessary for employing the statistical analysis cannot be met: no current measures are adequate indices of the relevant variables; the variables cannot be made independent of one another; and there is no way of specifying all the critical variables that should be included. The political problems are even more formidable. If the teachers' organizations are anything like the rascals I know them to be, they would never allow such a thing.

But I must confess I am intrigued by the prospect of Mr. Jones's sabotaging Mrs. Smith's lesson plans so he can pick up a few points on her. Or the eleventh grade algebra class's organizing to throw the math. test and send the despised Mr. Harms into bankruptcy. My mind slips back to those exciting days of comparative anatomy practical exams when the desperately competitive pre-meds would pull the numbered pins from one part of the cat's brain and stick them into another in order to fool their rivals.

Although such schemes are not going to be widely employed, this conception of accountability is so widely accepted that I would not be surprised to read in an education newsletter that the superintendent in Lockjaw, California, or Bone Gap, Illinois, having secured a batch of army surplus tests and a slide rule for the business manager to work the regression equations on, has decided to institute the system. (I also cannot help remarking that, after years of making the world safe for the American air force, the Rand Corporation is in serious financial difficulty. Let me be the first to recommend to the Rand administrators that they employ this very same technique to determine which of their economists are contributing to their productivity.)

The point I am trying to make is that discussions of accountability always lead us down this dismal road. In fact, we are so far down the road that it is impossible for many people to even imagine another type of accountability. For the dominant theme today is economic efficiency and its purpose is control—control over the behavior of pupils, control over the behavior of the staff, control over schooling.

At the risk of oversimplification let me outline this mode of accountability, which I call economic accountability. It is an economist's view of the world. Basically it presumes that the purpose of education is to supply manpower to other institutions of the society, particularly the economic ones. The skills needed to run the social machinery can be formulated in specific terms, so educational goals are mandated by technological demands. The goals being specific and set, the job of educators is to maximize these goals (usually forms of student achievement), with the greatest efficiency possible. Ultimately then the goals of education become economic and the attendant accountability system is economic.

Economic analysis always has to do with maximization of *known* objectives (Brandl 1970). It provides a descriptive theory of how maximization will happen or a prescriptive analysis of how to get it to happen. Thus we get analytic tools such as systems analysis, cost-benefit analysis, PPBS, and performance contracting. Perhaps the technique par excellence is regression analysis against a production function, in which the most efficient combination of inputs is related to output.

Now there are serious problems in applying economic analysis to education in a pluralist society. Where objectives or outcomes are not known, economic theory offers no way of determining them. And where there are competing viewpoints of what education should be doing, the maximizing solution does not even apply. In a pluralist society such as ours, there are irreconcilable differences as to what the outputs of education should be. At best one can compile a great list of possible outputs and try to relate inputs to them, thus establishing a collage. But this solution does not have much practical appeal to administrators who want to make decisions. For example, it would not tell them what would happen if an attempt were made to increase a particular output.

The alternative is to reconcile these differences into a few set goals—which is what I believe the demands for economic accountability are attempting to do. The ultimate form of accountability then is to tighten the system to the point at which each person is held personally accountable for his contribution to those few goals—just as the Rand economist suggested. In this scheme students are shaped to prespecified ends, educators are efficient at producing those ends, and education is more closely wired to the economic institutions of the society. The whole social system is more efficient, but the cost is terribly high: it is our cultural pluralism and our humanity. For this mode of accountability simply reduces to this: the individual is accountable to the institutions, but the institutions are not accountable to the individual.

THE DOMINANCE OF MANAGERIAL EDUCATION

Inextricably bound to economic accountability is what Green (1969) calls "managerial" education. The same principle of economic efficiency shapes both the accountability system and the nature of education. Managerial education dominates when the schools are assessed by the usefulness of their "product" to the dominant institutions of the society. In our society this means that the schools are held accountable for effectively and efficiently meeting the demands for educated manpower. To the extent that the economic institutions maintain their voracious appetite for technical skills and to the extent that school credentials become the primary means of placing people in the structure, managerial education will predominate.

Contrast this with humanistic education in which schools are assessed in terms of what they do for people—independent of their contribution to other institutions. The humanistic credo, often expressed as the impossible goal of "developing each individual to his fullest," is the official ideology of most educators. It seeks, not to shape the individual to a predetermined end, to some criterion of external utility, but to cultivate independence and individualism.

Yet, according to Green, in spite of this credo, managerial concerns now shape the schools and will increase their dominance substantially over the next two decades. One reason is that each lower educational level must at a minimum prepare its students for the next higher level and at the top of the pyramid are the graduate and professional schools, which feed the economic institutions.

Down this road in a few decades Green foresees a high level of managerial education for an elite and a lower level for the majority of people. To a certain extent this has already happened. As we investigated programs for gifted children across Illinois, we found gifted children being educated toward some kind of vocational marketability in the future. In shaping the child toward these distant and prespecified goals, the classes tended to be dull and repressive, often requiring that both teachers and parents exert great pressures on the child in order to get him to perform. The rationale underlying these classes was usually "This may be painful now but it will help the child when he wants to get ahead."

Here are some excerpts from one of our case studies. First, excerpts from an interview with the teacher Mr. Harms:

Q: What would you say your major goal is for this particular class?

Mr. Harms: I'd say the major goal is to prepare them for advanced math. Most of the students will probably go ahead and take college work in math. as either a science, math., or engineering major.

Q: What do the students do that is especially appropriate for the gifted?

Mr. Harms: It's primarily a matter of acceleration and an enrichment of mathematics. Projects are good but I feel that in math. there really is no substitute for hard work; there just isn't any royal road to mathematics. I'm afraid I probably assign more problems than some teachers do, but even the good students need practice.

Q: How would you describe a successful student in this class?

Mr. Harms: A successful student would be one that studies regularly every day, pays attention in class, does well in his tests, and does his homework pretty regularly.

I have some students that ask questions and others that don't. I believe that I like to have them ask questions but some students have gotten to the place where they get it pretty much on their own and they don't have to ask questions. Others don't ask questions because they're . . . well, they don't.

Q: What does it take to get an A?

Mr. Harms: Well, my feeling is you have to be pretty good to get an A. You have to be an outstanding student, have to almost have an A on every test. It depends somewhat on how many tests we have during the quarter but unfortunately with an A, you don't have a grade above the A to average with one below to bring it up, and so it's a little tough.

The students' enthusiasm was extremely low, and, what is rare for a gifted group, there was no humor in the class. Here is a brief excerpt from an interview with Donna, the best student in the class:

Q: What kinds of things do you do in this class?

Donna: Mr. Harms will ask us if we have any questions over the problems we did, and if we do, he'll discuss them and write them on the board. He'll also give us at least one proof a day. And he kind of yells at us a little because we don't like them. But he keeps saying that we should like them, and we should do them because that's all we're going to do in college.

Q: What kinds of things are you supposed to learn in this class?

Donna: I think we're supposed to learn the generalities with proofs and just learn the technique of proving. He doesn't give us too much busy work, like some teachers do. He is concerned about us knowing proofs because he keeps saying we have to know this for college.
We have to learn how to do the proofs; we are going to have to realize that we can't skip over them. Some of us work the problems and don't have enough time to get to all of them so we'll do the rest of the problems and skip the proofs. And say we didn't get them because we probably wouldn't get them anyway.

Q: Do you get graded in this class?

Donna: Yes, and I need to be graded so that I have some drive to get me going. It makes me feel real good when I can bring home an A and my Dad is real proud of me.

Finally here's part of our interpretation:

"Mr. Harm's class is the stereotyped math. class that students through the years have come to dislike intensely. Of more than 100 classes examined, this one is lowest on student enthusiasm. The unremitting aim of the teacher is to ingrain the subject matter into the heads of his students so that they can "get ahead" vocationally. This future orientation of the teacher and the degree to which he impresses it on the students is a significant feature of the class. The rationale for the future utility of the subject attempts to mitigate against current unpleasantness.

"To the teacher's credit he does manage to teach for the higher thought process of analysis. This emphasis occurs in all math. classes we have studied. In all probability, the students will perform well on the Advanced Placement tests he keeps reminding them about. Since this is the main goal, the class may be a success in that regard. The cost is high, however. The strict humorless classroom atmosphere and total domination of the class by the teacher results in a particularly uninspiring class. There is no joking, no questioning—only the grimmest pursuit of subject matter. When he wishes to "enrich" the class he does so by showing the students other ways of solving equations. His pathetic attempts at "making the students independent" consist of occasionally not giving them any help on their homework.

"When Mr. Harms tries to start a discussion in class, he asks recall questions that leave nothing to discuss and that no one cares to answer. In addition, he is a very hard grader. The extreme emphasis on grades is strong in the entire school—quite typical of all the middle-class suburbs studied—and the teacher manifests these pressures. The severe competitive environment is very real to the students. There is one thing that the students like about his class—he doesn't collect and check their homework. However, unknown to them, he does check on them covertly.

"Even the best student stresses the dullness of the class and claims that the only thing that keeps her going is pressure from her father to make good grades. At best the other students are resigned. As a helpful crutch, Mr. Harms relies on his ultimate rationale—that learning math. is unenjoyable. ('There is no royal road') but one must do it in order to get ahead in college and eventually gain a competitive advantage in the job market. The philosophy of the community is embodied in the classroom of the teacher—learning is not intrinsically worthwhile but is unpleasantly necessary to success. The honors classes reveal a considerable trace of elitism. Parents and students see the classes as quite a status symbol.

"In summary, strong community pressure for competition and success, a subject difficult to teach enjoyably, and a teacher who has little flexibility, humor, or ability to enliven the class combine for an unhappy learning experience and a negative feeling toward the subject. As one of Mr. Harms' students says, 'Math. is a lot more "cut and dried" than most subjects. I'm sorry to say it seems mostly dried, and I don't think anything can help.' "

Atkin (1970) has called attention to the paradigm of this type of education in which educational services are perceived as products to be mass-produced. This production-line model calls for elaborate prespecification and quality control. Emphasis is placed on that which is replicable, easily quantifiable, readily discernible, and unambiguous. Education becomes engineering and, finally, industrial production. Evaluation becomes greatly simplified: one need only compare the prespecification to the final product.

PPBS—AN ACCOUNTANT'S DREAM

Thus we get simple business management tools applied to education—as in the PPB system California is implementing. The system promises no less than the

> information necessary (1) for planning educational
> programs that will meet the needs of the community;
> and (2) for choosing among the alternative ways in
> which a school district can allocate resources to
> achieve its goals and objectives (California State De-
> partment of Education 1969).

According to the state's lucid and well-written manual here's how the system works:

The school arrives at a set of *goals,* which are the cornerstone of the system. From the goals is derived a set of objectives, which must be measurable. Based on these objectives the *program* is developed, which is a group of activities to accomplish the objectives including attendant resources and schedules. This completes the program development. Then the *program description package* is drawn up, which includes the course content, objectives, and method of evaluation. Then the *program structure* is set up which is a hierarchical arrangement of programs. (The system is permeated by hierarchies: about fifteen of the eighteen charts in the book show some kind of hierarchy.)

Finally the *program code* is built, which means each program is assigned a number, the *program budget* is completed, and the *multi-year financial plan*, a five-year cost projection, is constructed. All is neatly rational and internally consistent—if you believe in an abstract "economic man." Actually any relation between the PPB *system* and reality will be purely coincidental.

The problem of defining goals in a pluralist society has already been noted. The PPBS manual spends no time explaining how to arrive at goals, and with good reason. Defining goals is a political, not an economic, process. Empirical studies of business organizations have shown that their goals are changing, multiple, inconsistent—and the organizations survive quite nicely (March 1966). Upon close inspection even the profit goal in business organizations turns out to be quite elusive.

Assuming that the goal problem is overcome, one must then develop a set of objectives that are measurable—the old behavioral objectives problem. Here is a behavioral objective for students from *Educational Technology* (Kapfer 1968):

> The student will be given a problem which is totally unfamiliar to him. He will be able to respond by stating ideas or solutions to the problem. The responses (as measured by a choice of checklists, teacher observations, teacher evaluation, and teacher-made exercises) will be rated on the basis of newness and uniqueness.

How many of these would one have to write to cover fully what a child should be doing? One Office of Education project set out to compile a complete set of behavioral objectives for the high school. Before it was abandoned, the last I heard was that they had twenty thousand. Teachers must teach and measure each one. No wonder they want a raise.

There are many other objections to behavioral objectives, most of which revolve around the impossibility of specifying a complete set for anyone and the difficulty of specifying any but the most trivial tasks. I might add that, of all the gifted programs we investigated in Illinois, not one employed a set of behavioral objectives.

The program description package is prepared after the program has been "developed." A sample is illustrated in figure 19:1. If you compare the simplicity of this program description with even the brief excerpts from our case study example, you will see how something as complex as a classroom cannot be reduced to a ledger

---

FIGURE 19:1. PPBS ELEMENT FORM

Goal Statement

To provide all students the opportunity to develop skills in typing, shorthand, bookkeeping, and office machine operation.

DEVELOPED BY _____

Objective Statement and Evaluative Criteria

Ninety percent of graduating Business Curriculum students shall meet the following standards:

Typing—70 words per minute as measured by the IBM Test with 90 percent accuracy

Shorthand—100 words per minute as measured by the Gregg test.

Bookkeeping—Demonstrate understanding of journals, income statements, and balance sheets as determined by decision tests.

Office Machine Operation—Mean score equal to national average on NCR test.

DEVELOPED BY _____

Program Description Summary

This program is designed to allow students to develop skills in the areas of typing, shorthand, bookkeeping, and office machine operation sufficient to gain employment using these skills. This program will include practice with typical problems and situations found in actual employment situations. Contacts will be maintained with the local business community to aid students in obtaining employment.

DEVELOPED BY _____

PROGRAM TITLE _____

PROGRAM ID. NO. _____ PROGRAM NO. _____

SUPPORTED PROGRAMS _____ PROGRAM LEVEL _____

SUPPORTING PROGRAMS _____

sheet. I submit that, with this form completed, you would know almost nothing worthwhile about any program. Here is also implicit the interesting idea that "program development" is completed when these activities are specified. This is not how good programs develop. Our own data indicate that program development is a complicated process that occurs when an "advocate," perhaps a parent or teacher, becomes interested in developing a program for children. This advocate organizes a group of people, secures resources, and proceeds to build a program. The development of the program is never complete. (House, Steele, and Kerins 1970).

Finally these artifacts are coded and related to the budget—which I suspect was the purpose all along. The code numbers can then be manipulated as if they meant something—which they clearly do not. The manual is peppered with statements such as "Assessment of results is essential" and other exhortations to evaluate these programs, do cost-benefit analyses, and so on. But actual procedures for doing so are glossed over at great speed. Well they might be, for there is absolutely no legitimate way now in existence to collect the measures and make the comparisons the system demands.

The end result is what I always find in dealing with systems analysis—a lot of hazy generalizations that seem reasonable on the surface but are actually impossible to implement. All the objections to this system that I have raised are based on either empirical evidence or experience. But one thing I have found with the systems people is that they are never disturbed by data. They simply say "You aren't doing it right," which means that people are not behaving in accordance with the rationalist-economic model that underlies the system. If they did behave properly the model would work—a brilliant piece of circular logic.

In short this system seems to me to be an accountant's dream of how the world should work. Its implicit message is economic efficiency, promoting economic rationality at the expense of other human characteristics such as political rationality (Wildavsky 1968). Significantly, the California system was drawn up by an accounting and budgeting commission and almost all the examples used are in business education.

My prognosis is something like this. My worst fears are that the system will actually succeed in doing what I see as its real design. In that case, we will have a high level of managerial education. The repression and dullness of the classroom will increase and we will have succeeded in crucifying our children on the cross of economic efficiency. My most hopeful prediction is that people will realize the restrictiveness of this system and subvert it into an information system that attends to the needs of the children instead of simply shaping them to the needs of the institutions.

But I do not think that either of these projections is likely in the near future. I think the schools will stay pretty much as they are now. Schoolmen will get by just as they got through chemistry lab.—by filling out forms the way they are expected to regardless of what is happening in reality. In California the PPB system will take more people to fill out the forms, more destroyed trees to provide the paper, and more people in Sacramento to shuffle them around. As one economist says, most PPB systems have culminated in "sterile accounting schemes (Brandl 1970)." But I can see the public and certain government leaders providing more money for the schools now that "sound business procedures" have been adopted. The end result will be a slightly less efficient system that looks more efficient. But even that is certainly preferable to the first choice I outlined.

INSTITUTIONAL ACCOUNTABILITY

The headlines of an article in *The Wall Street Journal,* dated 24 June 1970, datelined San Francisco, read:

EDUCATED DROPOUTS
COLLEGE-TRAINED YOUTHS
SHUN THE PROFESSIONS
FOR A FREE-FORM LIFE
John Spitzer of Harvard Is
Cabbie; Clara Perkinson,
Smith, Carries the Mail
OPTING OUT OF 'THE SYSTEM'

The article goes on to say that increasing numbers of highly talented and educated young people do not want to join the system. John Spitzer says, "When I was a senior, Dylan's 'Subterranean Homesick Blues' came out. Remember that's the one when he says 'twenty years in school and then they put you on the day shift.' That touched so many nerves for so many people; that said it all." Although we might not agree on the problem, on whether those children are refuse or martyrs, saboteurs or saviors, we would agree that PPBS is not going to solve the problem. In fact, it would make the situation worse.

I wish I had a well-worked out alternative to economic accounta-bility that would solve all our problems. I do not. But let me suggest a different mode of accountability in which institutions are account-able to persons rather than persons accountable to the institution. Such an accountability scheme would provide feedback on the clients' well-being instead of just how well they are "shaping up." Teachers might be responsible to students and administrators to teachers. The information system for this accountability would re-volve around the question "Is this information going to help the institution adjust to characteristics of the student or will it result in shaping the student to the demands of the institution?"

With this in mind here are some recommendations for dealing with any kind of information system:

1. *Examine the function of the system, not just its rationale.* The true nature of the system is revealed by how it works, not by what it promises.

2. *Try to respect the complexity of reality.* Good programs do not result from establishing a few objectives and selecting appropriate activities. Establishing any program successfully necessitates com-plex political processes. Any model of development that denies this is dysfunctional.

3. *Insist on multiple outcomes.* No educational program should be judged on the basis of one or two measures. Resist attempts to reduce educational output to simple achievement scores.

4. *Look at classroom transactions.* Regardless of outcomes, the at-mosphere in which a child spends a good portion of his life is important. Many instruments for doing this are available.

5. *Collect many different kinds of data.* In light of all the above, the more kinds of data the better. Testimonials, interviews, classroom interaction analysis, objective tests—almost all data are appropri-ate. They provide a picture of the richness of classroom life and mitigate against making decisions based on highly abstract infor-mation. One thing we did in a recent evaluation was to combine twenty-five different kinds of information to produce a case study of the class. The resulting image of the class was much superior to that produced by combining just a few kinds of data.

6. *Collect data from different sources.* It is especially important to find out what students are thinking, even if one asks only "What are the three things in this class you would like to change most?" Students can give as good a reading of what is going on as anyone else. Information should also be collected from parents and other groups.

7. *Report to different audiences.* For example, parents have a right to know something about what is going on in class. So do many other people.

8. *Rely on intuition and professional judgments.* Many experts on PPBS emphasize that analytic tools should only provide assistance to intuition. There is no substitute for human judgment.

9. *Promote diversity within the system.* The most difficult task for organizations is to generate alternative ways of doing things. (March 1966). An information system should promote the development of divergent ideas, not inhibit them. There are many places where even economic efficiency should be the criterion. For example, recently we did a cost-benefit analysis in comparing the efficacy of demonstration centers and summer training institutes. But the circumstances were proper—a few short-range goals were at stake. Ordinarily, life is not that simple.

Breaking the exclusive hold of economic accountability is not easy to do. I hope that economists and those who control our economic institutions will stop maximizing economic gains long enough to assess the long-range consequences of doing so. There is some hope. Even an economist has remarked, "When my son Christopher got all As in first grade but found school repressive and dull, the arguments that his grades indicated a successful and lucrative future was little consolation to him or to me (Brandl 1970)."

REFERENCES

Atkin, J. Myron. "Curriculum Design: The Central Development Group and the Local Teacher." Paper prepared for the Institute fur die Padagozik der Naturwissenschaften Invitational Symposium, 14 October 1970, Kiel, West Germany.

Barro, Stephen M. "An Approach to Developing Accountability Measures for the Public Schools." *Phi Delta Kappan* 52, no. 4 (1970): 196-205.

Brandl, John E. "Public Service Outputs of Higher Education: An Exploratory Essay." In *The Outputs of Higher Education: Their Identification, Measurement, and Evaluation,* edited by Ben Lawrence; George Weathersby; and Virginia Patterson. Boulder, Colo.: Western Interstate Commission for Higher Education, 1970.

California State Department of Education. *Conceptual Design for a Planning, Programming, Budgeting System for California School Districts.* Sacramento: 1969.

Green, Tomas F. "Schools and Communities: A Look Forward." *Community and the Schools.* Harvard Educational Review Reprint, no. 3, 1969.

House, Ernest R.; Steele, Joe M.; and Kerins, Thomas. "The Development of Educational Programs: Advocacy in a Non-Rational System." Mimeographed. University of Illinois, Center for Instructional Research and Curriculum Evaluation, 1970.

Kapfer, Miriam B. "Behavioral Objectives and the Gifted." *Educational Technology* (15 June 1968).

March, Jones G. "Organizational Factors in Supervision." In *The Supervisor: Agent for Change in Teaching*, edited by James Raths and Robert Leeper. National Education Association, Association for Supervision and Curriculum Development, 1966.

Steele, Joe M.; House, Ernest R.; Lapan, Stephen; and Kerins, Thomas. "Instructional Climate in Illinois Gifted Classes." Mimeographed. University of Illinois, Center for Instructional Research and Curriculum Evaluation, 1970.

Wildavsky, Aaron. "The Political Economy of Efficiency: Cost-Benefit Analysis, Systems Analysis, and Program Budgeting." In *Planning, Programming, Budgeting: A Systems Approach to Management*, edited by Fremont J. Leyden and Ernest R. Miller. Chicago: Markham Publishing, 1968.

V

IF NOBODY AGREES . . .

Evaluation without a Consensus on Goals

In view of the great conflicts swirling around the school, it would seem that people do not always agree on the aims of public education. There are, in fact, great differences of value. If agreement on goals cannot be assumed, must one abandon attempts to evaluate? Newer than the evaluation systems that assume consensus are several approaches that do not. One approach is to measure the extent to which goal consensus exists. Evaluation then becomes a matter of collecting data about the goals themselves. It is a way of *ascertaining* the goals instead of assuming their existence.

In the first chapter in this section, Stake and Gooler contend that, in a pluralist community, different audiences place varying importance on goals. Priorities will indicate what emphasis will be given each goal. "Needs assessments," often mandated by federal programs, are attempts to define those public priorities. However, the authors contend that the diversity of responses, rather than simply the majority's opinions, should be reported. Also people order priorities in different ways and priorities change over time. The most important priorities will not necessarily require the greatest amount of school time. Hence, one should solicit information about their priorities from various groups, such as teachers, parents, and students, and these priorities should be expressed at varying levels of abstraction. Stake and Gooler present a model for doing so. They also find that teachers, citizens, and administrators have difficulty in thinking about the curriculum as a whole and feel that they lack the information to do so.

The Delphi technique, reported by Cyphert and Gant, is a method of intentionally striving for consensus. Ordinarily a small group of experts on a specific topic is identified. Their opinions are solicited and then fed back to them as group data. All this is done by mailed questionnaires so that each person is unaware of who else is responding and so that no single strong personality shapes the group as happens in a committee meeting. After repeated questionnaires, the group's opinion usually comes to reach more of a consensus.

For example, the original Delphi study was made to determine how many nuclear devices would be needed to destroy basic industry in the United States. The original range of estimates, from a few dozen to several hundred, was greatly reduced within the responding group. The Delphi technique in Cyphert's and Gant's study was used to arrive at some goal consensus for a college of education. Faculty, student teachers, administrators, public school teachers, legislators, and other public leaders were included among the respondents.

The group was sent four questionnaires. The first asked what the primary targets of the school of education should be during the next decade. The second questionnaire asked the respondents to rate each of these items on a priority scale. The third questionnaire fed back the group consensus and asked for another rating. If a respondent's answer fell outside the consensus, he was asked to give a reason. On the fourth questionnaire the dissenting opinions were fed back. Most opinion change occurred on the third questionnaire.

The last three selections are perhaps the most radical propositions in the book. If we assume that there is no definable consensus, what can be done? Three clear alternatives are presented. Each has been or is being tried somewhere. Each is quite different from the way evaluation is currently being done in schools. Each opens the school to divergent information and possibly conflict. Each makes the school less closed and more vulnerable than it is now.

The chapter by Owens deals directly with goal conflict. It institutionalizes the conflict by managing it in a quasi-judicial framework. The adversary proceeding from law is used as the model. Evidence for and against the curriculum is presented by different sides. As Owens points out, this is not a new way of collecting and analyzing evaluative data but it is a new way of interpreting, synthesizing, and reporting it.

Instead of allowing most data to pass unchallenged, as is usually the case, the adversary hearing allows for competitive consideration of alternatives. It exposes values inherent in the program; it considers the congruence between the program and the system it is to fit into; it reveals how different people may interpret the same data; and it provides a way of resolving disputes.

Such a hearing was actually tried out in Hawaii. The question was

"Should a certain social studies curriculum be adopted for the schools in Hawaii?" The two-hour hearing produced great excitement and the consensus that much was learned. On its usefulness as a device for making decisions, the opinion of the participants was split. Some felt that too much important information was excluded from the hearing. As an evaluative tool, though, the hearing offers promise.

Gooler defines evaluation as being a set of procedures designed to provide a capacity for greater understanding. He makes three assumptions: that it is possible and desirable for various public groups to understand education institutions; that it is possible and desirable for the public to have access to policy-making power; and that increased public involvement is good. To achieve this enlightenment, the public must seek data, synthesize the data, fill in gaps where no data exist, and judge the school on the basis of the data.

Behind this argument is the realization that public control of the institution is limited by access to data, and, in the past, small groups who do possess such data have controlled the schools, often to their own advantage. Such an emphasis on public disclosure leads to the need for some commonly accepted indicators. Gooler sees these as coalescing around a few questions. What is being done? How well is it being done? What are the trade offs? What is the cost?

The mechanism Gooler proposes to handle this is a public education information agency—a consumer agency for education. Its function would be to aid the public in understanding the schools and to aid the schools in finding out what the public thinks. Obviously the schools would be opened up to more public scrutiny than ever before.

Scriven's approach is to subject the program to the critical intelligence of the professional evaluator—unbiased by the intentions of the program developers. In a dialogue between evaluator and client, Scriven indicates that one cannot simultaneously both evaluate achievement objectively and be indoctrinated by the program's goals. His solution is studiously to avoid the goals. It is the evaluator's job to investigate the *effects*, especially those not expected by the developers. These are more important than the original intentions.

To the client's objection that it is not practical for the evaluator to investigate all possible outcomes, Scriven's evaluator replies that knowledge of the treatment itself greatly reduces the search for data. Often, even though the developer is not producing all that is called for in the contract, the evaluation may show that he is doing well in unexpected directions. To the client's contention that it would be more useful to tell the producer how well he has achieved his stated goals, the evaluator replies that it is his job to assess merit, not simply consonance with preset goals.

Even though eventually the evaluator may be able to infer the program goals, the point is that he not get locked in too soon. One should choose an evaluator according to his past experience. In formative evaluation, the evaluator should not play the role of the consultant by helping define behavioral objectives, and so on. Rather he should attend to the business of generating and testing hypotheses about the program effects. At no time should he interfere with the creative or exploratory process. Hence, in this approach, the problem about goals is avoided by referring the evaluation to the critical intelligence and technical judgment of the professional evaluator.

20

MEASURING EDUCATIONAL PRIORITIES

Robert E. Stake & Dennis D. Gooler

There are two specialists in education who are seldom in communication with each other: the curriculum specialist and the instructional researcher. They have a common concern about many aspects of the school situation, but they seldom work together. There are probably several reasons for this noncommunication, but one, we believe, is the insistence of the instructional researcher on acting as if there will be a *small* number of goals for teacher and learner to pursue. The instructional researcher assumes that a reasonable amount of time and support will be available for at least a few major goals.

In contrast, the curriculum specialist attends more to the facts that the goals of education are infinitely numerous, that the school serves a pluralistic and aspiring community, and that adequate time and support for mastery of top goals is not available. The curriculum specialist ponders the multitude of learning tasks within a subject matter—noting that many cut across subject matters and that the responsibility for developing these skills is shared by many teachers. He realizes that the teacher can concentrate on only a few topics at a time; she is forced by custom and the press of time to move on to other topics. Each topic calls for intertwining understandings and skills—the goal of mastery is not a very realistic goal in the eyes of the curriculum specialist. A lot of topics must be touched upon; none will be mastered.

The instructional researcher usually assumes that mastery of a few lessons is educationally preferable to acquaintance with many

Reprinted from *Educational Technology* 11, no. 9 (September 1971): 44-48.
Copyright 1971 by Educational Technology Magazine.

lessons. He enters the scene assuming that the critical learning tasks have already been selected and resources allocated to them.

Our point in identifying this dilemma is not to repair the lines of communication between instructional researcher and curriculum developer but to point out that, partly because neither acknowledges the relevance and contribution of the other, both fail to insist on an improvement in the statement of educational priorities. The technologically oriented researcher knows that techniques *are* available for assessing the strength of personal preference and group pressures. He has little interest in an argument about the curriculum with philosophers, teacher trainers, and spokesmen for the formal disciplines. But some encounter is essential to his work. Almost every instructional researcher fails to recognize the irrationality of careful specification of objectives without careful specification of the importance of the objectives. To what caprice will classroom time and effort be allocated if the teacher has no more in her blueprint than a specification of criterion behavior?

The curriculum specialist has become acquainted in small ways with educational technology. He encounters standardized tests, programmed instruction, microteaching, computerized class scheduling, and the like. These he finds sometimes helpful, sometimes aggravating. He discerns that none of them is central to the problem of *what curriculum the schools should offer.*

What help could he get from the technologist? The educational technologist, as we view him, is a specialist in routines, in standard procedures, in systematic ways of operating. Often less wise, less theoretical, even less mathematical than other educators, the technologist's special talent is that he knows that many things can be done better if a carefully developed routine is followed. The routine may involve words or it may not; it may involve numbers, "initial teaching alphabet," traffic patterns, or electronic computers. The important thing is that it will standardize an operation. The payoff may be efficiency, it may be a decrease in error, it may be doing the same work with fewer highly talented people. That is what the technologist has to offer.

What specifically does the technologist have to offer the curriculum specialist? First, he has a storehouse of languages, quantitative scales, and symbols that can aid in the specification of curricular goals, as the behaviorist has often reminded us. But, perhaps even more important, the technologist has access to methods for measuring preferences. The technologist could gather the data of which priorities are made.

Priorities are data. Priorities are indications of value or importance as seen and expressed by somebody. Like other judgment data, like objectives themselves, like ideals and standards and needs, priorities are data. Although priorities are highly subjective, they are susceptible to objective treatment. Borrowing from the methods of the social psychologist, the educational technologist could investigate the priorities held by various groups in the community and in the schools. Priorities are attitudes—we have attitude scales. Priorities are preferences—we have polls. Priorities are manifest behaviors—we have observation schedules. Priorities are documents—we have natural-language-processing routines. Stake dealt with these methodological choices at greater length in the April 1970 AERA *Review of Educational Research*.

The literal meaning of *priority* indicates "what comes first in a sequence of events," but the meaning of priority here concerns relative importance. A list of objectives implies priorities; the objectives expressed in that list have been considered to be more important than certain other unexpressed objectives. The author of that list made a crude dichotomy. A statement of priorities usually makes finer gradations of importance. Priorities usually indicate what kinds and amounts of emphasis will be given each objective.

If there were unlimited resources or if all objectives were attainable in the time available, it would not be important to recognize priorities. In every classroom it *is* important to allocate scarce resources to each of the several objectives. Of course, instructors, professors, and teachers do give priority to objectives. They do it intuitively. Perhaps they should do it more systematically.

Dorothy Fraser (1963), widely respected curriculum specialist, gave us little encouragement several years ago. Speaking for the National Committee of the NEA Project on Instruction, she recognized the criticality of *priorities*. But to the question of how to obtain priorities for a particular school she said, "There is no set of specifications . . . which can be applied to every school in the United States, just as there is no uniform prescription to determine what should be included and excluded from the school program." We cannot accept the idea that *How*-to-translate-local-objectives-into-local-programs is only a local matter. Dorothy Fraser's committee pleaded for "balance" in the curriculum but ignored the question, "How can the profession help the community see and adjust any such *balance*?" Any operationalization of "curricular balance" is a statement of priorities.

In the administration of Title III programs for educational

innovation and supplementary services, the U.S. Office of Education has paid increasing attention to "Needs Assessment." It has mandated state-by-state studies. What children need will get priority funding, is the promise. Some efforts to generate statements of state needs are being made as if *need* were a fixed and nonreactive characteristic (such as age, geographic location, or loudness). But a statement of need is the *reaction* of a person or many persons to something. To describe need is not only to describe that something but to describe the persons who see the need. People see need differently. The needs assessor has no obligation to find consensus. In fact, he is acting improperly if he does not report the diversity of viewpoints of needs. The developers of a state plan do have to find a compromise. In our opinion, Pennsylvania and Florida have done some of the best work toward a needs-assessment plan (Educational Testing Service 1965; Florida Educational Research and Development Council 1968).

James Popham, a respected instructional researcher, recognized the important need (in needs assessment) for empirical data on preferences. He equated critical needs with discrepancies between preferences of items from the UCLA Objectives Exchange and performance levels on still-to-be-constructed-or-selected National-Assessment-like criterion-referenced achievement items (see Popham and Skager 1968; Department of Elementary School Principals 1967). These discrepancies are important data for a needs-assessment study—but we object to the idea implicit in the Popham formula that the larger the discrepancy, the higher the priority. High priorities should be assigned to what people see as most critically needed. We have no satisfactory unit for directly comparing achievement discrepancies.

It would be nice if the teacher had systematic and logical procedures to translate educational objectives into teaching processes. Such a procedure would probably be sensitive to a statement of needs, an array of priorities, the ledger of educational resources, and some knowledge of probable success for each of the alternate instructional tactics. Since there is no calculus, no book of formulas, or no technological routines for deriving the best teaching tactic, we are forced to rely on experience, and intuition, and luck. We might add, the result is certainly not all bad.

But we would like it to be better. We do believe that a more careful consideration of the learning situation (against a background of research findings and experience) will give us a better basis for selecting teaching processes. One of the principal ingredients of that learning situation is priorities. We can anticipate neither a rational nor an intuitive solution to the choice of curricular pathways unless we appreciate the importance that people give to goals. What do the teachers want? What do lay leaders want? What do students want?

The technologist should help the educator decide *whose* preferences should be weighed: students', parents', citizens', national and community leaders', curriculum specialists', school administrators', or teachers'. Most people seem to think that the teachers should decide on priorities—with the expectation that the community will set them straight, if need be. But many a teacher feels he does not have the wisdom or time to decide, and he defers to textbook and syllabus writers, to college professors, or others. It is not our purpose to condemn the sources of preference that presently dictate priorities but to say that the people should know who the priority setters are and what the alternatives are. We have the technology. This could happen.

Would it bring curriculum specialists and instructional researchers into conversation? Probably not—because it would ease the burden on neither. Would an improved specification of priorities contribute to the improvement of education? We have doubts that it would. But we should find out.

Few investigators have examined empirically the relationship among values, objectives, and priorities. Maguire and Taylor are two who did. Maguire (1968) obtained teacher value-ratings of a heterogeneous set of objectives; then, from the same teachers got different expressions of the priorities that should be given to these objectives. He found that the teachers perceived the objectives in at least four dimensions: subject matter value, motivational qualities, ease of implementation, and statement (semantic) properties. In another study, Taylor and Maguire (1967) obtained value-ratings of high school biology objectives from three important groups: subject matter experts, curriculum writers, and biology teachers. The investigation found substantial agreement in group viewpoint, but with experts and teachers least alike.

Downey (1960) examined the different priorities given to sixteen general educational objectives. He found substantial differences between Canadian and U.S. respondents.

STUDY OF EDUCATIONAL PRIORITIES: A DESIGN

There are few people living in any community who are not in some way affected by the educational system within the community. How many of these people affect the educational system is another question. Our design for studying educational priorities calls first for attention to all individuals and groups in the community, both those intimately involved with the functioning of the school (that is, teachers, students) and those more remotely associated with the school (that is, the bond-issue voter). For our first collection of data we have asked high school teachers and a women's group in a small town for an expression of their priorities.

A second dimension of our design concerns the "Real-Ideal" dichotomy. Most people have ideas as to what, *ideally,* the school should be treating as important. These same people also view what the school is *actually* treating as important. The two statements of "priorities" may be quite different. We are particularly interested in any discrepancies that may exist between observed and desired priorities from each of the viewpoints (sources of data).

To explain the third dimension of our design it is necessary to consider how priorities are to be stated. We have suggested that priorities should indicate amount of importance. We could say that the importance of writing good essays is 19, but that is not very meaningful. We could say that the importance of writing good essays is 19 times greater than the importance of writing good budgets, but even that is not very meaningful. Nineteen is a very precise amount, but we do not know what it is an amount of. We do not have a meaningful scale for expressing our priorities. One way to solve this measurement problem would be to shun the use of scales and to express each and every performance objective as being simply more or less desirable than the others. We would have a preference hierarchy of goals (quite unlike Gagné's hierarchy of goals), and the teacher could work hardest at the more popular goals.

This would prove to be unworkable due to different preferences, and all persons change their preferences from time to time. Some common scales, some standard operationalizations of priorities, have to be developed. We have to specify more precisely what we mean by priority. Maguire's work (1968) has helped us raise these operational questions:

1. How much is accomplishment of this goal worth in money?
2. How much school time should be spent in pursuit of this goal?
3. If this goal is not met, how much should be spent in remediation?
4. If this goal is not met, how upset should the school people be?

While these questions fall something short of operational definitions, they do suggest that a high spot on a list of objectives or a simple indication of high priority can have different implications for different readers.

We hypothesize that people may reorder their priorities differently when asked to express them in these various ways. That is, a person may regard a particular aim of the school as a most important aim for the school to pursue. When asked to allot time to pursue that aim, knowing that not all things may be accomplished by the school in the time available, that person may not be willing to devote a great deal of time to pursuing the aim. In our present design, we look at importance as a school concern and allotment of time as a medium for the expression of priorities.

So far we have suggested various ways in which we plan to look at educational priorities. All of the preceding discussion assumes there is something to which priorities are assigned. Our design requires that we conceptualize the educational system in terms of its broad educational aims, the courses and activities it offers, and the behavioral goals or specific outcomes it seeks to foster.

Three broad educational aims, or orientations, have been identified: the *human* purpose of education, the *knowledge* purpose of education and the *career* purpose of education. Each is present in any teacher's teaching to some extent. Each purpose differs from the others to some extent. We are seeking to put priority values on these three aims of education.

At a more detailed and operational level we can identify school courses, content, and activities. Still, it is a broad umbrella, covering items as diverse as Afro-American studies and girls' intramural softball, chemistry and morality, interpersonal relations and the stamp club. It is by these subtitles that the school is most easily recognized by the public. School—by this definition—is the courses taken by students. What priorities do the courses and activities get?

There is a still more detailed and operational level. Most educational spokesmen have some rather specific behaviors they would like students to have as a result of their exposure to the system. These behavioral goals—usually subsumed under the broad aims of education but more specific than those aims—reflect desired outcomes of the educational program. The behaviors vary widely: students will respond appreciatively to good literature; the student will be able to identify three causes for the Civil War; the student will be able to write a business letter; the student will be able to get a good job. People value these abilities and skills differently. How to represent their different values is what this study of priorities is aimed at.

Figure 20:1 represents the overall design of our present studies. What we hope to learn is not so much what their priorities are but how we may communicate with them as to what their priorities are.

FIGURE 20:1. DESIGN FOR A STUDY OF
EDUCATIONAL PRIORITIES

Scale for Priorities

		Time Import		Time Import	
To which Priorities Are Given	Aims	A	D	G	J
Broad educational aims					
School courses, content,					
and activities	Courses,				
Behavioral goals	Activities	B	E	H	K
Viewpoints					
Citizens'					
Teachers'	Behavioral				
Administrators'	Goals				
Parents'					
Students'		C	F	I	L

THE TEACHER'S VIEWPOINT

Scales for Indicating Priority	Aims	A	D	G	J
Importance					
Time allotment	Courses,				
Cash allotment	Activities				
Vigor of efforts to reme-		B	E	H	K
diate					
Real—Ideal Perspective	Behavioral				
That which is observed	Goals				
That which is desired		C	F	I	L

THE CITIZEN'S VIEWPOINT

Ideal   **Real**

When we asked a pilot group of eleven teachers and eleven laymen about allocation of faculty time for the three principal aims (see figure 20:2), we found higher priority given by the laymen to vocational education. This is summarized in table 20:1. As the teachers saw it, the actual allocation now is about 30 percent, 30 percent and 40 percent, respectively.

When our scale of priorities shifted from use of time to the more general attribute, importance, we found these few teachers clearly

FIGURE 20:2. THE PRINCIPAL AIMS OF EDUCATION
AS SEEN BY RESPONDENTS

The HUMAN Purpose of Education	The KNOWLEDGE Purpose of Education	The CAREER Purpose of Education
The main responsibility of the schools should be to examine what man is—his history, his values, his work and play, his arts and his sciences, what he has accomplished and what he has failed to accomplish. The schools should give students the opportunity to be a participant in the human experience, the aesthetic and emotional experience as well as the intellectual experience.	The main responsibility of the schools should be to help young men and young women know all about the world. Each student should have maximum opportunity to understand nature, technology, commerce, the languages, the fine arts, and practical arts. Facing the knowledge explosion, the schools should help young men and women build skills for understanding—and even discovering—new knowledge.	The main responsibility of the schools should be to prepare young people for their life-work. Though most careers require training on the job and continuing education throughout life, the schools should lay the foundation for successful work. For students who will take further training in a technical and professional area, the schools should emphasize entrance requirements and preparatory skills.

saying that the knowledge purpose was the *most* important task of the schools. The laymen were evenly split on this question between the knowledge purpose and the career purpose. Although these small samples cannot be taken as representative, our hunch is still alive: that different ways of operationalizing priorities may lead to quite different school procedures.

TABLE 20:1. DIFFERENCES BETWEEN TEACHERS'
AND CITIZENS' PRIORITIES

Of the total faculty working time . . .	Teachers wanted	Citizens wanted	
	36%	20%	. . . oriented to the *Human* purpose
	33%	35%	. . . oriented to the *Knowledge* purpose
	31%	45%	. . . oriented to the *Career* purpose

Using the ideal priorities to prove importance, we found rather different rankings of courses, content areas, or activities in our small group of teachers and citizens, as illustrated in figure 20:3.

FIGURE 20:3. RANKING OF COURSES

	Teachers	Citizens
Extremely important:	Family life and sex educa-tion Forms of government Physical education and ath-letics Morality Rapid reading	Forms of government Chemistry Sociology World history Bookkeeping Rapid reading Morality
Somewhat important:	Consumer buying Sociology Bookkeeping Chemistry Public speaking World history Interpersonal relations Painting, drawing, sculpture Afro-American studies	Public speaking Physical education and ath-letics Religious history Family life and sex educa-tion Consumer buying Interpersonal relations Painting, drawing, sculpture Afro-American studies
Unimportant:	Religious history	

When the teachers were asked to allocate faculty time to these subjects, they awarded the largest blocks to chemistry, physical education and athletics, and bookkeeping and shorthand. Even with these meager results, we believe we are headed for an obvious but easily overlooked conclusion: *that the most important objectives in school will not and should not necessarily require the greatest amount of school time.*

There are three magnificent and interrelated obstacles to success-ful measurement of school priorities—at least, that is the number presently apparent to us. First of all, the conceptual scope of the task is too great; second, people are not capable of giving absolute priority information that is meaningful; and third, there is such a marvelous redundancy in a total education system that estimating the priority for any one sector is not really meaningful without knowledge of the cumulative priorities of thousands of other sectors.

We first found one obstacle that we expected to find: our teachers and citizens—not unlike our instructional researchers—have a great deal of difficulty thinking about the school curriculum as a whole. They appear to be devoid of the information needed to make judgments about the importance of the work of even a major subdivision of the curriculum, such as the science department or the athletic department. They do not know what the total effort to teach social responsibility is, and they feel most uncomfortable making even the crudest estimate of resources that might best be allocated to it. Part of the problem is that for a particular school or school district no one, including the superintendent of schools, thinks very much about the total curriculum. That conceptual realm is pretty much virgin territory. Adding to the problem is the shortage of terms and graphics that would give concrete form to the total curricular responsibility of the schools.

We were not unprepared for this finding. Just as it is too much to try to get an estimate of personal intelligence with one item, or to learn of social disadvantage with one anecdote, it is too much to try to get an idea of need for vocational emphasis with a single question. Our remedy, of course, is to ask about priorities of smaller scope—of intermediate goals of specific tasks—and hope to aggregate item responses into meaningful holistic descriptions.

The second obstacle is the difficulty of working with absolute estimates of priority. For some items we used total faculty workload to represent the total emphasis that could be allocated. For example, in a school with fifty faculty members, should the geometry course load absorb 1.2 full-time equivalents? The respondents found this task onerous. We indicated that we were primarily interested in the relative emphasis on world history versus geometry and the like, but staff time allocations was not their way to do it. In our reflections, we concluded that it might be necessary to relate all our questions to the status quo, to rely on the respondents' acquaintance with present operation: would you like to see a greater emphasis on leadership training than there is at present? We believe that the respondents would be able to handle such questions better, but the usefulness of the information would be more limited. Outsiders would have little idea of the status quo and could learn relatively little about what the staff would like the curriculum to be.

The third obstacle was the redundancy of the school curriculum. The same things are taught many times, many ways. That may be good or bad. Personal initiative is taught in public speaking, and in social studies. Reading is taught in arithmetic class as well as in reading class. Different people have different expectations as to what will be accomplished by a course, and different expectations as to the uniqueness of loss if that course is not taught. In the same course, at the same time, using the same resource allocation, the teacher can be simultaneously

1. teaching facts about the Civil War,
2. developing attitudes toward the South,
3. fostering listening skills,
4. serving as a model narrator of human events,
5. demonstrating a style of narration of human events,
6. orienting children to a particular reward schedule,
7. teaching about ethical compromise.

What does it mean to give priority to these goals if they can be accomplished simultaneously and with the same resources? Yet people do have ideas about the importance of each of them.

It is apparent to us that there is a need for ways of expressing what people want schools to be doing. *We do have priorities. What we fail to have are ways of representing them.* Each of us operates within a framework of personal preferences for each of the persons we work with. What we fail to have are suitable ways for representing those priorities. We have heard that the squeaking wheel gets oiled. We are looking for better ways of squeaking.

REFERENCES

Department of Elementary School Principals, National Education Association. *National Assessment of Educational Progress: Some Questions and Comments.* Washington, D.C.: National Education Association, 1967.

Downey, Lawrence W. "The Task of Public Education: The Perceptions of People." Chicago: University of Chicago, Midwest Administration Center, 1960.

Educational Testing Service. *A Plan for Evaluating the Quality of Educational Programs in Pennsylvania—Highlights.* Princeton, N. J.: Educational Testing Service, 1965.

Fraser, Dorothy. *Deciding What to Teach.* Washington, D.C.: National Education Association, 1963.

Maguire, Thomas O. "Value Components of Teachers' Judgments of Educational Objectives." *A-V Communication Review* (1968): 63-86.

Popham, W. James, and Skager, Rodney. "Instructional Objectives Measurement Systems." In *Progress in Evaluation Study*, Third Annual Report to the U.S. Office of Education. Los Angeles: University of California, Center for the Study of Evaluation, 1968.

Taylor, Peter A., and Maguire, Thomas O. "Perceptions of Some Objectives for a Science Curriculum." *Science Education* 51 (1967): 488-493.

21

THE DELPHI TECHNIQUE

Frederick R. Cyphert & Walter L. Gant

Most schools of education and most universities operate on the apparent assumption that persons inside the organization control its destiny. While no one can deny the influence of students, faculty, and administration on the organization's welfare and mission, it is equally fallacious to ignore the impact of persons outside the organization. Perhaps one reason why schools of education have not received the support they desire on either a moral or a fiscal level is that they have not accurately assessed the judgments made about them by others. If schools of education are to increase their effectiveness, they need to give fresh attention to the clarification and ordering of their goals.

THE DELPHI TECHNIQUE

Traditionally, the method for achieving consensus is a round table discussion among individuals who arrive at a group position. There are a number of objections to this procedure. The final position, usually a compromise, is often derived under the undue influence of certain psychological factors, such as specious persuasion by the group member with the greatest supposed authority or even merely the loudest voice, an unwillingness to abandon publicly expressed opinions, and the bandwagon effect of majority opinion. In contrast, with the Delphi Technique an attempt is made to overcome these factors by not bringing the participants together in one place and by not reporting individual opinions (Helmer 1967). This eliminates committee activity and replaces it with a carefully designed program of sequential interrogations (with questionnaires) interspersed with information and opinion feedback.

For example, a study of short-term predictions was conducted with twenty graduate business students at the University of California in Los Angeles during the fall of 1965. They were asked to forecast gross national product, defense expenditures, and fourteen other business indices. A general consensus was reached after a series of four questionnaires. Forecasts were later checked with the actual happenings. Although consensus varied greatly from what actually occurred in certain indices, predictions were better on thirteen of the sixteen items than the predictions of twenty graduate students who were not involved in the process (Pfeiffer 1968).

The Institute of Government and Public Affairs at the University of California in Los Angeles used the Delphi Technique in an attempt to generate some useful perspectives on changes in American education. The authors of the study felt that the procedure was regarded by almost all of the participants as potentially useful in educational planning at all levels (Adelson 1967). Scientific assessment of the needs, desires, and opinions of clientele was the motivation behind the use, here described, of the Delphi Technique by the School of Education at the University of Virginia.

IMPLEMENTING THE SURVEY

Sample selection involved a rather arbitrary definition of the "power structure" of the Commonwealth of Virginia in relation to the School of Education. Six major categories of persons were included: 1) the faculty of the School of Education and selected student leaders from the graduate and undergraduate populations; 2) deans, the president's cabinet, and the elected members of the university faculty senate. Off-campus elements incorporated into the sample included: 3) educators, that is, elementary and secondary school teachers and administrators who held elective office in statewide professional organizations and the deans of the state's major schools of education; 4) organizational leaders, such as the officers of the Virginia School Boards Association, the Virginia PTA, the State Council of Higher Education, and the State Board of Education; 5) persons of influence in political circles, for example, the education committees of the Virginia House and Senate, U.S. senators and representatives, the governor, and so on; and 6) leading newspaper editors and persons dealing with education in such groups as the Virginia AFL-CIO, NAACP, and chamber of commerce. It was decided to seek perspective by including a seventh group of selected teacher educators of national reputation from across the nation. The initial sample included a total of 421 persons. No person was informed of the classification which was the basis for his inclusion or of the groups and other individuals involved in the survey.

Respondents were asked to suggest prime targets on which the School of Education should concentrate its energies and resources in the next decade. Questionnaire I was returned by 68 percent of the sample and the more than 750 individual suggestions were reduced to 61 generic statements.

Questionnaire II contained a random listing of the sixty-one items with a five-point grid for rating each on a priority continuum. Questionnaire III differed from its predecessor only in that it reported both the group consensus and the respondent's prior rating for each item. Respondents were asked to re-rate all items in light of the additional information concerning group feeling. For all items where the participant wished to remain outside the consensus, he was asked to state his primary reason for so doing.

Ratings on Questionnaire III were computed to determine any changes that had occurred in the distribution of priorities. Questionnaire IV was then constructed, containing as before the mode for each item, the respondents' prior ratings, and, in addition, a list of the major "dissenting opinions." Final ratings were based upon the respondents' own values and a knowledge of majority and minority views. Final ranking of items was tabulated on the basis of 262 returns (or 62 percent of the original population). Of these, 194 had changed ratings on Questionnaire IV.

CONCLUSIONS REGARDING THE TECHNIQUE

There were several differences in the way this study applied the Delphi Technique in comparison with its use in preceding studies. First, the technique has usually been used with groups of 50 or fewer respondents rather than with the 400 involved in the present survey. Second, most participants in prior studies have felt a greater degree of expertise in the field being surveyed. Third, and perhaps most significant, the technique has generally been used to predict what *will* happen rather than to seek agreement concerning what *should* happen. Fourth, consensus in this study was defined as the mode of the distribution of ratings on each goal, whereas other studies defined consensus as the interquartile range. However, several significant generalizations concerning the Delphi Technique grew out of this experience:

1. Prospective participants must be made to feel that their response is valid so that they will take part.
2. The variation in agreement with the consensus rating on all the goals by individuals ranged from less than 20 percent to agreement with 100 percent of the consensus ratings.
3. A bogus item, which read, "Emphasizing the production of doctoral graduates who can improve the programs in schools of medicine, law, nursing, and engineering," was initially rated below average. However, when the feedback was distorted to reflect a high ranking, the participants then rated the item considerably above average, although it was not among the ten highest-ranked targets. The hypothesis that the technique can be used to mold opinion as well as to collect it was supported.
4. When respondents disagreed with the consensus rating of a goal, they tended to attribute the consensus to a group of which they were not a member.
5. Virtually all (99 percent) of the respondents' changes in opinion occurred on Questionnaire III which informed them of the first "consensus" reached by the group. With hindsight, one can seriously question the need for going beyond Questionnaire III. The university family made the greatest change in ratings throughout the study, while the off-campus educators modified their original ratings least.

In conclusion, besides giving the satisfaction of planning the future with the assistance of data, this survey made the influential persons in the commonwealth aware of the school's existence and gave them a vested interest in its future accomplishments.

REFERENCES

Adelson, Marvin. "Planning Education for the Future: Comments on a Pilot Study." *American Behavioral Scientist* 10, no. 7 (March 1967): 1-31.

Helmer, Olaf. *Analysis of the Future: The Delphi Method.* Santa Monica, Ca.: Rand Corporation, 1967.

Pfeiffer, John. *New Look at Education.* Poughkeepsie, N.Y.: Odyssey Press, 1968.

22

EDUCATIONAL EVALUATION BY ADVERSARY PROCEEDING

Thomas R. Owens

Within the last ten years the concept of educational evaluation has undergone an interesting expansion beyond that of judging the final outcomes of an endeavor to that of providing information to decision makers for planning projects, implementing them, and judging their intended and unintended effects. Much of the methodology of evaluation, however, has not kept pace with the expanded concept of its broader functions.

A frequently cited weakness of educational evaluation today is its reliance upon the psychological testing model. Such evaluations usually avoid questioning the value of the objectives of a new project or curriculum and instead focus upon judging the extent to which a project has achieved its stated objectives. Scriven and others have emphasized the need to examine critically the assumptions and objectives upon which a project is based (Scriven 1967). Unfortunately, few, if any, methods exist for judging the values of a project in terms of its benefit either to individual students or to society.

A second limitation to the psychological testing model for evaluation is that it is more suited for research, that is, the creation of new knowledge, than it is for practical decision making. For example, although one instructional strategy may be found, with certain types of students, to produce academic gains that are statistically more significant than a second instructional strategy, it does not automatically follow that the first strategy should be employed. Thus, a gap exists between empirical findings and administrative decisions to implement certain practices. A third limitation to the psychological testing model is that it tends to limit sharply the variables to be examined. Educational evaluation is seldom related directly to practical decision making because evaluation often emphasizes the easily quantifiable aspects of a project and neglects the less tangible aspects that are often more directly related to decision making. For example, the decision whether to adopt a new school curriculum is seldom based solely upon the research data related to the students' academic performance. Other variables, such as the congruence of the new curriculum with the existing school curriculum and facilities, the willingness of the school board to fund the new curriculum, and the estimated level of acceptance of the project by students, educators, and the community, must also be considered.

ADVERSARY PROCEEDING

One model that can handle the interpretation of both qualitative and quantitative information comes from the field of law. The adversary proceeding has been established as an administrative hearing process for judging the merits of a case involving opposing parties. The hearings officer sometimes serves the combined roles of judge and representative for the litigants. At other times the prosecution, defense, hearings officer, and jury may be different. The system of litigation is based on the *fight* theory, which states that "the facts in a case can best be ascertained if each side strives as hard as it can, in a keenly partisan spirit, to bring to the court's attention the evidence favorable to that side (Auerbach 1961)." Judge Jerome Frank has argued that, although this has invaluable qualities with which we cannot afford to dispense, "the partisanship of the opposing lawyers blocks the uncovering of vital evidence or leads to a presentation of vital testimony in a way that distorts it (Frank 1949, p. 81)." Frank discusses in detail some factors that strengthen and weaken the fight theory.

Some characteristics of the adversary proceedings make them more appropriate than either a criminal or civil court model would be for educational decision making. For example:
1. The rules established for handling the adversary proceedings are quite flexible.
2. Complex rules of evidence are replaced by a free evaluation of evidence based solely upon whether the evidence is considered by the hearings officer to be relevant.
3. Both parties can be required before the trial to inform the hearings officer of all relevant facts, means of proof, and names of witnesses.

4. A copy of the charges is furnished to the hearings officer and defendant before the trial and the defendant has the option of admitting in advance to certain charges and challenging others.
5. Witnesses are allowed to testify more freely and to be cross-examined.
6. Experts are often called upon to testify even before the trial.
7. Pretrial conferences of the hearings officer with both parties tend to make the trial less a battle of wits and more of a search for relevant facts.
8. In addition to the two parties involved, other interested groups may be permitted to participate.

Applications to Educational Evaluation

Adversary proceedings in educational decision making are not intended to replace existing designs for collecting and analyzing data, but to provide an alternative way of interpreting, synthesizing, and reporting evidence. At present many of the underlying assumptions, rationales, methods of data collection, or analysis of evaluation reports are allowed to pass unchallenged. The adversary system allows for the competitive consideration of an alternative proposal or at least a devil's advocate to keep the evaluation intellectually honest.

Specifically, the adversary system could be used to: explore the values of a new or existing curriculum; select new textbooks; estimate the congruence between an innovation and the existing system; reveal the different interpretations of the same data by various representatives; inform teachers, supervisors, and administrators; resolve disputes about performance contracts; and arrive at the decision to be implemented.

Exploring the values of a new or existing curriculum. A problem of most comparative evaluations is the failure to specify the theory or rationale behind the curricula and the assumptions implicit in the evaluation design. For example, a typical pre-post design, in which the measures are administered in September and May, assumes that the expected changes will occur within one school year. Actually, this may contradict the rationale of some long-term curricula intended to produce a significant change only after several years. A frank debate about the relevance of a particular curriculum to children's present or future needs, social needs, or disciplinary integrity may be a useful step before deciding whether or not it is wise to develop or implement the curriculum.

Selecting new textbooks. Rather than have a school district's text-books selected on the basis of the curriculum director's hasty choice, the popularity of the book salesman, or the advertising appeal of the publishing company, it might be useful to have a selection committee of teachers participate in an adversary hearing. Teachers who had perhaps examined alternative textbooks only cursorily could listen to extensive arguments presented for and against each alternative before reaching their verdict.

Estimating the congruence between an innovation and the existing system. Often innovations are initiated without regard to their con-sequences for the existing structure. In an adversary proceeding the evidence citing the potentially detrimental effect of an innovation on an existing system could be systematically presented and debated, and reveal potential barriers to the success of the innovation in time to avert or overcome them.

Revealing the different interpretations of the same data by various representatives. A jury could represent students, teachers, adminis-trators, parents, and the community. Although the same data might be presented to each juror, his interpretation of them might be completely different. If the interpretations were made known to the decision maker, it could improve his communication with the groups. He might also choose to include the groups in joint decisions. The implications of this process for community involvement are far reaching. From both a practical and a research point of view it would be interesting to learn what criteria and types of evidence are considered important by different groups in reaching their verdicts.

Informing teachers, supervisors, and administrators. Educators who could observe or participate in such a trial would gain new insight into the advantages and limitations of a particular topic. Recently, at an administrators' conference in California, the adversary proceed-ings were suggested as a novel way to introduce the controversies surrounding year-round school.

Resolving disputes about performance contracts. With the spread in popularity of performance contracts, by which a company is paid only for those students who reach a predetermined level guaranteed in advance by the company, disputes over the successful completion of such contracts are likely to arise. The adversary proceedings would probably resolve the dispute effectively. Undoubtedly a wide variety of evidence and expert testimony would be used.

Arriving at the decision to be implemented. The exact relationship of the adversary proceedings to the actual making of decisions could take the several forms suggested in the five uses already mentioned. The educational decision maker may, in fact, serve as the hearings officer; his verdict could be the decision itself. He might wish to share his decision-making powers with several other jurors such as representatives of the students, teachers, or community, and give each one including himself, one vote. Or the decision maker may wish simply to accept the findings of the jury as one additional piece of data, coupled with the actual evidence presented in the trial. Both types of information would then serve as inputs into his decision making.

The use of the adversary proceedings is especially relevant in implementing three evaluation models developed by Daniel Stufflebeam, Robert Stake, and Malcolm Provus. The Stufflebeam evaluation model is based upon the concept of evaluation as a process by which "to acquire and use information for making decisions associated with planning, programming, implementing, and recycling program activities (Stufflebeam 1967, p. 126)." Planning decisions are those that focus on needed improvements by specifying the domain, major goals, and specific objectives to be served. Programming or structuring decisions specify procedure, personnel facilities, budget, and time requirements for implementing planned activities. Recycling decisions include terminating, continuing, evolving, or drastically modifying activities. Of these four types of decisions, planning and recycling decisions focus more upon ends than upon means and could be profitably assisted by the thorough examination of the issues that occurs in adversary proceedings. Further discussion of this model and its relation to decision making may be found in the report by the Phi Delta Kappa National Study Committee on Evaluation (Stufflebeam 1971).

The Stake evaluation model (Stake 1967) stresses description and judgment as the essential elements of an evaluation. After describing the congruence between the intents and observations of a project, he states that judgments are made by comparing the descriptive data from one program either with some absolute standard of excellence or with some relative comparison such as data from other programs. The interpretation of such comparisons becomes more credible if they are systematically and thoroughly analyzed as they would be in adversary proceedings.

The Provus evaluation model, operating in the Pittsburgh public schools, is divided into five stages (Provus 1971). The first stage serves to assess viability and feasibility of the program design; the second to assess the installation of the program and the validity of program assumptions; the third to assess the fidelity of the operating program to the program design, and to assess the relationship between process and interim products; the fourth to compare the terminal products with the program design; and the fifth to compare the cost of the program being evaluated with that of other programs with the same goals. The adversary system would appear to be a feasible strategy for any of the five stages.

A TRIAL RUN IN HAWAII

After several meetings to discuss the potential of adversary proceedings for educational evaluation, to which a lawyer and several consultants were invited, a decision was made by a group of curriculum specialists, teachers, and evaluators from the Hawaii Curriculum Center at the University of Hawaii to hold such a hearing. The Hawaii Curriculum Center was formed to develop new curricula and to field test and evaluate selected curricula developed in other parts of the country. The hearing, held in February 1970, was to explore the technique of a modified judicial model, the administrative adversary hearing, as an aid to curriculum evaluation. The focus was on exploring the technique rather than on the substantive concern, so a hypothetical issue was used. The hearing was to decide whether the curriculum *Man: A Course of Study,* developed by the Educational Development Center in Massachusetts, should be adopted for the public schools in Hawaii.

The chairman of the Social Science department at the University Laboratory School, who had had extensive experience in teaching and evaluating this course was selected to present the case for the adoption of the curriculum. The former chairman of that department, who had also taught and evaluated the course, presented the case for its rejection. An experienced curriculum planner and administrator at the Center, who had formerly been the Director of Research for the Hawaii Department of Education, served as the hearings officer. Three judges were appointed for this hearing: a public school sixth grade social studies teacher who had never taught the curriculum, the state Department of Education's program specialist in social studies, and a university evaluation officer. I served as a special assistant to the hearings officer to obtain feedback on the experimental use of the hearing for curriculum evaluation. Approximately forty members of the University faculty and the state Department of Education accepted an open invitation to observe and comment upon the hearing.

The hearing officer organized the pretrial conferences with the defense and prosecution, established flexible rules of operation, required that a written outline of the arguments against the adoption of the curriculum be given to the defense and to himself before the hearing, conducted the hearing, ruled on the admissibility of evidence and the propriety and relevance of questions if objections were raised by either party, limited the hearing to two hours, and specified which points were in contention at any time during the hearing.

Several weeks of part-time work were involved in the preparation of the case by the defense and prosecution, both of whom had had some law school training. Both felt that they did not have enough time to prepare their cases properly, but were persuaded to do their best within the two weeks allotted.

The agenda for the hearing contained the following items:

1. A call to order, review of procedures, and introduction of participants by the hearings officer.

2. Technical instructions to the jury by the special assistant to the hearings officer. These instructions stated that, since this was the first time an adversary hearing had been attempted as part of a curriculum evaluation, a written statement was desired after the hearing summarizing the separate verdicts based upon the evidence presented at the hearing. Their evaluation of the hearing itself was also requested.

3. Recommendation for the adoption of the curriculum with background and description of the course (including excerpts from a tape-recorded talk by Jerome Bruner, who was instrumental in the development of the curriculum), by the defense.

4. The introduction and main points in the case against the adoption of the curriculum into the public schools of Hawaii presented by the prosecution. The main points of the prosecution's argument were:

   A. The rationale for including the course in the social studies program was weak: it was irrelevant to the goals of democratic citizenship; it failed to meet the minimum coverage required by the state for the social studies program; and it bore no relationship to the Hawaii state curriculum program in social studies.

    B. The theoretical foundation of the curriculum was dubious: its ethology lacked theoretic structure; its anthropological notions had not demonstrated analytical power *vis-à-vis* contemporary, large-scale social phenomena; its conjunction of animal and human studies, and the simplistic notions it taught, were bound to implant theoretical confusion; its conceptions of structural and personal knowledge were at war with each other; its content was utterly remote from the experience of Hawaiian children; its notion that the curriculum materials enabled the children to empathize with strange cultural behavior was probably naive.

    C. The objectives of the curriculum are nebulous in the extreme, and cannot be specified in terms of student performance. Hence the curriculum cannot be evaluated.

    D. Practical considerations, such as the bizarre subject matter, the lack of durability, and expense of the materials, made the curriculum's successful implementation doubtful.

5. Points conceded by the defense. These were points about the bizarre subject matter and the expensive materials.

6. Point by point charges by the prosecution. After each charge was presented there was a rebuttal by the defense. Several witnesses, including a curriculum theorist and a social studies teacher at the university, were called to testify.

7. After each rebuttal there was an opportunity for direct questions by the prosecution to the defense and/or his witnesses. Redirected questions to the witnesses by the defense, or a final response by the defense if no witnesses were called were allowed.

8. Summaries by the prosecution and by the defense.

9. Report by the three jurors and an open discussion with the audience on the process of the case.

10. Adjournment by the hearings officer.

Reactions to the Hearings

A great deal of excitement was generated by the proceedings. The consensus of the participants and audience was that the two hours of hearings had served as an excellent way of learning the many facets of a new curriculum. The majority felt that two hours was insufficient time in which to reach a verdict. Suggestions were made to: reduce the scope of the points to be covered in any single hearing; reduce the debate between the prosecution and defense and make the hearing less dominated by personalities; rely more upon documents, printed evaluation data, and the testimony of witnesses; have the defense's argument in writing before the hearing; open the hearing to points of view expressed by the audience; lengthen the duration of the hearing or have several short hearings each on a different aspect of the issue; be more flexible in deviating from established procedures when the situation warrants; and have the actual decision makers participate actively in the hearings rather than simply review the jury's verdict.

At the heart of the discussion after the hearing was whether the procedure should be used to delve into the facts and produce new information about the issue or whether it should serve as the decision-making mechanism itself. Opinion on this question was split. The disadvantage seen in using the hearing as the decision-making mechanism itself is that some factors that the decision maker may need to consider before reaching a decision may not be touched upon in the hearing. If the hearing were to be used as a decision-making mechanism, however, it would seem appropriate for the decision maker to serve as hearing officer and/or judge.

POTENTIAL LIMITATIONS

Although the adversary proceeding has considerable potential as one strategy for educational evaluation, there are several possible limitations that need to be considered. The first is the potential entanglement in legal technicalities. A second and bigger danger in using the adversary system is the jury's tendency to become more influenced by the rhetoric of the prosecution, defense, or expert witnesses than by the substantive data. Associated with this is the personal identification of the prosecution and defense with the educational issue being argued. This could lead to a feeling that an individual is on trial rather than an educational issue. In a few circumstances, however, the issue may be the professional accountability of an individual or of an entire project staff. A third limitation is the amount of time required to adequately prepare and conduct such a hearing. But several weeks of preparation and hearings may be reasonable compared with the alternative of hastily made decisions that prove unwise in the future because relevant factors were not considered.

The state program specialist in social studies who served as one of the jurors in the hearing summarized her reactions to the hearing:

> I believe the adversary hearing is a meaningful way to assist in making curriculum decisions. Perhaps it is a more meaningful experience for curriculum and program specialists who must consider the substantive merits of the curriculum as primary, and other more practical considerations in implementation as secondary, concerns. I say this because in areas such as the rational and theoretical basis of a curriculum, such a hearing can bring together much of what [a] specialist [may] have heard or read at various times and put things in a total perspective, giving due emphasis to various aspects of the curriculum. For decision makers who must consider fiscal and other constraints, this might be a valuable experience, especially if these considerations are part of the hearing.

The experimental use of the adversary proceedings in Hawaii as one strategy for educational evaluation and decision making has indicated a strong potential for the method. It is hoped that this strategy will be creatively applied to other educational decision-making situations in other parts of the country and the results reported so that a variation of procedures might be documented and used more widely.

FIGURE 22:1. APPLICATIONS AND DIMENSIONS OF
THE ADVERSARY PROCEEDINGS

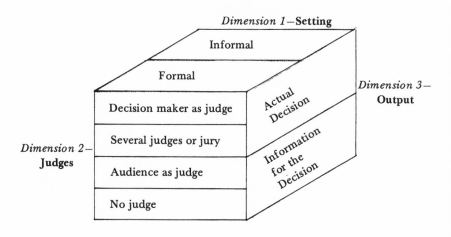

The cube illustrated in figure 22:1 might suggest new applications of the adversary proceedings. Along the first dimension of setting, the hearings could range from informal to highly structured and formal. Usually this would depend upon the subject under consideration and the use to which the verdict might be put. The second dimension deals with the nature of the judges involved in the hearing. At least four possibilities exist. The decision maker, for instance a district superintendent, could serve as the sole judge, or several judges or a jury could participate. In a less formal setting, the entire audience might vote on an issue such as the selection of a new textbook. On occasions meant mainly to be informational, it might be appropriate not to have a judge. The third dimension considers the output of the adversary proceedings. The output could serve to provide only information for a future decision or could result in the actual decision.

FOOTNOTE

The author wishes to express appreciation to Dr. Egon Guba, Associate Dean of the College of Education at Indiana University, for his critique of an earlier draft of this paper, which was presented at the American Educational Research Association Convention in February 1971.

REFERENCES

Auerbach, C.; Garrison, L. K.; Hurst, W.; and Mermin, S. "The Adversary System." In *The Legal Process.* San Francisco: Chandler, 1961.

Frank, J. N. *Courts on Trial.* Princeton, N. J.: Princeton University Press, 1949.

Provus, Malcolm. *Discrepancy Evaluation.* Berkeley, Ca.: McCutchan, 1971.

Scriven, Michael. "The Methodology of Evaluation." In *Perspectives of Curriculum Evaluation,* edited by R. E. Stake. Chicago: Rand McNally, 1967.

Stake, R. E. "The Countenance of Educational Evaluation." *Teachers College Record* 68 (April 1967): 523-540.

Stufflebeam, Daniel. "The Use and Abuse of Evaluation in Title III." *Theory into Practice* 6 (June 1967): 126-133.

Stufflebeam, D.; Foley, W.; Gephart, W.; Guba, E.; Hammond, R.; Merriman, H.; and Provus, M. *Educational Evaluation and Decision Making.* Itasca, Ill.: Peacock, 1971.

23

EVALUATION AND THE PUBLIC

Dennis D. Gooler

Most administrators have a pretty good sense of what is going on in the system they are responsible for. Survival demands a sensitive finger on the pulse of the system. Not all of the people affected by or involved in an educational system, however, share the same sense of what is going on. Does that matter?

There are some interesting pressures developing for the establishment of community. Such pressures are certainly not new, but the present emphasis on smallness and togetherness appears to be springing from a revulsion toward bigness and impersonality, a longing for some sense of control while in the midst of things and ideas of a size that seems to mitigate against anyone's being able to control anything that affects him. Americans formed large urban areas for the opportunities and advantages of economy, but are now questioning the trade offs they have made in achieving that economy. And so we have the establishment of New Towns, most of which are planned for active communities, so that the citizenry may govern itself.

One of the obvious places for renewed involvement of citizens is in one of the most pervasive agencies in any community: the educating agency. This agency serves various public groups, each of whom would have the school accomplish some goals (not always the same), using some particular procedures (about which there is often disagreement), with a minimum of unnecessary public expenditure (here there is general agreement). There is growing thought that these things cannot be adequately accomplished without the public's considerable involvement in policy formulation.

The purpose of increased involvement is associated with the political clout obtained from being involved. But one of the principles underlying widespread involvement has to do with our understanding of the systems that govern us. If we understand, we are in a better position to make wise decisions, or to respond more adequately to decisions that are made for us. It is difficult to control what is not understood. And it is important from the viewpoint of a quest for quality of life that we are able to feel we are a part of the process of control. Evaluation can be thought of as a set of procedures designed to provide a capacity for greater understanding.

What follows is a set of ideas about publics, and understanding, and involvement. The ideas are based on a set of assumptions that not everyone will be willing to accept as worthwhile or possible, or desirable. The major assumptions of my thesis are that: it is possible and desirable for the public to understand more thoroughly what goes on in formal educating institutions; it is possible and desirable for the public to have clear and reasonable access to the policy-making processes; increased involvement of people in the organizing and implementing of educational endeavors is in itself desirable, even if inefficiency should ensue; some people *would* like to be more involved in their schools, if they knew how; evaluation practices might be useful in accomplishing these purposes.

DISCLOSURE AND UNDERSTANDING

Historically, many methods have been used by educational agencies to inform people about what happens in schools: report cards, parent-teacher conferences, public relations newsletters, evaluation reports, research studies. Most efforts have been random and incomplete. It remains difficult for any member of the public to understand the educating system in all its complexity. Evaluation is a technique designed to help.

What must each of the public groups do with these various efforts to help them understand the education situation? It appears that any group would have to perform four tasks with the kinds of information that might be obtained. First, an individual or a group must actively *seek* the data it needs to understand an education situation. There is little to suggest that appropriate useful data are automatically forthcoming to everyone. It is true that report cards come home, and that conferences are held. But the average consumer has little opportunity to come across research data, or the data supplied by national efforts.

Second, each interested public group must learn to *synthesize* the data obtained from a variety of sources. There appear to be few agencies, organizations, or methodologies that will do this. This represents a most difficult task. It takes a sophisticated individual to put together the often disparate findings from a variety of sources, so that the results make some sense.

Third, the public must learn to *fill in the gaps* that are clearly present in existing data. Not all the questions will be answered by the data. A consumer of information must learn how to ask questions, and must learn of whom to ask them. This is no easy task.

Fourth, it appears that each group must learn how to *judge* the school on the basis of the information it has. Judgment is difficult even when *all* the facts are known, but increasingly difficult when large gaps exist. Yet, if any public group is to exercise effective involvement in the school system, it must be able to make judgments, and to determine how to act upon those judgments.

These tasks are formidable indeed. It is easy to understand why most public groups simply do not try to understand the education system.

Disclosure is a central issue in any society. Those who interact must have some sense of what the others are about. Disclosure clearly centers about the exchange of information. The assumption is that some use will be made of this information, and further, it is assumed that more adequate disclosure will yield a more complete understanding of the situation. The disclosure thought of here is defined in part by the kind of information traditionally made available to people, but the idea must be expanded to the development of indicators that will enable any of the various public groups to understand where the school stands on the goals that the public deems desirable. A broadened notion of disclosure would enable us to gain greater insight into the presence or absence in the educational situation of those principles and procedures someone thinks should be found in the system.

Potency is a human necessity. It is essential for every human to feel an ability to control some aspects of his own destiny. Schooling systems, particularly because of their pervasive nature, are prime institutions for either limiting or expanding opportunities for individuals to exercise potency. Schools are complex, affording many entry points for people to exercise some control. That same complexity can function as a shield, however, such that no one can determine how to get a "handle" on the system.

The effectiveness of any public control over education systems is limited by the amount and kind of information about the system available to the public. I suggest that the various public groups need to have information about what the school is doing, how well it is doing it, who is receiving what, and what it is costing the public to support the system. Without this information the public will not know how to deal with the institutions, its potency will not be felt, and the schools may not be required to attend the needs and values of the public.

Historically, schools have been controlled by a small number of kinds of people, people who *were* able to get a handle on the system. If indicators of the work of the schools were made available to other public groups in a form they could understand, those groups could more effectively control the system that affects their lives in so many ways.

Not only must people feel a sense of potency, but they must also possess the capacity for initiative—they must see a way in which their potency can be translated into action. Education systems can enhance feelings of potency while precluding the capacity for initiative. Parents are often invited to visit schools, but once there, have little idea of what to look for, what questions to ask, what demands to make. Students feel a sense of power, but do not know how and where to exercise it. Increased information may be a necessary, if not sufficient, condition for understanding the nature of schooling, and for enhancing the capacity for initiative.

In that light, it is argued that if various public groups were able to understand how well the school is achieving high priority goals, these groups might have a better handle on the educating system. Policies and procedures can be developed so that specific public groups *can* understand what the educating system is doing about the purposes and goals that the public views as desirable.

Finally, it is argued that disclosure in education, as in other situations, is a two-way process. The school must learn how to tell its story as completely as possible, and in a manner understandable to diverse public groups. But so also must the society more adequately disclose its needs, values, and priorities to the educating system. This cooperative disclosure may culminate in more satisfactory cooperative policy making. Various public groups may be able to exercise a greater role in policy making, because they understand what the present school system is about, and in what directions it is moving. Conversely, the school may be able to make sounder decisions with information about what its constituency regards as important. Equally possible is a rise in the conflict between the school and the community. The community may protest vigorously when it learns more about its schools. The school may refuse to meet particular community needs. In either case, it would appear that increased disclosure will lead *away* from unilateral policy making.

Disclosure of What?

A plea for greater disclosure cannot be made without some indication of what is to be disclosed. The case for increased disclosure is built on the assumption that greater amounts and kinds of information will lead to a better understanding. Traditionally, the public receives a small amount of information, primarily directed at the outcomes of learning and matters concerning the administration or the facilities. Are alternatives or additions needed?

What is being done? It is reasonable to begin by asking what the school does. An answer requires more than a description of the outcomes of an educational program. Full disclosure of what is being done requires disclosure about what is going into the educating system. What are the skills and resources made available to those in the educating system? What kinds of students do we have in our schools? What are they able to do? What are they not able to do? What is the profile of our faculty and our administrators? What kinds of inputs do community members make? A list of questions about inputs could go on considerably longer. The point is that the nature of any educational enterprise is determined in part by the nature of its input. Those who wish to exercise some control over the educating system must have an understanding of the nature of the input.

In addition, disclosure must be made about the *processes* of education. That is, what kinds of activities are engaged in? How do the attributes of individuals in the program interact with the attributes of the school, or school district? How do students learn in this educational system? How are the inputs processed? Questions of this nature require disclosure about pedagogical theories, relationships among students, and among faculty and students, and so on. A study of educational processes is an important one, and one that is seldom open to those public groups interested in education.

Outcomes. Outcomes continue to be significant. The public must understand what the outcomes resulting from the educational process are. But it might be emphasized that disclosure requires disclosure, not just about certain cognitive outcomes, but about attitudinal outcomes, and the effects of various outcomes on other people and other institutions. Disclosure demands that the unintended, as well as the intended, be described and that the description of outcomes be made in many different ways. For some, reporting on the results of a standardized reading test constitutes a meaningful set of data. For others, standardized reading test results have little meaning. Perhaps the number of books going in and out of the library has meaning. Or perhaps an indicator of the interest that a student shows in reading while he is at home is important. The point is simply that disclosure may require a description of input, processes, and outcomes, rendered in many different ways.

How well is it being done? It is one thing to talk about what is being done and another to talk about how well it is being done. Questions of "how well" entail descriptions of effectiveness and efficiency. Full disclosure requires an accounting of how effectively goals are being achieved. Many members of the public will want to know whether their tax dollars are being spent in the most effective way possible. They will want to know if the school is wisely allocating its resources to those goals and endeavors that really matter.

The public will want to know about the effectiveness of the goal selection processes in the school. How well things are being done may be related to how well goals are being selected. Are there alternative goals for alternative needs, interests, and capabilities? Can any public see the goals it desires being perceived as important in the school? With what effectiveness are the goals being met? The question of how well something is being done is a question of standards. Individuals will have particular standards for the educational enterprise, and they will determine how well the school is doing its job by determining the extent to which those standards are being met. *How well* is both an economic and a social question. Disclosure must aim at describing how well things are being done.

Who gains or loses what? Because there are many kinds of people involved in and affected by education, it is reasonable to speculate that not all of those people will win all of the time. Disclosure should seek to describe as accurately as possible what is being gained and what is being lost, and by whom.

This is a particularly difficult task for the school to undertake. Disclosure of this kind almost insures that certain public groups will become more alienated or more distraught with the schools. However, if these groups come to understand just what is being lost and what is being gained, they will have greater opportunity to exercise the kind of initiative that will either continue to enhance or correct the present state of affairs.

Schooling has theoretically been thought of by many as an enterprise in which everyone wins. When there was a consensus on the goals of education this was particularly true. However, it now appears that there is a substantial portion of the population that is using schools for purposes of their own, not necessarily the purposes which some had originally intended for the schools. The question of who gains and who loses thus grows in importance.

What does it cost? The question of cost pervades all the previous questions. It is unlikely that a system that produces good results, yet is financially impossible to support, will survive. The public wants to know what it costs to run its education enterprise, and whether it is getting the maximum profit from its dollars. It is going to want to know whether instructional technique A provides a greater benefit for the dollars than does instructional product or process B. These are extremely difficult questions to answer. Extensive work has begun on cost-effectiveness ratios, and other means of understanding the financial aspects of education, but we have a long way to go.

Disclosure, if it is to have any usefulness or credibility, will need to take the cost factor into account. Ways must be devised so that each of the various public groups can understand the economic situation as a part of the educational enterprise.

A VEHICLE FOR DISCLOSURE

There are undoubtedly a variety of ways in which greater disclosure between the school and the public could be achieved. What follows is a description of one possible vehicle for disclosure.

A Public Education Information Agency

It is proposed that an intermediate agency be established to facilitate two-way information exchange, and to monitor the subsequent implications of this exchange for both schools and multiple publics. The primary intent of this agency would be to develop in educators and the public skills needed for information gathering and interpretation. Thus, the agency's role would be to aid the public in understanding its own needs in relation to the school's program, to aid the schools in dispensing information that is helpful to various public groups, and to aid the schools in interpreting responses from the public, as well as helping them assess its various priorities. What is involved is the exchange of evaluation information. The agency must be independent, but might reasonably be situated in an existing institution. It will be crucial for such an agency to establish credibility and rapport with both the school and the community. Therefore, the choice of its situation is highly critical for its success.

The word *agency* often conjures up images of yet another bureaucracy. Such an interpretation is not intended. By agency, I mean a series of functions to be performed, by someone somewhere. *Agency* is merely used here to signify a process. Nonetheless, in some instances the more traditional notion of agency might describe the most efficient way to accomplish the purposes.

The purposes of the agency, wherever it might be physically situated, would be to make the schools and their communities mutually comprehensible, able to seek and use new data, and to understand the role of parents.

Mutual comprehension. Often, members of the public affected by educational decisions lack the legal or technical vocabulary to understand the education news they receive. For example, when a bill with important implications for local education is proposed, legal jargon often prevents the lay person from understanding its consequences. When teachers tell parents their child's achievement scores, parents are unsure what the significance is, whether these scores reflect badly upon the school or individual child, and what they might do to improve matters. When school boards make decisions about resource allocations, parents often cannot penetrate the jargon to understand the implications of the choices being made.

The agency would assist the lay person in translating these various "languages" into terms he could understand. This would be done through assistance in acquiring background information, analyzing ambiguities, considering possible consequences, or examining implications. The agency's role would not consist solely in translating information for the public; it would also train them to do it for themselves.

Likewise, school people are often unsure how to interpret information they have about the people who make up the community they serve. What do the ethnic backgrounds, voting patterns, occupational clusters, or value differences imply for the educator? The agency's role would be in giving schoolmen the skills to translate available data about various public groups into implications for educational decision making.

New data. Community members at all levels lack adequate information about their schools. The agency would increase their capacity to obtain such information by helping to answer the following questions:

What are the sources of information (local media, local educational leaders, national media with good educational coverage, such as the *Saturday Review,* school board members, lay advisory committees, reformers in education)?

What are the questions to ask (about determining curriculum, about appropriating and allocating funds, about hiring and removing teachers, principals, and supervisors, about policy plans for the future)?

Where should these questions be asked (at school board meetings, at small discussion groups of concerned community and school members, in letters to the editor, on local television forums)?

How may new data sources be created (requesting more educational coverage from local media, creating a school-community information exchange board, holding open forums on educational issues)?

What are some important skills in gathering new kinds of information about schools (observation techniques, surveys and interviews, development of multiple criteria and indicators for a variety of educational goals)?

Likewise, schoolmen need new tools for assessing the stances of the public. Much conventional wisdom about the goals of parents for their children turns out to be based on faulty assumptions when closer communication is achieved. The agency would assist school people to answer the above questions when gathering information from and about the public.

Using data. Once parents have gathered data from relevant sources and have developed new sources, and once they understand and can interpret the data, they must use the data so that they may have a positive effect upon educational decision making. To do so, they need decision making and political strategies. Assisting in the acquiring of these strategies is another important purpose of the agency.

The use of data includes:

Formulating intentions (how can values, concerns, ideas about education be formulated into practical educational programs?);

Clarifying goals (distinguishing between the problem and its symptoms; dealing with root issues rather than with peripheral concerns or transitory crises);

Determining priorities (improving reading scores, emphasizing affective areas such as self-concept, ego development, values, attitudes, aspirations, providing an "action-rich" environment; equipping children for competition and survival in adult life);

Anticipating and projecting consequences of action on behalf of these goals (what might be the unintended consequences? Would alternatives serve better?);

Discovering the points of leverage in the educational bureaucracy (where and how to make their voices heard).

Parents' role. Although the American school system is based upon the notion of lay influence through the school board, few parents, especially the poor, really understand what the schools are trying to do or how the parents might help. One purpose of the agency would be to increase the parents' capacity to contribute to and be a part of their children's education by: encouraging activities at home that would complement and support the children's growth and development; becoming involved in some way as a resource person for the school; sharing information with teachers about the children's capabilities, interests, and problems.

These purposes represent a substantial range of activities. The role of evaluation is evident in most of them. The establishment of such an agency would be instrumental in calling attention to alternative kinds of evaluation strategies.

It is impossible to describe exactly how the agency would be organized or to detail its specific procedures. These matters will vary with locale, context, and the state of existing relations between the school and community, and should be determined largely by the community. The agency might perform a number of functions in a variety of settings.

Achievement tests. Standard achievement tests are given throughout the district upon the opening of the school session. The test results are not generally made available to parents except upon special request. The agency would help parents obtain and decipher test scores. It would help parents formulate questions to ask of school officials, about the interpretation of the results and the school's use of this information.

Parent conferences. Parent conferences are held twice a year. This is the only time parents visit the school or discuss their children with the teachers. Many feel inhibited at these conferences and doubt that much useful information is shared. The agency would help parents

develop questions to ask the teachers about their children's achievement, feelings about school, relationships with others. It would help
parents identify the kinds of information useful to the teacher and
might suggest a format for sharing such information.

Referenda. The voters must decide whether to approve a bond issue
for the school. The agency would assist parents and community
people to translate the language of the bill, to ask the right questions
about the request for money, and to examine the future consequences of such a commitment.

Curricula. A segment of the community is discontented with a
particular part of the curriculum and wants to protest its continua-
tion. The agency would help the parents develop a method of
inquiring into the issue and of checking the reliability and validity of
their own information. It would suggest procedures for entering the
complaint and would help define alternatives that might be offered.

Tracking criteria. Students are tracked by counselors and teachers,
but the criteria for selection are not made public, nor are the benefits
of the policy evaluated. The agency will assist parents in asking for
pertinent information and in assessing its relevance. Data concerning
tracking and an analysis of its possible consequences will be provided
to the public.

Qualifications. There is community concern about the adequacy of
the teaching staff. The agency would help teachers report on their
own successes and failures. It would help parents become more
tolerant of some inadequacies, less tolerant of others.

Special programs. The school is uncertain about a new special program. The agency would assist the school in feeling the pulse of the
community; in identifying pockets of resistance and support. It
would help the parents articulate their points of view about the
consequences they would desire from such a program.

Resources. The school has become aware that the community is a
vast sea of resources but is unsure how to tap the talent. The
agency would help set up the means of dialogue whereby needs could
be matched with resources.

Student opinion. Students are convinced that the school should be
dealing with their own life styles and the nature of the society in

which they live. The agency would help the students articulate their case, and would suggest whom they should contact, in what form, and when.

Grades. Schools issue report cards and parents typically treat them as objective assessments of their children's performance. The problems of grading, the meaning of grades and their usefulness will be explained. Alternatives to current practice will be described.

Reform. Reformers within the district are pushing for open elementary schools. The agency will assist parents in assessing such programs, comparing the objectives and known effects with the parent's goals, and putting them into comparative perspective by examining alternatives.

Implications

If such an agency were to become a reality, school personnel would need to consider the collection of evaluation data on a broad range of topics. School administrators would need to become much more adept at translating what the school does into languages comprehensible to a variety of people. Such demands could have implications for school staffing and resource allocation.

The public also would assume new responsibilities. It might no longer be feasible to argue that the school does not tell what it does, and is therefore not to be supported. There might be increased responsibilities for making choices. Presently, most members of the public do not need to make many choices about their schools. More disclosure may require more and harder choices.

It is reasonable to question whether the public or schools really *want* to know more about each other. I do not know how many people do want to know more. Some people would benefit from less evaluation information. Openness may breed conflict. The concepts of Reich's "Consciousness III," Ocean Hill—Brownsville community's decision making, Perrone's "Parents as Partners," and the public's growing concern for accountability seem to indicate a growing awareness among public groups of their rights—their educational rights—and the desire of these groups to participate and have an impact on the educational decision making process. Not all people possess that desire.

There are also some hard questions to be raised about our capacity to help people translate information. Even the experts often have difficulty knowing what to ask and when, and how to interpret the replies.

Despite these and a host of other problems, the agency described above promises to increase our understanding of the school and its role in society. The idea of the agency further underscores a fundamental belief in public participation in government. It should be tried. Evaluation, I believe, is a way of thinking, a social process. The administrator who regards evaluation in this frame of reference should feel less threatened and more receptive to the idea of disclosure.

FOOTNOTE

Portions of the section *A Vehicle for Disclosure* are taken from an internally-circulated draft working paper entitled "A Capacity for Choice: Toward Enlightened Participation in Education." My thanks to Clem Chow, Tom Corcoran, Connie Leean, and Penny Richardson, colleagues at The Educational Policy Research Center, Syracuse University.

24

GOAL-FREE EVALUATION

Michael Scriven

Suppose the client is an agency that wishes to get an independent evaluation of a project done under contract. To illustrate the radical approach to which the title refers, consider the goal-free evaluator at his first interview with the client.

IN THE SUMMATIVE CONTEXT

Client: Well, we're very glad you were able to take this on for us. We consider this program in reading for the disadvantaged to be one of the most important we have ever funded. I expect you'ld like to get together with the project staff as soon as possible—the director is here now—and of course, there's quite a collection of documents covering the background of the project that you'll need. We've assembled a set of these for you to take back with you tonight.

Goal-Free Evaluator: Thanks, but I think I'll pass on meeting the staff and on the materials. I *will* have my secretary get in touch with the director soon, though, if you can give me the phone numbers.

Client: You mean you're planning to see them *later*? But you've got so little time—we thought that bringing the director in would really speed things up. Maybe you'd *better* see him—I'm afraid he'll be pretty upset about making the trip for nothing. Besides, he's understandably nervous about the whole evaluation. I think his team is worried that you won't really appreciate their approach unless you spend a good deal of time with them.

Evaluator: Unfortunately, I can't *both* evaluate their achievements with reasonable objectivity and also go through a lengthy indoctrination session with them.

Client: Well, surely you want to know what they are trying to do—what's distinctive about their approach?

Evaluator: I already know more than I need to know about their goals—teaching reading to disadvantaged youngsters, right?

Client: But that's so vague—why, they developed their own instruments, and a *very* detailed curriculum. You can't cut yourself off from *that*! Otherwise, you'll finish up criticizing them for failing to do what they never tried to do. I can't let you do that. In fact, I'm getting a little nervous about letting you go any further with the whole thing. Aren't you going to see them *at all*? You're proposing to evaluate a $3 million project without even *looking* at it?

Evaluator: As far as possible, yes. Of course, I'm handicapped by being brought in so late and under a tight deadline, so I may have to make some compromises. On the general issue, I think you're suffering from some misconception about evaluation. You're used to the rather cozy relationship which often—in my view—contaminates the objectivity of the evaluator. You should think about the evaluation of drugs by the double-blind approach . . .

Client: But even there, the evaluator has to know the intended effect of the drug in order to set up the tests. In the educational field, it's much harder to pin down goals and that's where you'll *have* to get together with the developers.

Evaluator: The drug evaluator and the educational evaluator do not even have to know the *direction* of the intended effect, stated in very general terms, let alone the intended extent of success. It's the evaluator's job to *find out* what effects the drug has, and to assess them. If he or she is told in which direction to look, that's a handy hint but it's potentially prejudicial. One of the evaluator's most useful contributions may be to reconceptualize the effects, rather than to regurgitate the experimenter's conception of them.

Client: This is too far-out altogether. What are you suggesting the evaluator do—test for effects on every possible variable? He can't do that.

Evaluator: Oh, but he has to do that *anyway*. I'm not adding to his burden. How do you suppose he picks up side effects? Asks the experimenter for a list? That *would* be cozy. It's the evaluator's job to look out for effects the experimenter (or producer, etc.) *did not expect or notice*. The so-called side effects, whether good or bad, often wholly determine the outcome of the evaluation. It's absolutely irrelevant to the evaluator whether these are side or main effects: that language refers to the *intentions* of the producer and the evaluator isn't evaluating intentions but *achievements*. In fact, it's risky to hear even general descriptions of the intentions, because it focuses your attention away from the side effects and tends to make you overlook or down-weight them.

Client: You still haven't answered the *practical* question. You can't test for all possible effects. So this posture is absurd. It's much more useful to tell the producer how well he's achieved what he set out to achieve.

Evaluator: The producer undoubtedly set out to do something really worthwhile in education. That's the really significant formulation of his goals and it's to that formulation the evaluator addresses himself, if to any. There's also a highly particularized description of the goals—or there should be—and the producer may need some technical help in deciding whether he got there, but that certainly isn't what *you*, as the dispenser of taxpayer's funds, need to know. You need to know if the money was wasted or well-spent, etc.

Client: Look, I already *had* advice on the goals. That's what my advisory panel tells me when it recommends which proposal to fund. What I'm paying *you* for is to judge success, not legitimacy of the direction of effort.

Evaluator: Unfortunately for that way of dividing the pie, your panel couldn't tell what *configuration* of *actual* effects would result, and what that would be worth, and that's what I'm here to assess. Moreover, your panel is just part of the whole process that led to this product. They're not immune to criticism, nor are you, and nor is the producer. Nor am I. Right now, you have—with assistance—produced something, and I am going to try to determine whether it has any merit. When I've produced my evaluation, you can switch roles and evaluate *that*—or get someone else to do so. But it's neither possible nor proper for an evaluator to get by without assessing the *merits* of what has been done, not just its consonance with what *someone else* thought was meritorious. It isn't proper because it's passing the buck, dodging the issue, or one of them. It isn't possible because it's almost certain that no one else *has* laid down the merits of what has *actually* happened. It's very unlikely, you'll agree, that the producer has achieved exactly the original goals, without shortfall, overrun or side effects. So—unless you want to abrogate the contract we have just signed—you really have to face the fact that I shall be passing on the *merits* of whatever has been done—as well as determining exactly what that is.

Client: I'm thinking of at least getting someone else in to do it too—someone with a less peculiar notion of evaluation.

Evaluator: I certainly hope you do. There's very little evidence about the interjudge reliability of evaluators. I would of course cooperate fully in any such arrangement by refraining from any communication whatsoever with the other evaluator.

Client: I'm beginning to get the feeling you get paid rather well for speaking to no one. Will you kindly explain how you're going to check on all variables? Or are you going to take advantage of the fact that I have told you it's a reading program—I'm beginning to feel that I let slip some classified information. What's your idea of an ideal evaluation situation—one where you don't know what you're evaluating?

Evaluator: In evaluation, blind is beautiful. Remember that Justice herself is blind, and good medical research is double blind. The educational evaluator is severely handicapped by the impossibility of double-blind conditions in most educational contexts. But he or she must still work very hard at keeping out prejudicial information. You can't do an evaluation without knowing what it is you're supposed to evaluate—the treatment—but you do not need or want to know what it's supposed to do. You've already told me too much in that direction. I still need to know some things about the nature of the treatment itself, and I'll find those out from the director, via my secretary, who can filter out surplus data on intentions, and so on, before relaying it to me. *That data on the treatment is what cuts the problem down to size.* I have the knowledge about probable or possible effects of treatments like that, from the research and evaluation literature and from my experience, that enables me to avoid the necessity for examining *all* possible variants.

Client: Given the weakness of research in this area, aren't you still pretty vulnerable to missing an unprecedented effect?

Evaluator: Somewhat, but I have a series of procedures for picking these up, from participant observation to teacher interview to sampling from a list of educational variables. I don't doubt I slip up, too. But I'm willing to bet I miss less *overall* than anyone sloshing through the swamp toward goal achievement. I really think you should hire someone else to do it independently.

Client: We really don't have the budget for it . . . maybe you *can* do something your way. But I don't know how I'm going to reassure the project staff. This is going to seem a very alien, threatening approach to them, I'm afraid.

Evaluator: People who feel threatened by referees who won't accept their hospitality don't understand about impartiality. This isn't support for the enemy, it's neutrality. I don't want to penalize them for failing to reach overambitious goals. I want to give them credit for doing something worthwhile in getting halfway to those goals. I don't want to restrict them to credit for their announced contracts. Educators often do more good in unexpected directions than the intended ones. My approach preserves their chances in those directions. In my experience, interviews with project staff are excessively concerned with explanations of shortfall. But shortfall has no significance for me at all. It has some for you, because it's a measure of the reliability of the projections the staff will make in the future. If I were evaluating them as a production team, I'd look at that as part of the track record. But right now I'm evaluating their product—a reading program. It may be the best in the world even if it's only half as good as they intended. No, I'm not working in a way that's prejudiced against them.

Client: I'm still haunted by a feeling this is an unrealistic approach. For example, how the devil would I ever know who to get as an evaluator except in terms of goal-loaded descriptions. I got you—in fact, I invited you on the phone—to handle a "reading program for disadvantaged kids" that is goal loaded. I couldn't even have worked out whether you'd had any experience in this area except by using that description. Do you think evaluators should be *universal* geniuses? How can they avoid goal-laden language in describing themselves?

Evaluator: There's nothing wrong with classifying evaluators by their *past* performance. You only risk contamination when you tell them what you want them to do *this* time, using the goals of *this* project as you do so. There's nothing unrealistic about the alternative, any more than there is about cutting names off scientific papers when you, as an editor, send them out to be refereed. You could perfectly well have asked me if I were free to take on an evaluation task in an area of previous experience—a particularly important one, you could have added—requiring, as it seemed to you, about so much time and such and such a fee. I could have accepted tentatively and then come in to look into details, as I did today.

Client: *What* details can you look at?

Evaluator: Sample materials, or descriptions by an observer of the classroom process, the availability of controls, time constraints, and so on. What I found today made it clear that you simply wanted the best that could be done in a very limited time, and I took it on that basis—details later. Of course, it probably won't answer some of the crucial evaluation questions, but to do that you should have brought someone in at the beginning. Your best plan would have been to send me reasonably typical materials and tell me how long the treatment runs. That would have let me form my own tentative framework. But no evaluator gets perfect conditions. The trouble is that the loss is not his, it's the consumer's. And that means he's usually not very motivated to preserve his objectivity. It's more fun and less strain to be on friendly terms with the project people. By the way, the project I'm on for you *is* hard to describe concisely in goal-free language, but that's not true in all cases. I often do CAI evaluations, for example, and other educational technology cases, where the description of the project isn't goal loaded.

Client: Look, how long after you've looked at materials before you form a pretty good idea about the goals of the project? Isn't it a bit absurd to fight over hearing it a little earlier?

Evaluator: The important question is not whether I do infer the goals but whether I may infer some other possible effects before I am locked in to a 'set' towards the project's own goals. For example, I've looked at elementary school materials and thought to myself—vocabulary, spelling, general knowledge, two-dimensional representation conventions, book-orientation, reading skills, independent study capacity, and so on. It isn't important which of these is the main goal. If the authors have made any significant headway on it, it will show up; I'm not likely to miss it altogether. And the other dimensions are not masked by your 'set' if you don't have one. Remember that, even if a single side effect doesn't swamp the intended effect, the *totality* of them may give a real advantage to this program by comparison with others which do about as well on the intended effect and on cost. *After* I've looked at materials (not including teachers' handbooks, and so on), I look at *their* tests. Of course, looking at materials is a little corrupting, too, if you want to talk about pure approaches. What I should really be looking at is *students*—especially *changes* in students, and even more especially, changes *due to* these materials. (I'm quite happy to be looking at *their* test results, for example.) But the evaluator usually has to work pretty hard before he can establish cause. It's worth realizing, however, that if he *had* all that, his job is not yet half done. But I guess the most important practical argument for goal-free evaluation is one we haven't touched yet.

Client: Namely?

Evaluator: Goals from the project staff are a mess. They're usually the slogans of the project, not the real (that is, the realistic and implicit, rather than the idealistic and explicit) goals. They are often at odds with the goals of the funding agency, though supposedly consistent and believed by all parties to be consistent. The same holds true for goals of consumers, taxpayers, the community, and so on. They usually involve a jargon, or a hidden jargon, that is, special uses of ordinary terms. Absolutely the worst part of the problem of evaluation, they are also unnecessary. What a tremendous argument for avoiding them! They are the ladder by which we climb up in the production process, but which we should throw away when we turn to summative evaluation.

IN THE FORMATIVE CONTEXT

It is a commonplace complaint about or by evaluators that the usual experimental design locks them in too soon. For example, Provus, in *Discrepancy Evaluation* (1971), uses this as an argument for moving to his own system of extremely detailed monitoring against a very detailed program plan. In particular, locking occurs because an evaluator will want to set up pretests on criterion behavior and, if the goals are changed, he won't have a baseline from which to calculate change. Again, if the treatment is not kept standard across the groups of experimental students, he cannot tell what produced the effects, if any. Hence creative experimentation by teachers is damaging and anytime you're set up so that creativity is damaging, you are likely to be unpopular.

To some extent, this problem can be handled by clearly distinguishing formative and summative evaluation. In the early days of a new approach, there should be no thought of *proving* anything to the external world, but only the idea of *exploring* and *experimenting*. The evaluator is there to give the best possible feedback about the relative success of the experiments. Of course, he is severely limited by the constraints of time (no follow-up), sample size, instrumentation, and poor controls. But a good evaluator in that position should most certainly pick up side effects the experimenter has overlooked and be able to identify some promising practices. There has to be *some* gear-shifting later if a serious attempt is to be made to prove to a funding agency or a prospective consumer that something worthwhile and exportable has been developed. But it is still a trade-off situation; depending on what the project's ambitions are, the staff can trade retained flexibility for external validity. If each teacher in the pilot run being evaluated is told to extemporize when she feels like it, one is evaluating the use of these materials with those instructions and the only problem is sample size. (It would be very important to have classroom observers and/or a diary system.) This can be conceived of as a hybrid formative-summative situation, and it may be a realistic picture of what usually happens in supposedly more standardized situations.

Frequently, of course, the problem is really one of convincing teachers of the importance *to them* of reliable knowledge about the effects of certain approaches. Sometimes that is something that requires a completely different approach at the teachers' college level or before, not something that can be corrected later. Without long training it is not usual to find someone more rewarded by making *a* contribution to a *team* effort to pin down a *little* knowledge about the *relative* merits of *one* textbook (or teaching method, and so on) than by the pleasures of classroom response to a spontaneous innovation.

But there is something else one can do to improve flexibility—not much, but something. That is to divorce evaluation from goals. Goals are necessary for effective planning and implementation. They are *not* necessary for evaluation (as our friend the goal-free evaluator argued). Suppose that we apply the doctrine to formative evaluation. The implication is that we should use *broad-spectrum* tests, not (initial) goal-focused tests. There's no need to use math. pretests for French, but the necessity for picking up what the project staff would regard as side effects guarantees wide coverage. As long as subsequent switches in goals keep the effects within that spectrum, the evaluation framework can operate unperturbed. This does nothing for the problem of variability among teachers, but provides a good deal of latitude for shifts in project goals.

Strictly speaking, it is unfair to claim this as an advantage for the goal-free approach, since a good goal-achievement evaluator should surely cover himself against side effects. But the ideology of the two approaches is very different. The goal-free evaluator (GFE) is a hunter out alone and goes over the ground very carefully, looking for signs of any kind of game, setting speculative snares when in doubt. The goal-based evaluator, given a map that, supposedly, shows the main game trails, finds it hard to work quite so hard in the rest of the jungle.

The GFE can work in the formative role as well as in the summative—but will not be doing what most formative evaluators do, that is, spending much time helping the project staff convert their plans into behavioral objectives, and advising them on probable mismatches between their abstract goals and some implicit commitments of their materials, or constructing biserial correlation matrices for item analysis on their quizzes. The GFE will simply get a look at the materials plus procedures (or descriptions of what they will be like) and a deadline by which time evaluative feedback must be put into the rewriting and replanning process. The GFE will go out and set up some snares, develop special instruments, set up controls, and so on, if granted the resources and time.

Of course, the other tasks are likely to be within the evaluator's field of expertise. But to get into them, is to be co-opted. *Those* tasks should be done by an evaluation *consultant,* but not by an evaluator, even a formative evaluator. Its natural to form instant opinions about the format or content or use of materials, based on previous experience, but such judgments should be withheld till they can be as fully tested as is possible in the formative phase. For test construction, the project could well use a tests specialist; for content, subject-matter consultants; for evaluation, an evaluator who should try to avoid using the implicit power of the role to affect the creative, exploratory process, even if asked.

Usually, in practice, the request is for a hybrid or nonevaluative role, either through confusion or budget exigencies. The evaluator has to clarify the trade offs in role-switching and pinch-hitting and then do whatever he can do well. But too many doors on too many projects say "Evaluation Staff" and contain people whose only function is writing tests and digesting data. That is tolerable if one thinks of the evaluation task as being that of evaluating the *students*. But those same projects often have no other evaluation staff at all and, even if you feel that the students are progressing well toward your goals, your judgment (and that of anyone whose ego and job are involved in the project) is no more reliable than that of four scientists assessing the success of the same four scientists. If you are really interested in success, rather than in the feeling of success, you have to bring independents in to look.

Properly speaking, formative evaluation ought to be set up so as to give a preview of what a summative evaluation would look like, without getting into the whole scene. To be done at all well, this necessitates the separation of an "external" team (or series of teams) for formative evaluation from an "internal" team. The former simulate a—relatively crude—summative evaluation, but report to the project, not to the funding or consumer agency. They should consider goal-free methodology as the sole, or as a supplementary, procedure. The latter, who design the project's own instruments, translate goals into forms that may be tested, and so on, rapidly become quasi producers, ego-involved in the project. They should not be relied on to provide a satisfactory forewarning of summative evaluation. The loss of independence is like pregnancy—good intentions are bad insurance.

FOOTNOTE

This chapter describes work done under a National Institute of Education Planning Team grant. Some criticism of this approach and a somewhat different treatment of it by the author may be found in the December 1972 issue of *Evaluation Comment*, published by the Center for the Study of Evaluation at the University of California at Los Angeles.

REFERENCE

Provus, Malcolm. *Discrepancy Evaluation for Educational Program Improvement and Assessment.* Berkeley, Ca.: McCutchan, 1971.

EPILOGUE

Can Public Schools Be Evaluated?

This book began with an analysis of how vulnerable the school is to public pressure and its consequent reluctance to evaluate itself. The book ends with three radical propositions, any of which might expose the school to intense criticism. Perhaps some explanation is in order.

It is clear from several selections that teachers and administrators do not want to be evaluated or to expose their programs to public scrutiny, except in the most favorable light. If such exposure exacerbates the value conflicts inherent in American society, the repercussions would be damaging indeed. While conflict is often productive, in fact, essential, there is no doubt that excessive amounts can be destructive for education.

Administrators have for too long avoided any and all conflict, and have treated conflict, and even conflicting ideas, as a disease. Feverish attempts have been made to present the school district as a happy family. Those days are gone for good. Among other things, organizations of teachers, voters' disenchantment with rising taxes, and the cries of awakened minorities have shattered the school community. Behind these lies the fragmentation of the larger community. There is no easy way to get it back together. Having lost their implicit faith and trust in the existing school system, people now want proof and demonstration of good works. It is here that evaluation may play a role.

One choice is the tight managerial model of evaluation in which goals are agreed upon and the behavior of administrators, teachers, and students is monitored to insure compliance with a master plan. The result is a highly centralized system of control. Such decisiveness often seems attractive in the face of a fragmented and politicized community. One longs for a new unifying authority that will restore order. Accountability advocates often promulgate such an approach, and usually choose the systems analysis type of evaluation.

But this tack is sterile and uncreative in the long run. Ideological considerations aside, and even though the object of such approaches is greater efficiency, it is by no means proven that such gains are forthcoming. In fact, experience with federal programs the last decade would indicate the opposite. None of the highly centralized and massive evaluation schemes has worked. Most have resulted in fiascoes, and with good reason. Aggregating problems into massive centralized piles does not solve them. The talents of the men who must deal with them is not increased correspondingly. The result is that men with very modest talents face demanding problems.

Neither are evaluative techniques powerful enough to perform such a service. The techniques of systems analysis are considerably weaker, offering more promise than performance, more froth than substance. If they did work, they would make our institutions even more impersonal and inflexible than they are now. There is no real alternative. The decision maker is going to have to struggle with a considerably smaller arsenal. When he tells the PTA that his new program is raising achievement, one mother is going to ask for data about personality development. Grandiose evaluation schemes cannot substitute for negotiation, compromise, personal influence, and other manifestations of political rationality.

But if his weapons are humble, the decision maker is not totally disarmed. Various techniques exist for evaluating instruction, determining public opinion, and even cutting costs. The trick is not to find the quickest way of justifying decisions that will take the heat off, though that is tempting, but to find ways of promoting a more viable community. Evaluation can help one group communicate with another. It can help the administrator justify his program to various public groups. It can help him understand those groups. But it can only help.

All these functions can exist under a dispersal and separation of powers within the schools. The teachers can possess considerable autonomy in how they operate. At the same time the administrator may be justified in seeking some evidence of good works—and so would the public from him. But this evidence should be gathered in modest proportions. A good motto in evaluation is "think small," both in terms of results and of what it is possible to do.

Can public schools be evaluated? Certainly, in terms of any of a dozen sets of standards, many of which conflict with one another.

Can they be evaluated unequivocally? No, there is always a criterion omitted, a sample misdrawn, a statistic misused. Can they be evaluated decisively? Occasionally they can, and even favorably, for selected audiences. Can they be evaluated successfully? Yes, but it must be with modest expectations. Can they be evaluated helpfully? Yes. Immersed as the school is in a political context, it is neither possible nor desirable that it be run entirely on deliberate rational grounds. But it can be self-critical part of the time. It can try to assure me as a parent that my five-year-old daughter, whom I sent away to school for the first time this year, is getting good treatment.